Philip Guston Retrospective

Philip Guston Retrospective

Organized by Michael Auping

With essays by Dore Ashton / Michael Auping / Bill Berkson /
Andrew Graham-Dixon / Philip Guston / Joseph Rishel / Michael E. Shapiro

 Thames & Hudson   Modern Art Museum of Fort Worth

Frontispiece: Detail of *To Fellini*, 1958
(See plate 46)

Contents

This exhibition and catalogue
are made possible by
The Burnett Foundation and
special funding from Gerald L. Lennard

Modern Art Museum of Fort Worth
March 30 – June 8, 2003

San Francisco Museum of Modern Art
June 28 – September 27, 2003

The Metropolitan Museum of Art
October 27, 2003 – January 4, 2004

Royal Academy of Arts
January 24 – April 12, 2004

Foreword

Philip Guston's importance to the history of American art is by now a matter of fact. For half a century, Guston's innovations altered the way we see American culture, and still stand as important guideposts in its continued development. Few artists are fortunate enough to have such long careers, and fewer still are able to create intensely powerful works throughout each decade, particularly their last. Indeed, the last decade of his life stands as one of Guston's most important bursts of creativity, reminding us that age and the creative impulse are not always contradictory experiences.

The Modern Art Museum of Fort Worth's commitment to Guston's work has been considerable. In 1994 the Museum purchased *Wharf*, 1976, a grand drama picturing the artist and his wife, Musa, in a rising sea, keeping their heads above water, while Guston continues to paint. Three years ago, with the help and support of the Estate of the artist, the Museum acquired five more works: three abstract ink drawings; a major abstract painting, *The Light*, 1964; and the powerful and provocative *Painter's Forms II*, 1978. Each of these works speaks to the varied impulses that fueled the artist's imagination. This exhibition—the most comprehensive view of the artist's career to date—continues our commitment to Philip Guston's art.

This presentation and this book would not have been possible without the energy and dedication of our Chief Curator, Michael Auping. He has committed himself to studying the artist's work with a rare degree of curiosity and insight, and the results are apparent in both the exhibition and this illuminating book of essays. We are also grateful to Thames & Hudson for their collaboration on this important publication.

The opportunity to have this exhibition travel to both coasts of the United States and to England has been made possible by our museum colleagues, and we are most appreciative for all their efforts and support. At the San Francisco Museum of Modern Art, where the exhibition travels after its opening in Fort Worth, I would like to thank David Ross, former Director, and Neal Benezra, Director. At The Metropolitan Museum of Art, New York, we are grateful for the early and continued support of Philippe de Montebello, Director; William S. Lieberman, the Jacques & Natasha Gelman Chairman of 20th-Century Art; Nan Rosenthal, Senior Consultant, Department of Modern Art; and Mahrukh Tarapor, Associate Director of Exhibitions. In London, we are particularly grateful to Norman Rosenthal, Director of the Royal Academy of Arts, for bringing our presentation to a vibrant cultural center and city teeming with artists, many of whom admire Guston's work but have not had the opportunity to see it in such depth.

The kind cooperation of all the lenders to the exhibition has been invaluable. They have worked patiently and graciously with us on all arrangements for photography and shipping, and are parting with their works for more than a year so that this exhibition can be seen in three other major cities.

Philip Guston Retrospective is the inaugural special exhibition to be organized in our new building designed by Tadao Ando. If it is a model for exhibitions to come, we look forward to a very successful future.

Marla Price *Director*

Acknowledgments

Certain artists inspire a longer commitment to their art. Philip Guston is one of those artists. His is a complex and intelligent vision—as lush and visually compelling as it is demanding. Organizing a Guston exhibition, particularly a retrospective, without the benefit of time to reflect and consider would be a disservice to the artist's work, as well as a lost opportunity to learn the many things that Guston's fifty-year career can teach.

This exhibition has been a number of years in the making, and over that period I have been the beneficiary of the support of many individuals. First and foremost, I must acknowledge the contributions of David McKee. Guston's dealer from 1974 until the artist's death in 1980, he has been central to the success of this exhibition. Over many lunches, trips to Woodstock, and visits to collectors' homes, he has offered his insights and his files, both of which have been invaluable. His support and friendship, and that of his wife Renee, and the help of the McKee Gallery staff (Anders Bergstrom and Kendra McLaughlin, in particular) have made my task especially rewarding.

Musa Guston Mayer, the artist's daughter, has also been remarkably generous. Opening her father's studio in Woodstock, which she has kept essentially as he left it in 1980, she allowed me full access to its contents, including many paintings that are housed in its racks. Her book *Night Studio*, a biography of her father, has offered all of us a poignant and illuminating view inside a complex individual. Given her insider's knowledge of my subject, one of her greatest generosities has been her supportive distance, allowing me to think for myself and make my own choices.

The preparation of this exhibition and publication have drawn on the resources of virtually every department of the Modern Art Museum of Fort Worth. My foremost thanks go to the Director, Marla Price, for her early encouragement and continued support during difficult moments of the exhibition's organization. The Museum's Registrar, Rick Floyd, has assumed the considerable burden of coordinating the safe shipment of the works of art smoothly and skillfully. As always, my Administrative Assistant, Susan Colegrove, when she is not singing country blues, has helped keep me organized, asking me to address issues I would prefer to ignore.

In organizing this publication, I have called upon the scholarship and insights of a number of highly recognized and very busy individuals for whose time and contributions I am especially grateful: Dore Ashton (who uses a manual typewriter!), Bill Berkson, Andrew Graham-Dixon, Joseph Rishel, and Michael Shapiro. I also want to acknowledge the various research and editorial contributions, particularly in regard to the chronology, of Arden Decker, Research Assistant, and Andrea Karnes, Associate Curator. The preparation of these manuscripts and the accompanying illustrations has been an enormous task, and I am deeply grateful for the dedication, precision, and good spirits of Pam Hatley, Museum Editor. As he has done on so many occasions, Peter B. Willberg has organized these pictures and words into an elegant and vibrant design. Susanna Friedman has worked diligently to ensure that the reproductions are of the highest quality. Nikos Stangos and Susan Dwyer have championed this project at Thames & Hudson, and I am grateful for their support.

This exhibition would, of course, not be possible without the support of the many lenders, private and institutional, who have generously agreed to part with their paintings or drawings for months so that Guston's achievements can be seen by a broad and international public. Their dedication to the artist is seen throughout this presentation.

I met Guston only once, around the time of the opening of a major survey of his work at the San Francisco Museum of Modern Art. A young and embarrassingly brash curator, I was intent on speaking with the artist whose "Klan" paintings had offended all of the critics I disliked and inspired so many of the artists I admired. He was in a wheelchair due to a weakened heart (but definitely not a weakened spirit). I told him how much I liked the exhibition, and that I was the "contemporary" curator from across the Bay in Berkeley. He thanked me and asked what a contemporary curator did. I said something like "Mostly the newest things." His response was, "So they don't really let you learn that much." Well, almost twenty-five years later and at the tail end of a Guston retrospective, I can only say, "You'd be surprised."

M. A.

Philip Guston in 1976

Introduction

This book and the presentation it accompanies have been organized with a number of goals in mind. Beginning with the earliest works from 1930 and continuing to the artist's last small paintings, completed just before his death in 1980, it is an attempt to chart and analyze the complete arc of Philip Guston's development. Our objective is to show the artist's career "whole," and the artistic whole, like a life, is often as varied in its path as it is revealing and threaded. At issue here is not the construction of smooth story lines, but the presentation of a credible and real picture of an artist who constantly questioned every aspect of the creative process and its relevance to him and the world around him.

Included are classic Guston images from each stage of the artist's career: *Porch No. 2*, 1947 and *The Tormentors*, 1947–48, which initiated Guston's transition from Symbolic Realism into abstraction; *Painting*, 1954 and *Zone*, 1953–54, examples of the extremely nuanced abstractions John Cage referred to as "that beautiful land"; *Edge of Town*, 1969, *The Law*, 1969, *The Studio*, 1969, and *Courtroom*, 1970, iconic representations of the artist's troubling Klan paintings that were debuted in his controversial 1970 Marlborough Gallery exhibition; and *Wharf*, 1976, *Painting, Smoking, Eating*, 1973, and *Talking*, 1979, which reflect Guston's powerful autobiographical symbolism.

There are also a number of surprises in the form of works that have seldom been seen or reproduced. An intriguing drawing of hanging parachutes commissioned by *Fortune* magazine in the forties to illustrate war training programs bears a menacing resemblance to a congregation of hoods. The exhibition also includes a survey of drawings completed throughout the artist's career. Rarely shown in relation to his paintings, they demonstrate not only his skill and inventiveness as a draftsman, but the dialogue that took place between drawing and painting in his development.

A work such as *By the Window*, 1969 from the artist's Marlborough exhibition shows the more intimate and reflective side of his Klan images. One of the most painterly canvases from the Marlborough show, *Blackboard*, 1969, is being shown for the first time since that presentation. Painted in thick layers of black, pink, and red—it has, in fact, only recently dried—*Blackboard* announces the rich surfaces that would distinguish the artist's subsequent paintings. Also included are some of the so-called "one-shot" paintings the artist produced in the mid-1970s, each of which was painted in one intense session with the canvas, demonstrating what might be thought of as the far edge of Guston's self-mocking side. The most poignant of these, *Street II*, 1977, is a street scene painted from the perspective of a dog in the gutter eating out of a discarded can of beans. This is the flip side of the Metropolitan Museum's powerful battle scene *The Street*, 1977. Guston's rarely seen painting of

Philip Guston in 1923, age 10

1 Morton Feldman in conversation with the author, May 20, 1986.
2 Musa Mayer, *Night Studio: A Memoir of Philip Guston* (New York: Alfred A. Knopf, 1988): 11–12.
3 Ross Feld, "Philip Guston: An Essay by Ross Feld," in *Philip Guston* (New York and San Francisco: George Braziller in association with the San Francisco Museum of Modern Art, 1980): 12.

Richard Nixon, *San Clemente*, 1975, which depicts the ex-President with a bulbous and bandaged phlebitic leg, demonstrates the artist's frustration with American politics in the late sixties and early seventies.

The two earliest works in this exhibition date from 1930, when the artist was seventeen years old. While this might seem like a premature beginning, these paintings can be seen as containing the broad parameters of Guston's vision. Painted with Dutch Boy house paint, *Mother and Child* depicts two swelling, Picassoid figures in the form of a secular Madonna and Child placed in a lonely de Chiricoesque environment. The seated female figure tilts its head in contemplation of the rambunctious and needy child. *Drawing for Conspirators* employs a surprisingly similar compositional format; however, the "mother" figure is wearing a hood in the manner of a Klansman and holding a rope, while in the background a black man is being lynched. This main figure has turned its back on the action, suggesting indecision, if not remorse for its complicity. In these surprisingly sophisticated images for a seventeen-year-old, it is not difficult to see this figure as Guston's first surrogate self-portrait, and an early indication of the moral intensity and self-reflection he would bring to his art. Experiencing these early works in relation to the artist's late figurative paintings gives a sense of the

elliptical character of Guston's ultimate vision. In Guston's development, the end is never far away from the beginning.

The youngest of seven children, Philip Guston was born Philip Goldstein in Montreal, Canada in 1913, in what one of his friends called "one of the better Jewish ghettos in North America, but a ghetto nonetheless."[1] His mother and father had immigrated from Odessa, Russia looking for a better life. They didn't find it in Montreal.

The family moved to the greater Los Angeles area seven years later. The weather improved, but their financial situation did not. The adjustment was difficult, particularly for Guston's father, Louis, a blacksmith who had trouble finding work and who reluctantly worked as a junkman collecting refuse in a horse-drawn wagon. As the elder Guston's state of mind worsened, he developed an overwhelming depression, eventually committing suicide. Guston's daughter recounts the event: "My grandfather's despair worsened until finally, in 1923 or 1924 (the exact date isn't certain), he took his own life. It was my father, then ten or eleven, who found his father, the body hanging from a rope thrown over the rafter of a shed."[2]

Guston's mother, Rachel, was left to raise and support seven children. In the case of Philip, that involved nurturing his interest and skills in drawing. As his friend the poet Ross Feld put it, Guston "literally drew a distance for himself away from the family's shock and grief."[3] His favorite refuge was a large closet illuminated by a single light bulb. Guston spent hours

PHILIP GUSTON RETROSPECTIVE

Guston with his mother and his older brother Nat

there in isolation, inventing cartoons. The light bulb, a multivalent symbol of Guston's childhood, would show up in many of his later paintings. By the age of twelve, Guston had become a serious draftsman, and for his thirteenth birthday, his mother gave him a year's correspondence course to the Cleveland School of Cartooning. As an aspiring artist, one of his first influences was George Herriman, the creator of the comic strip *Krazy Kat*. Herriman's strip, which began in 1914, revolved around the unlikely story of a large black cat who had fallen madly in love with a wisecracking mouse who does not return its affections, but instead sends bricks flying at the cat's head, which the cat inexplicably interprets as flirtation. At thirteen years old, Guston was not yet making distinctions between the daily comics and the art of museums. He also followed the antics of Bud Fisher's *Mutt and Jeff*, but Herriman was his favorite, and was a shrewd choice, as he ended up producing one of the most sophisticated and subversive comic strips in the history of the genre.

As Bill Berkson points out in the following pages, many would-be artists of Guston's generation engaged the comic strip with the intensity children now give

to video games. On the one hand, it was a matter of expediency; an avenue for a youngster to channel his as yet untrained skills in drawing and dramatic composition. Guston never forgot the strength and clarity of Herriman's compositions and iconography, particularly the barren, surreal backdrops that would be echoed in a number of Guston's late figurative works. At the same time, the cartoons were a means of nurturing the young artist's early political instincts. Guston intuitively felt that cartoons were not simply entertainment, but expressions of societal and political structures. As an adult, he certainly became aware of Herriman's outsider status as a black man in a white man's profession. Berkson, a poet and close friend of the artist, navigates through Guston's attraction to "the funnies," as well as his continued interest in caricature, political and otherwise, throughout his career.

At Manual Arts High School, Guston and his classmate and friend Jackson Pollock were introduced to modern European art, as well as Oriental philosophy, theosophy, and mystic literature, through their instructor Frederick John de St. Vrain Schwankovsky. Along with his newfound interest in modern art, sketching and drawing remained an important part of Guston's activities, and he produced drawings for the student publication *Weekly* and won a sketching contest run by the Los Angeles *Times*. Guston and Pollock were also politically active in their support of art education at a school that was fast becoming a hotbed of talented high school athletes. Their activity reached a climax when they were expelled for

4 Dore Ashton, *A Critical Study of Philip Guston* (Berkeley, Los Angeles, and Oxford: University of California Press, 1990): 19; first published as *Yes, But . . . : A Critical Study of Philip Guston* (New York: Viking Press, 1976).

publishing and distributing leaflets against the popularity of high school sports. Pollock returned to finish high school; Guston, however, did not.

A couple of years later, Guston was granted a scholarship to study at the Otis Art League in Los Angeles, but he dropped out after only three months, deciding he was better off on his own. Guston found the methods at Otis too traditional, involving drawing problems he had already mastered. Ironically, after leaving Otis, he engaged an even more rigorous and traditional form of study, carefully analyzing and then copying book and magazine reproductions of works of the Old Masters. He would eventually discourse for hours on the technical and formal characteristics that distinguished Michelangelo, Giotto, Masaccio (he carefully copied each head in Masaccio's *Tribute Money*), Signorelli, Mantegna, and arguably his favorites, Uccello and Piero della Francesca.[4] Throughout his career, Guston's use of art history was exceptionally knowing and complex. Few artists of his generation (with the possible exception of de Kooning) were as sophisticated in this regard. In his essay in the following pages, Joseph Rishel, Senior Curator of European Painting and Sculpture before 1900 at the Philadelphia Museum of Art, explores Guston's astute and wide-ranging historical interests.

What Guston needed was a way of bringing the past and the present together, and this ambition would fuel his thinking for much of his career. One of the best things that came out of his brief experience at Otis—along with meeting his future wife, Musa McKim—was his acquaintanceship with Lorser

Feitelson and Rueben Kadish. Feitelson, a prominent Surrealist, helped expose the young painter to recent developments in European art, taking him to see the Walter and Louise Arensberg collection, where he saw works by Picasso and de Chirico in the flesh for the first time. (The composition of both *Mother and Child* and *Conspirators* owes a debt to de Chirico's *The Poet and His Muse*, c. 1925, a part of the Arensberg collection.)

Kadish and Guston became friends and collaborators, investigating various theories of Marxism and questioning the idea of "art for art's sake." Art and politics were close bedfellows in 1930s America, and Guston's political instincts developed as quickly as his artistic interests. In New York, *Partisan Review* and other left-wing publications were proposing a socialist agenda in which art would play a central role in political activism. The logical role models for similarly aspiring artists working in southern California were the Mexican muralists David Alfaro Siqueiros, Diego Rivera, and José Clemente Orozco. Guston became interested in mural painting and went with Pollock to watch Orozco work on his fresco *Prometheus* at Pomona College in Claremont, California. In 1934 he traveled to Mexico with Kadish and art critic Jules Langsner to serve as a mural assistant to Siqueiros.

At the time, Guston supported himself working odd jobs in an atmosphere when unionist and anti-unionist sentiments struggled for power. As Guston remembered it, "The police department had what they called the Red Squad, the main purpose of which

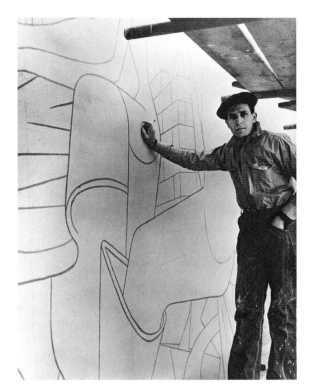

Guston in 1935

Guston working on his mural for the 1939 World's Fair in New York

5 Quoted in "Philip Guston Talking," ed. Renee McKee, in *Philip Guston: Paintings 1969–1980* (London: Whitechapel Art Gallery, 1982): 52. Taken from a lecture originally given at the University of Minnesota in March 1978.

6 David M. Chalmers, *Hooded Americanism: The History of the Ku Klux Klan*, second ed. (New York: New Viewpoints, 1981): 119.

was to break up any attempts at unionizing. Remember this was 1932, 1933. I was working in a factory and became involved in a strike. The KKK helped in strike breaking so I did a whole series of paintings on the KKK. In fact I had a show of them in a bookshop in Hollywood, where I was working at that time. Some members of the Klan walked in, took the paintings off the wall and slashed them. Two were mutilated. This was the beginning."[5]

The Ku Klux Klan, also known as the Invisible Empire, had a significant membership in California in the 1930s and 1940s, and Los Angeles County was its most active Klavern.[6] Guston and several of his friends also painted portable murals for the John Reed Club on the theme of "The American Negro." Guston's submission was particularly volatile. Based on the Scottsboro case, in which nine black men were sentenced (many said on false and circumstantial evidence) to life in prison for raping a white girl, Guston's mural depicted a group of hooded figures whipping a black man. The murals were eventually attacked and defaced by a band of "unidentified" vandals. The experience of seeing the effect of art on life and life on art never left Guston, and the

unsettling image of the hooded figure was branded into his visual imagination.

In late 1935, at Pollock's urging, Guston moved to New York, where he joined the mural section of the Federal Arts Project (FAP), launched as part of Roosevelt's New Deal Program through the Works Progress Administration (WPA) to create murals in American cities to boost public morale during the Depression, and at the same time to provide modest funding for artists with no means of support. He was selected to do his first major mural commission for the facade of the WPA building at the New York World's Fair in 1939, which won first prize in the outdoor mural category. Through this and other projects, he was put in contact with James Brooks, Stuart Davis, Willem de Kooning, Burgoyne Diller, Arshile Gorky, and Conrad Marca-Relli. Along with Pollock, and Kline, Rothko, and Newman, whom he would also soon meet, this group had an immense impact on American art in the 1940s, becoming the nucleus of what would soon be known as Abstract Expressionism.

The late 1930s and 1940s constitute a critical stage in Guston's career, a period when he shifted from public murals to private studio work. The latter coincided with his acceptance of various teaching positions in Iowa, Minnesota, and St. Louis. In St. Louis, the artist became familiar with that city's great collections of the works of Max Beckmann,

7 Feldman, conversation with the author, May 20, 1986.

offering the model of an artist keenly interested in presenting the psychological face, as it were, of humanity. This period in Guston's development is explored in Michael Shapiro's well-researched essay "The Early Years, 1930–1945." It is during this time that the artist established many of the themes that occupy his subject matter later in life.

The phenomenon of abstraction, which had its beginnings in Europe and Russia in the early part of the century, was by the 1940s being reinvented with dazzling intensity in New York. Even Guston, whose works to that point had been thoroughly based on figurative compositions, found his way into the drama of "non-objective" painting. Perhaps because of his rigorous, self-taught understanding of the traditional genres, Guston came to abstraction slightly late in the game. When he did so, however, he created an imagery that was as complex and powerful as any works produced under the sign of Abstract Expressionism. Indeed, Guston's abstractions remain one of the best-kept secrets of that groundbreaking movement and one of the least understood aspects of the artist's development. The essay "Impure Thoughts: On Guston's Abstractions" addresses this important body of paintings from the 1950s and early 1960s and their relationship to the works of the other Abstract Expressionists.

From the Vietnam War, continued racial tensions, the moon walk, through the Nixon presidency and resignation, the late 1960s and early 1970s was a turbulent period of conflict and reevaluation in America, and Guston's imagery would engage both impulses with a boldness that shook even the generally glib art world. Guston's 1970 exhibition at Marlborough Gallery in New York was one of those events that people tend to remember, especially if they weren't there. It had the immediate impact of legend. What Guston unveiled on that October evening were images of strange hooded figures huddled in discussions, drinking and eating, and driving around desolate streets in cartoon cars. The fallout from these pictures and those that would follow over the next decade was considerable. What to one generation, mostly those born before 1930, was a slap in the face was to a younger generation a wake-up call.

Guston's new work made the former group more than a little nervous, demonstrated by the reaction of one of the artist's best friends, the avant-garde composer Morton Feldman. "I couldn't see it. I just felt the abstract work from the fifties was so important—and now he abandoned it for the Pop art thing."[7] To complicate matters, Guston's work didn't look or read like Pop art, which by that time was establishing its place in postwar art history. Guston's images of hooded protagonists were variously too personal and generally too subversive, sliding under the radar of Pop art's sparkling media-based theatrics. The late sixties was a time of cool strategies in the art world, with the aloof abstractions of Color Field painting sharing the limelight with Pop art's reflective gaze. Following the Marlborough show—without waiting for the reviews—Guston left for Rome, clearing his head of "contemporary art" to engage his beloved Old Masters. This was the arena in which he felt he needed to operate. As Guston put it, "To paint

Guston's studio, 1979

8 Philip Guston, "Faith, Hope, and Impossibility," *Art News Annual* XXXI, 1966 (October 1965): 101, 153.

is always to start at the beginning again. . . . I do not think of modern art as Modern Art. The problem started long ago. . . ."[8]

Guston's transition from abstraction back to figurative imagery in the late 1960s and 1970s constituted a grand and provocative synthesis. The exceptional qualities of touch and structure that developed in his abstract works were now invested in monumental portraits, still lifes, and landscapes. Characters and symbolic objects appear, disappear, and reappear in Guston's paintings of the 1970s like actors on a stage. The proscenium that had been introduced in such early paintings as *If This Be Not I* of 1945 has opened onto a broad, Beckett-like landscape. Guston's late paintings constitute some of the most poignant autobiographical images in postwar art. As he was pointing a finger at the Klan and the Nixon administration, he was also boldly revealing his own vulnerabilities and doubts. Andrew Graham-Dixon, a British writer who has followed Guston's work for many years, points out in his essay here that Guston's ambition was as broad as it was personal, a successful struggle to depict "the ills of his time head-on."

Many of Guston's late paintings are frankly confessional, questioning the personal habits of the artist and the seemingly indulgent and mysterious act of painting. Guston was a master of self-investigation, always sticking to basic human needs, concerns, and dilemmas, images of which surface in his paintings with a phenomenal sense of painterly obsession and self-doubt. In a series of long and revealing letters to his friend the artist Mercedes Matter, Guston describes his state of mind:

Of course it is all internal, private and silent. All having to do with painting—creating, *overwhelming* self-doubt in spite of the fact that I've never painted so much as I have this year. I try desperately to put everything else aside in order to concentrate— concentrate, which is to say, TO LIVE THE PAINTING—what a difficult state of *being* to move into—it is totally another way of life than what we all are accustomed to ordinarily! And yet, if I have one good day in ten, I am fortunate—the rest is torment and a shambles—and debilitating self torture and disgust. After so many years of work,

9 Quoted from a letter to Mercedes Matter dated November 13, 1975, with the kind permission of Alex Matter.

10 Guston left David McKee Gallery for six months, returning December 13, 1977.

I feel I know nothing at all—so very little—in front of the canvas or the drawing paper, I feel like an innocent—a beginner—a primitive. Also there is the anxiety—a *fierce one*—of *time*—a dominating feeling of getting old puts me in the worst depressive states I've ever been in. I know this isn't unique—I know. Yet experiencing life, *to oneself, in oneself* has nothing to do with knowing, or rationalizing about it all.

In the same letter, the artist writes of reconciling his current feelings with his early inspirations:

This past year, I've done a lot of reading and looking (*Books* and *Museums*) of my favorite masters, and it all feels newer and *stranger* than ever! I've *never* felt more remote from what's called "Modern art." What a *fabulous* source of inspiration the past is!

I feel like I've made—travelled over a vast circle—when I was a boy of 17 or so, all I could look at was Piero, Masaccio, and other later masters, and here I am back again for the last ten years or so, but with greater intensity and in a renewed *alive* way. . . . When I am faced with an Italian master work, I am put deeply in a state of anxiety, almost painful and ecstatic at once—their particular—special, rare mixture of the *ideal*—the *optimum* order, going *together* with the "human," the *observed* tangibilities of life. I think finally it possesses the aspects of the dream—a plastic dream—and this *strangeness* is what makes me feel so faint.[9]

By 1977, Guston had become so reclusively ensconced in his studio that he told his friend and dealer David McKee that he was leaving the gallery.[10] The following year, he wrote:

11 Quoted from a letter to Mercedes Matter dated July 7, 1978, with the kind permission of Alex Matter.

We are living now in near *total* isolation. . . . I think this is the first letter I've written in many months. Musa shows me the mail at the end of the week. But this is only part of the story. I am so *deep* in what I am painting now and it takes such concentration that I've never felt before.[11]

In the latter half of the 1970s, having survived a heart attack, the artist focused in on issues of death and desire to reinvent himself. He and his wife, Musa, are pictured huddled together in bed, protecting each other as they ride out the storm. More often, however, they are seen cast about in a turbulent sea. These "deluge" paintings suggest an artist tossed by waves of turmoil and emotion. In many societies, a deluge suggests a clearing away in preparation for a new beginning. For Guston, these paintings were an acknowledgment that even late in a successful career an artist must navigate a sea of fear and doubt in order to see things anew.

In the small gouaches he would produce the year of his death, Guston once again reviews the imagistic parameters of his psyche, from the immediacy of a pile of fresh cherries on the kitchen table, or a thick and juicy half-eaten sandwich, to an uphill landscape being climbed by Guston's battered and bandaged head, or a pair of those familiar legs attempting to climb a ladder they are nailed to. Until the very end, Guston would continue to fight for the imaginative life at the same time he depicted it, in all its ironies and complexities.

Although these paintings have diverse subjects and formats, they are united by Guston's very particular ways of using paint and emphasizing structure and composition. And in each instance, the way he has done so has grown directly out of his response to both his subject matter and his ongoing engagement with the history of painting; from the works of Uccello to Piero della Francesca, and Goya to Cézanne and Picasso.

The late paintings also reflect the artist's library. A high school dropout, Guston devoured literature as the self-educated often do. He was attracted to those writers who trafficked in the existential complexities of human nature and the creative process. His reading often entered his paintings, sometimes directly, more often obliquely. Dore Ashton, a longtime friend of the artist and a bookhound in her own right, tracks Guston's literary wanderings and their role in his imagery. Ashton reveals the painter as a reader and conversationalist "always after what quickens the mind and emotions." She details Guston's early and sustained interest in Russian writers, especially Isaac Babel and Boris Pasternak, drawing parallels from those writers' works to images in his late paintings. She explores the influence on Guston of poets, essayists, and novelists—from Rainer Maria Rilke, Nathanael West, and Franz Kafka to Samuel Beckett, Paul Valéry, Wallace Stevens, and T. S. Eliot—and details his late friendships with younger poets, such as Clark Coolidge, and novelists, including Philip Roth. She concludes with a discussion of Guston's affinity for the poetry of the Surrealist Louis Aragon, with whom he felt a great communion.

Guston was himself a thoughtful and penetrating writer and speaker, and therefore this book would not be complete without the experience of Guston in his own words. We have chosen for inclusion here one of the artist's most thought-provoking texts. "Faith, Hope, and Impossibility" conjures the heart and soul of the image-making process. Rather than rhetorical proclamation, it is a profoundly honest self-evaluation of the strange need to apply paint to canvas.

Significant artists are often those figures who make bold and difficult transitions throughout their career, and in that process synthesize vast territories of art history. These are artists whose works reflect not only the aspirations and anxieties of their own generation, but of those that came before and after. In the twentieth century, one thinks of Kandinsky, Picasso, and Mondrian, among others. In the era of postwar art, Guston's ability to grow and invent throughout his long career must be reckoned with on similar terms. Having helped to define the one great movement associated with American art, Abstract Expressionism, he also had the boldness and skill to carve his way out of it. In this sense, Guston is like Cézanne, having greater relevance to succeeding generations perhaps than to his own.

Indeed, if the respect of other artists is any indication of Guston's significance, he is already an important marker on the path of art history. Guston's imagery oscillated in so many different directions and has been so subtly pervasive that it is impossible to pin down the exact range of his influence. Nonetheless, it would be hard not to see an echo of Guston's abstractions in the work of Robert Ryman or Sean Scully (who owns an abstract work by the artist). The initial generation that blossomed in the wake of Guston's late figurative work—Jonathan Borofsky, Neil Jenny, Susan Rothenberg, Elizabeth Murray, et al.— readily acknowledge the inspiration his work provided. The balance that Guston often achieved between irony and romantic quest is one that many emerging artists are searching for today. We should not be surprised, then, to find so many artists in their twenties and thirties who proudly announce that it is their generation that has discovered Guston. The following pages reveal the complex puzzle that is the imagery and life of Philip Guston, an artist whose significance seems to swell with each succeeding generation.

Michael Auping

The Early Years, 1930–1945

Before Philip Guston was an easel painter, he was a muralist. From his youthful days in Los Angeles until the early 1940s, the large flat surfaces of murals had absorbed his energies. He was inspired in part by his contacts with the Mexican muralists. His 1934 visit to Mexico to work with David Alfaro Siqueiros and his two pilgrimages—to the Los Angeles area to look at murals by Diego Rivera and to Dartmouth in 1937 to see those by Orozco—attest to his studiousness and devotion to the planar forms and social agenda that were part of the spirit of the muralist movement of the 1930s.[1] Guston's earliest major works in Los Angeles were in this medium, but the West Coast appeared to be less culturally promising than the East for the young muralist. During the Depression years, federally sponsored mural commissions were assigned from Washington and New York. Guston moved there in 1935 to be part of a large community of artists working on the WPA Art Project and to develop as an artist.

In 1939 Guston won a competition to paint a mural in the community room of the Queensbridge Housing Project in Long Island City. His successful proposal, entitled *Work and Play*, was executed under the auspices of the New York City Work Projects Administration Art Project, the New York City Housing Authority, and the Queensbridge Community Association. The mural illustrates healthful and wholesome activities for families and, in particular, children. The frieze of vignettes includes basketball, music, a doctor examining a young person, and people working, among other motifs.

One of these motifs is a make-believe battle between several youngsters seen against a backdrop of high brick walls (see plate 5). The grouping was characterized in the *New York Herald Tribune* and *The New York Times* as "children playing near a slum in the process of demolition."[2] The children, dressed in paper hats and armed with garbage-can lids as shields and homemade wooden swords and staffs, struggle with one another. The fight image, which Guston first expressed in visual terms in 1938, is a metaphor for much of his work in the forties and for years after. He saw battle as inherent in human and artistic life; children, fundamentally innocent in their play, confirm this notion of the naturalness of combat.

The Gladiators, 1938 (plate 6), an oil painting which Guston completed at the time of the Queensbridge mural, is a further development of the Queensbridge frieze. Four protagonists are arranged in interlocking pairs. A boy with a paper hat, who holds a long, broken piece of wood, fights with another boy wearing a kitchen pot for a helmet and using a garbage-can lid for a shield. An enormous, hooded figure in the background grabs a fallen warrior, who still clings to a homemade wooden sword. The

1 On Guston's trip to Mexico, he and fellow painter Reuben Kadish painted the mural *The Struggle Against Terror* in Morelia. Their work was reproduced in "On a Mexican Wall," *Time* (April 1, 1935): 48.

2 "Section of Mural to be Unveiled at Queens Houses," *New York Herald Tribune* (March 13, 1941).

Guston and Reuben Kadish
(with the poet Jules Langsner)
in front of their mural *The Struggle
Against Terror,* 1934, in Morelia,
Mexico

3 Horst W. Janson, "*Martial Memory*
by Philip Guston and American
Painting Today," *Bulletin of the City
Art Museum of St. Louis* 27
(December 1942): 41.

foursome, with their props and barking dog, are composed into a single energetic form.

In the first quarter of 1941, after completing the mural the previous year, Guston resigned from the New York City WPA Art Project and moved to the artists' colony of Woodstock, New York. In Woodstock (during the winter of 1941), Guston continued his theme of youthful combat in his first mature easel painting, *Martial Memory* (plate 7). In this work Guston differentiated his figures of children through the use of props. Rather than focusing on combat, he chose to represent a moment of classical repose. Three boys face out toward the viewer. Two others present their backs to us, facing the three. One wears a triangular paper hat, another has a paper bag over his head, and a third has a tea kettle rather improbably tied to his head with a piece of rope. The sole hatless lad looks outward and has winglike shields affixed to both arms. The boy with a bag on his head clasps a trash-can lid with his right hand. His left hand holds a staff-length piece of wood. The boys on either side of him carry crude wooden swords.

When Guston left Woodstock to teach at the University of Iowa, he took *Martial Memory* with him. It is likely that the row of brick buildings in the background, with their eyebrowlike trim around the windows, was added in Iowa City. If so, this final element of the composition would have been added between September and October of 1941, prior to sending the painting to exhibition. Similar buildings lined the Iowa City street on which Guston's studio was located, and they appear in various combinations

in the backgrounds of a number of Guston's paintings during his years in Iowa City and, later, St. Louis. *Martial Memory* was completed then, just before the United States entered World War II. It was included in *Directions in American Painting*, an important group exhibition held in October 1941 at the Carnegie Institute in Pittsburgh, where it was probably seen by Perry Rathbone, then director of the City Art Museum of St. Louis. In August 1942, Rathbone acquired *Martial Memory* for his museum. It was the first work by Guston to enter a museum collection and his first fully realized easel painting.

Professor Horst W. Janson wrote an article for the December 1942 issue of the *Bulletin of the City Art Museum of St. Louis* entitled "*Martial Memory* by Philip Guston and American Painting Today." Janson noted that the boys in the painting "display their weird accoutrements with an air of almost ceremonial solemnity." As a consequence, he says, the emphasis has been shifted from the physical to the spiritual aspect of the scene: "In the mock seriousness of these boys, Philip Guston has found the true image of this war-torn world, suggesting at once the tinsel glitter of martial trappings and the deep emotional crisis that underlies every human conflict."[3]

The word that best characterizes the achievement of *Martial Memory* and much of Guston's figurative work in the forties is *ambiguity*. The roots of ambiguity as a pictorial goal can be found in the works of two of Guston's earliest artistic heroes, Giorgio de Chirico and the American Surrealist Lorser Feitelson. In their works, creating a lack of certainty for the

Figure 1
Sunday Interior, 1941
Oil on canvas
38 × 24 inches (96.5 × 61 cm)
The Estate of Philip Guston
Courtesy McKee Gallery,
New York

4 For more information on Guston's early influences, refer to Horst W. Janson's "Philip Guston," *Magazine of Art* (February 1947): 56. Also Alison de Lima Greene's "The Artist as Performer, Philip Guston's Early Work," *Arts Magazine* (November 1988): 55–56.

5 See correspondence between Guston and Gruskin, Archives of American Art, Smithsonian Institution, Washington, D.C.

viewers was one of the artists' goals. Guston's feeling for the indeterminacy of Surrealism found its counterpoint in his simultaneous attraction to the balance of the Italian quattrocento, to the works of Paolo Uccello and Piero della Francesca, in particular.[4] His fascination with the orderly spatial compositions of the Renaissance led Guston to place his figures in definable and often compact spatial situations and to provide a strong compositional structure. There coexisted within him, however, the urge to express mystery in the subject and mood of painting.

A longtime friend of Guston's, the painter Fletcher Martin, helped Guston's career by recommending his work to Alan Gruskin, Martin's New York dealer. Gruskin's Midtown Galleries represented such figurative artists as Paul Cadmus, Isabel Bishop, and

Isaac Soyer. In January and February 1943, Gruskin and Guston reached an agreement, and the gallery represented Guston until early 1951.[5] Gruskin played an important part in placing Guston's paintings in major group exhibitions and in providing the artist with his first New York exhibitions in 1945 and 1948.

One of the paintings Guston completed during his first few months in Iowa City was *Sunday Interior* (figure 1). This 1941 painting depicts an African American man, holding a cigarette and sitting in a chair behind a plain wooden table. The impassive and narrow-faced subject looks directly at the viewer with the same wide-eyed stare as Ben Shahn's figures. He wears a white shirt and a narrow tie, and the only object on the table is a single pink shell. Behind him in the barren room is a window. A green shade with a

6 In 1945 he moved to 1428 East College Street.

long cord is drawn over the top half of the window. The view out the lower window reveals the facades of three brick buildings on the opposite street. A solitary figure smoking and staring ahead under the glare of a suspended light bulb is an image that Guston personalized late in his career. While the identity of the man in the painting is unknown, he is a lonely and anxious surrogate for the artist himself, perhaps as he felt shortly after his arrival in Iowa City.

Among Guston's colleagues at the University was the young art historian Horst W. Janson, one of a number of talented historians and artists recruited for Iowa by Lester Longman, head of the Department of Art. Janson played a significant role in Guston's early career. He was a modernist with whom Guston felt he could talk, and also an active and articulate advocate. Janson preceded Guston to his next two teaching appointments at Washington University in St. Louis and New York University. As curator of the Washington University Art Gallery, Janson acquired one of Guston's finest paintings, *If This Be Not I*, 1945 (plate 13), for the collection. And, finally, Janson published several of the first serious treatments of Guston's work.

Guston was an engaging and charismatic teacher. He talked with his students seriously and at length, not only in the painting studio but also in bars, in the homes of friends, and at his own small white clapboard house at 725 South Summit Street.[6] Among his graduate students were artists who developed distinguished careers of their own: Paul Brach, Stephen Greene, and Miriam Schapiro.

Among Guston's paintings of the period is a group of works that portray members of his family, fellow fine arts professors, and students. The paintings in this group are *Portrait of Shanah*, 1941; *The Art Student* (unlocated); *Musa McKim*, 1942; *The Sculptor*, 1944; *Sanctuary*, 1944; and *The Young Mother*, 1944. These works can be seen as portraits and also as an inventory of types of people—wife, mother, sculptor, model, student, artist. The subjects were close at hand and cumulatively formed a catalogue of his key relationships as husband, father, and teacher. Late in his career, his increasingly inward interests would more often be expressed as an inventory of types of objects—books, shoes, cigarettes, drink, paint— rather than individuals.

Musa McKim, 1942, is Guston's first painting of his wife. The two had met in Los Angeles at the Otis Art Institute in 1930 and were married in New York City seven years later. McKim was also an artist, and in the 1930s and early 1940s she often worked with her husband on mural commissions or made her own paintings. In Laconia, New Hampshire, the two worked side by side, each creating a mural for the U.S. Forestry Department in 1941 (see page 247).

Having arrived in Iowa, however, Musa put her art aside, choosing to focus her energies on supporting her husband and, soon, on raising their daughter. Musa was a quiet and gentle person, a dreamer who wrote poetry more for herself than for others. Her qualities of dreamy inwardness are evident in Guston's painting *Musa McKim*. In this picture she looks down at the seashells she has collected in her lap.

7 Michele Vishny, "On the Walls: Murals by Ben Shahn, Philip Guston and Seymour Fogel for the Social Security Building, Washington, D.C.," *Arts Magazine* (March 1987): 40, 42.

8 Archives of American Art, Smithsonian.

Her arms are crossed, her gaze is lowered, and she is lost in thought.

Three years later Guston turned again to his wife as a subject for *The Young Mother*. He had first painted a mother and child in 1930 when he was only seventeen years of age. Now, at age thirty-one, he painted his blond wife seated in a high-backed rocking chair and wearing a green hat, a blue-and-white striped shirt, and an orange skirt. Their child, Musa Jane, naked below the waist, stands on her mother's lap with arms extended outward. She wears a white jacket with gold trim and a gold-colored undershirt. The seated mother and the child on her lap are seen against a Midwestern background of barnlike structures, factories, and churches.

Some of Guston's fascination with depicting those close to him stemmed from traumatic events that affected family members early in his life. His father had hanged himself, and it was Philip who discovered the body. Also, his favorite brother, Nat, was killed in an automobile accident.

While Guston was painting pictures of his wife and daughter and the artists around him, he was also working on his last mural commission, which was awarded in 1941 by the Section of Fine Arts of the Public Buildings Administration. The mural was intended as a backdrop for the stage in the auditorium of the new Social Security Board Building in Washington, D.C. Immediately outside the auditorium was a recent mural by an artist Guston admired, Ben Shahn. The assigned topic for the mural competition was "Reconstruction and the Well-Being of the Family."[7]

Guston's mural was conceived as a triptych. The central panel portrays a family enjoying a picnic and their free time together, and the narrow flanking images depict rural and urban workers. The panel on the left shows three rural workers engaged in conservation work. In the foreground a boy and a young man stack logs, while behind a stone wall a man works in a barren landscape. The panel on the right depicts two urban laborers at work, while another worker, his back to the viewer, uses a jackhammer. In front of him a man digs with a shovel. The figures in the mural have the characteristic bearing of Guston's figure paintings during this period.

Public works murals typified one aspect of American art of the thirties. Guston's mural, begun just prior to America's involvement in World War II and installed midway through the war, represents both the end of Guston's mural painting and the virtual end of the WPA-sponsored mural movement in America. Before its demise, however, motivated by ambition and entrepreneurial instinct, Guston was able to link his art to the nation's war effort, even while living in the Midwest.

Guston executed the murals in 1942 in Iowa and sent them to Washington for approval in January 1943. He then traveled in late February 1943 to wartime Washington to install them. Museum professional Perry Rathbone, then a lieutenant in the Arts and Poster Division of the Navy, and Jane Watson, art critic for the *Washington Post*, went with Guston to admire the newly installed mural.[8]

War had been declared late in the first semester

9 Unpublished contract entitled "The State University of Iowa Description of Contract with United States Government for United States Navy Pre-Flight School," The University of Iowa Library, Special Collections.

10 "War Art Workshop Established to Make Posters, Visual Aids," *Daily Iowan* (November 22, 1942): 19.

11 Information on the Camp Dodge murals comes from unpublished correspondence between State University of Iowa faculty and Camp Dodge personnel concerning the execution of and payment for the murals, The University of Iowa Library, Special Collections.

12 "Collection of Work by Art Professor Will Be Exhibited," *Daily Iowan* (February 27, 1944).

13 See unpublished letter from Lester D. Longman to Earl E. Harper, Director of Fine Arts, Iowa Memorial Union, March 8, 1943, The University of Iowa Library, Special Collections.

that Guston was in Iowa City. And on April 9, 1942, the University had announced a contractual arrangement with the U.S. Navy making it a United States Naval Air Corps Training Station. The school was to be "primarily devoted to training in physical fitness, with some class work in mathematics and physics taught by instructors employed by the Navy."[9] The agreement meant the construction of a new classroom building and the remodeling of existing buildings to train thousands of future aviators.

In line with this call to arms, and with Guston's prompting and Lester Longman's support, the art department had developed a War Art Workshop in the fall semester of 1942. The goal of this initiative was to utilize the university's art faculty and students to create posters for the region's war effort, murals and sculpture for army camps, and visual aids for army and navy instruction.[10]

The first substantial project of the War Art Workshop was a series of murals and sculptures for the Camp Dodge Recreation Center, Des Moines, Iowa.[11] Guston's concurrent experience with the WPA aided him in planning and supervising the mural component of this student-executed commission. Guston created a large, instructional mural (now unlocated) for the teaching of celestial navigation at the new Pre-Flight building, which was constructed in 1943.[12]

Guston also sought to obtain a commission from the navy to document the Naval Air Corps Training Center through his own drawings. During his visit to Washington in late February 1943 to install his Social Security Administration murals, he met with Lieutenant Parsons, a U.S. Navy public relations officer with the Arts and Poster Division. Responding to the officer's enthusiasm for the proposed drawings, Guston returned to Iowa and immediately set to work making quick sketches.[13] He then enlarged several of them into finished ink-and-wash drawings portraying training activities at the school (see plate 9). He made drawings of parachute, flotation, and physical training and sent the finished drawings to Washington in early May. Unfortunately, after reviewing the drawings, the naval authorities thanked him for his efforts but declined to continue the project.

Guston's most substantial war-related project was a series of illustrations for three articles in *Fortune* magazine. The first focused on the Butler Manufacturing Company in Kansas City, Missouri, a company that produced the components for portable airplane hangers and runways. Guston traveled to Kansas City in the spring of 1943 to see the plant. The article in the August 1943 issue contained three black-and-white drawings by Guston. These drawings depicted men constructing mobile airplane hangers, welders adding attachments to mobile refueling units and hydraulic presses, and punching machines producing metal runway sections.

Following the success of this article, the *Fortune* editor asked Guston to illustrate two others. During the summer of 1943, he traveled to Tennessee to observe the Air-Troop Command's glider and paratrooper training. Six drawings were reproduced in the October 1943 issue of *Fortune* in an article entitled "Troop Carrier Command" (see plates 10 and 12).

14 Unpublished correspondence between Guston and Gruskin, Archives of American Art, Smithsonian.

15 "Air Corps Paintings by Art Professor to Appear in *Fortune*," *Daily Iowan* (January 27, 1944).

In that same month, Guston visited Matagorda Island off the Gulf Coast of Texas on his last assignment for *Fortune*. He then created six illustrations for a February 1944 article entitled "The Air Training Program" (see plates 8 and 11). Guston wrote enthusiastically to his dealer about his Texas experience: "I had a grand time, flying every day and in almost every kind of Army Bomber and Fighter plane."[14] He also commented on the experience to the University newspaper: "I wasn't so much interested in portraying the appearance of the nuts and bolts of the planes as I was in showing the faces of the men, their tenseness and determination."[15]

Guston did indeed create tautly composed images of pilots undergoing the serious business of war training. Eventually, his Pre-Flight School and *Fortune* magazine drawings played a substantial role in an exhibition of his works in the main lounge of the Iowa Memorial Union in March 1944. They also appeared in his first solo exhibition in New York, which took place at the Midtown Galleries in 1945.

The stoicism that informs Guston's figures in the Social Security murals and the *Fortune* magazine illustrations is also present in Guston's easel paintings of the period. For *The Sculptor*, Humbert Albrizio, a colleague in the art department, was the model. Albrizio, like Guston, had moved from New York to Iowa, arriving in 1942. He was a direct carver of wood and stone. In the painting he is shown as a powerfully built man working in his undershirt on a sculpture of a woman with her arms raised. He holds the chisel in place with one gloved hand while he prepares to lift the hammer with the other. Pervading the painting is the same calm and quiet integrity that characterize the workers in the Social Security murals of the previous year. Like some of the children in Guston's paintings of the forties, the Albrizio figure wears a paper hat. As with many sculptors, Albrizio actually wore a paper hat while working to keep the wood, stone, or plaster chips from lodging in his hair. The painting is not a strict likeness of the sculptor but rather a portrait of a sculptor as a dedicated worker.

Perhaps the tenderest of these paintings is *Sanctuary*, 1944 (figure 2). In this painting a sleeper appears startled into consciousness. He is wide eyed, his left arm raised to his head, his pink-and-white-striped pajamas opened to reveal his chest and the medallion he wears around his neck. His orange blanket, bedsheets, and pajamas are in disarray from a restless night. Behind him and beneath a blue-green sky is what can only be described as an Italianate view of Iowa City, with a basilica facade and a church spire. For Guston, the dream of Italy and, in particular, the work of Piero della Francesca were palpable presences in a dreamscape that lay just beyond the reality of bedstead, bureau, and mirror. With its richly dappled surface, the picture is painted as delicately as the sensibility that it attempts to convey.

Sanctuary and its drawing are the first images of a sleeping figure in Guston's work. This motif was continued in several larger works of the 1940s, notably in *If This Be Not I*, 1945. It also appears, perhaps most poignantly, in an untitled drawing of 1946. In this work a fine, nervous ink line defines the outline of a

Figure 2
Sanctuary, 1944
Oil on linen
22¹/₈ × 35⁷/₈ inches
(56.2 × 91.1 cm)
Private Collection

16 Guston to Gruskin, Archives of American Art, Smithsonian.

reclining, egg-shaped head. Just beneath the head are a pair of crossed legs wearing shoes. At the left edge of the drawing are circular, triangular, and oval forms. These cloudlike forms suggest the inchoate dream world of the sleeper in the foreground. The sleeping or dreaming figure became a central motif in Guston's late work, such as *Sleeping*, 1977 and *Couple in Bed*, 1977 (plates 107 and 108). The vigilant and anxious ancestors of these late paintings are found in Guston's paintings and drawings of the 1940s.

The best-known painting from 1944 is *Sentimental Moment*. It is similar in mood to *Musa McKim*, for both depict the single figure of a slightly melancholy woman. *Sentimental Moment* is a three-quarter-length view of a woman in a classical pose. She wears a pink-and-red-striped sleeveless shirt and a black skirt and holds a locket with a gold chain in her hands. She has heavy arms and fuzzy long hair and stands against a dappled, greenish background. The model is said to be Guston's student Miriam Schapiro. As in many of his paintings, the artist worked away from his model, moving to a more generic type rather than seeking an accurate likeness. According to reports, at one time Guston perched a dove on Schapiro's shoulder, but he subsequently painted it out.

Sentimental Moment was included in the Carnegie Institute's survey of American painting in 1945 and was selected by the jury as the grand prize winner.

As a result, Guston received an enormous amount of attention in the art press, though the reaction to the painting itself was mixed. The title may have been too accurate, and subsequently Guston was embarrassed by the picture itself.

Holiday, another 1944 painting is, according to the artist, "a city-scape or rather a small town-scape. . . . It is not a straight scene sort of thing: It is definitely a mood or 'idea' picture involving my reactions to middle western towns and their characteristic forms." [16] The painting depicts a wooden porch that extends from the doorway of a brick house. A green banister and post define the forward edge of the porch, whose roof is supported by a large, brown wooden column. The column is the element around which the composition is arranged. A small, barefooted boy wearing a pink beanie, tee shirt, and blue jeans emerges from the doorway and pauses, with his hands in his pockets, to observe the objects arrayed on the porch before him: a carousel horse, a round table covered with a pink cloth, newspapers, and a drum. A single pink rose lies on top of the drum. Beneath the drum, the anxious eyes and forehead of the artist, in a small self-portrait wedged between the drum and the table, peer out at the viewer. Just as the gentle child observes or imagines the objects before him, he too, appears to be observed. A woman, possibly the boy's mother, partially hidden by a green

17 Ibid.

18 Ibid. In St. Louis, Guston was friendly with William Inge, then a reporter for the *St. Louis Post-Dispatch*; Joseph Pulitzer, Jr., the collector and publisher; Perry Rathbone, director of the museum; and the Washington University faculty.

window shade, looks down from her second-story window. In the distance, behind the porch and the tattered flags and a network of telephone wires, is a cluster of buildings improbably brought together. They press upon one another and upon the open, relaxed, and wistful space of the foreground. The sky is punctuated on the left by a slender metal radio tower and on the right by the spire of St. Mary's church in Iowa City, a motif that Guston had used on several occasions. Some of the elements found in *Holiday* fully distill and summarize his artistic development in Iowa: the compositionally important column, the backdrop of brick buildings that pushes activity to the foreground of the painting, the assortment of inexplicable objects, and the important role of children as protagonists.

If This Be Not I, one of Guston's most important paintings of the period, is a horizontal frieze featuring nine children. They are arrayed among discarded kitchen pots, trash-can lids, ropes, doors, and newspapers. The central figure wears a paper bag on his head and a mask that covers his eyes and nose. He sits in a wooden chair borrowed from *The Young Mother*. The figure lying on the ground to the left wears a pajama top, like that worn by the figure in *Sanctuary*, and holds a light bulb in his hand. The smallest of the children, a little girl wearing a crown, is the artist's daughter, Musa. One child holds a blindfold in front of another, while still another, at the far right and seen from the back, appears to be putting on an adult's shirt or pajama top.

If This Be Not I is a richer, more atmospheric and deeply poetic painting than *Martial Memory*. In it an armistice has been declared: the children have ceased fighting and now are reflective, standing amid the rubble. *Martial Memory* and *If This Be Not I* frame the years of World War II as well as the artist's stay in Iowa. *If This Be Not I* was acquired by the Washington University Gallery of Art in St. Louis in October 1945 through the efforts of the gallery's curator, Horst W. Janson.

Partly at Janson's suggestion, Guston was offered a teaching position at Washington University. He received a two-year leave of absence from The University of Iowa, after convincing the faculty that "mainly I wanted a change and to live in a city for a while." [17] He went there thinking that "St. Louis is a stimulating town and I feel I will be more productive there considering everything. The museum is a good one and there are lots of people interested in the arts." [18]

During the summer of 1945, the Gustons made their move to St. Louis. Because of the flood of returning soldiers, it was extraordinarily difficult to find adequate housing. Eventually, they rented a flat in a two-story brick house at 2545 Bellevue Avenue in the suburb of Maplewood, a short drive from the University.

It was after Guston's arrival in St. Louis, in October 1945, that he received the cash prize at the Carnegie Institute's annual exhibition for *Sentimental Moment*. Since 1896, the Carnegie organized an international exhibition that during the war years had become a survey of contemporary American painting. The cash prize was a highly visible award for a young artist, and *Life* magazine published an illustrated article about Guston. Within the next fifteen months, he won two other awards, one from the Virginia Museum of Fine Arts for *The Sculptor*, and one from the National Academy of Design for *Holiday*.

In *The Porch*, 1946–47, Guston created a dense arrangement of five figures in shallow space. The three flanking figures each play musical instruments while the two central masked figures do not. The cross created by the intersection of the column and the banister provide a compositional armature for the figures arrayed around it. The central figure, a girl in a pink dress, holds a blindfold in front of her eyes, a pose which echoes that of one of the children in *If This Be Not I*. She and the drummer boy, who has his back to the viewer, are on the viewer's side of the banister.

Within the claustrophobic and compressed confines of the porch are three revelers: a cymbal player with bandaged legs at the left, a horn player with a gold crown in the center, and on the right-hand side, the strongest figure in the painting, a figure who wears a white circus costume and a pink mask. The egg-shaped, masked head is tilted to one side, and the figure's hand touches his mouth in a gesture that signifies both hesitation and anxiety. Both the position of the hand and the rendering of the head suggest that this is a self-portrait. The figure is also an allusion to Max Beckmann, an artist Guston admired and whose work he had seen at Curt Valentin's gallery in New York. Beckmann often inserted images of himself into his own densely packed paintings of enigmatic

revelers. Guston's figure in white has another significant detail that is prophetic of the artist's later work. His right leg is curiously raised, allowing the viewer to see the form of his heel, the sole of his shoe, and the outline of the nails that hold heel and sole to the body of the shoe. Just as the cord and light bulb in *Sunday Interior* reappear in the late work, so too would Guston return to the outlined shapes of shoes and their forms in his later work. This is the initial appearance of the shoe motif in Guston's painted work.

Guston's next major work, *Porch No. 2*, 1947 (plate 15), continues to synthesize and toughen the achievement of *The Porch*. *Porch No. 2* also has five figures and a wooden cruciform shape at the center. The central figure, and the only one that looks out at the viewer, appears to be another self-portrait. This figure supports himself with one arm while his other hand is placed next to his lips. The pose of the drummer in the earlier Porch painting is reused more schematically, this time in the form of a girl. In the second version, the porch is treated more abstractly, depth being suggested by the red horizontal form behind the figures. Several autobiographical references appear in this painting. On the far right, a taut rope leads to the closed-eyed musician, who holds his horn. Guston used rope horizontally in the earlier Porch painting to link two figures. Using it in a vertical arrangement, however, more clearly suggests hanging, the method of suicide his father had chosen. It might be too much to suggest, however, that cutting off the legs of the central figure in this painting suggests the automobile accident that crushed his

Figure 3
Sketch Book, 1947
Ink on paper
22$^1/_2$ × 29 inches
(57.2 × 73.7 cm)
Private Collection

19 Guston to Gruskin, Archives of
American Art, Smithsonian.

brother's legs. Here as well, the raised soles of the figure on the left and the two soles of the inverted figure on the right have expanded their role since the motif's appearance in the previous painting. In *Porch No. 2* Guston himself is the isolated figure, surrounded in part by memories of personal tragedy and probably contemplating his own condition. This was how Guston found himself in 1947, and these were the concerns he translated into paint for the remainder of his career. While his mature work broods powerfully on these themes, they were first posed by the artist in the 1940s.

In a letter to his dealer written from St. Louis, Guston communicated his anguished feelings: "I would give anything for a Guggenheim—one or two years of concentration in painting is the *only* thing I need and desire intensely. Teaching has gotten me into a terribly nervous state and it's just *impossible* for me to go on."[19] Guston's application to the Guggenheim Foundation was successful, and he spent 1947 to 1948 in Woodstock and New York City. This was an important year for Guston. He immersed himself in his own work and the work of his colleagues and moved strongly toward complete abstraction.

A drawing from this period, subsequently titled *Drawing for Tormentors (Drawing No. 1)*, 1947–48 (plate 17) is a study that sublimated the imagery of his earlier paintings. Near the left edge of the drawing is a fragment of a self-portrait. Near the face, an arm reaches outward. The right side of the drawing is less representational, with thin lines describing round and linear forms. The dash marks that appear in some of the lines appear to simulate stitch marks and derive from the upturned shoe that appears in earlier drawings and the Porch paintings. The stitches hold the forms together and provide a memory of earlier representational imagery, as well as creating an abstract shape. Another drawing from this same period, *Sketch Book*, 1947 (figure 3), is a large work with an inventory of forms: soles of shoes, a head wearing a crown, trumpets, and in the lower right-hand corner, a self-portrait drawing. In his later works Guston continued to inventory objects. These inventories repeat simple, understandable facts of importance to Guston—books, light bulbs, paintings, shoes—that have their source in his works of the forties.

To create his painting *The Tormentors*, 1947–48 (plate 18), Guston drained his canvas of color, allowing

20 See award letter Guston received, dated February 27, 1948, Archives of American Art, Smithsonian.
21 Telephone conversation between Heliker and the author.
22 Guston to Gruskin, Archives of American Art, Smithsonian.
23 Ibid.

black and red to predominate and more clearly concentrating on formal considerations. The quilt of shapes outlined by white lines forms a template. On the upper left is a triangular shape that might be the echo of a hood, while in the upper right a horseshoe shape looks like the neck of a shirt or the heel of a shoe. In the lower right a circular shape perhaps recalls the remains of a horn, and the stitched horseshoe in the upper center recalls a shoe sole.

To come into direct contact with the world of Renaissance Italy, which he knew largely from books and American museums, Guston applied for and received a fellowship to study at the American Academy in Rome for the 1948–49 academic year. Along with other fellows, he sailed on the *Vulcania* in September 1948.[20] The painter John Heliker, with whom Guston became friendly, sailed with him. It was their first trip to Europe and on their drive from Naples to Rome, both artists were shocked at the devastation from the war. On occasion, the two traveled together to see the Piero della Francescas in Arezzo and the Etruscan paintings in Tarquinia. Heliker recalls that Guston painted actively shortly after arriving, but he notes that there were periods when Guston was prone to substantial depressions.[21]

Guston wrote to his dealer in New York from Italy: "Well, Italy is a great thing for me! I've travelled a great deal, seen much and feel more stimulated than I've felt in years. I am now settling down to work and have several new things going."[22]

While in Italy, Guston had his dealer ship *The Tormentors* to him. He wrote, "I feel it's necessary to have some sort of continuity and I want to study it."[23] It is difficult to know what paintings were painted by Guston in Italy. Perhaps the most important is *Red Painting*, 1950 (plate 23). It is this painting that develops most directly out of *The Tormentors*. With this painting Guston would embark on a new journey into the ethereal realm of abstraction. For well over a decade he would wrestle with the subtle complexities of non-objective painting, only to emerge in the late 1960s with a new dedication to figuration. It is at that crucial moment that the artist would draw on his imagery of the 1940s, extending that imagery into new and unprecedented territory.

Michael E. Shapiro

A version of this essay appeared in the catalogue for *Philip Guston: Working through the Forties*, published in 1977 by The University of Iowa Museum of Art.

Impure Thoughts: On Guston's Abstractions

There is something ridiculous and miserly in the myth we inherit from abstract art—that painting is autonomous, pure and for itself, and therefore we habitually defined its ingredients and define its limits. But painting is "impure." It is the adjustment of impurities which forces painting's continuity. We are image-makers and image-ridden.[1]

PHILIP GUSTON, 1960

1 Musa Mayer, *Night Studio: A Memoir of Philip Guston* (New York: Alfred A. Knopf, 1988): 141.

2 Guston in *Philip Guston: A Life Lived, 1913–1980* (New York: Michael Blackwood Productions, 1980). Color film, 58 minutes.

3 See Robert Rosenblum, "The Abstract Sublime," *Art News* (February 1961): 38, and Lawrence Alloway, "The American Sublime," in *Topics in American Art Since 1945* (New York: W. W. Norton and Company, 1975): 31–41. These authors introduced a theme that over the years has become diluted and overused almost to the point of cliché.

4 Quoted in Bruce Glaser, "Questions to Stella and Judd," in Gregory Battcock, ed., *Minimal Art: A Critical Anthology* (New York: E. P. Dutton, 1968): 158.

5 Quoted in "Philip Guston Talking," ed. Renee McKee, in *Philip Guston: Paintings 1969–1980* (London: Whitechapel Art Gallery, 1982): 49. This is the transcript of a lecture given at the University of Minnesota, March 1978.

When Philip Guston wrote down some of his concerns about the prospect of abstract painting, he was making thoroughly beautiful and ever more refined abstract paintings. And he would do so for at least another eight years. Guston was not renouncing abstract art, although many have interpreted his statement in that way. He was simply, and eloquently, poking at its philosophical boundaries. Guston was a man who preferred the hard-fought question over the smooth and carefully orchestrated answer. If abstraction were to be his mode of working, he would need to subject it to the same difficult questioning that he would pose to any form of image-making. For Guston, abstraction was not a heavenly end game, but a practice that involved constant and at times contentious negotiations; what he called "a contest." As the artist put it, "a contest between a subject and the plastic forms it will result in."[2] It is in fact those subject-impurities that made Guston's abstractions unique within the pantheon of Abstract Expressionism.

Much of the literature we inherit on Abstract Expressionism assumes that the development of the movement was driven by some mysterious teleological force; in this case, an elegant fade from Surrealist figuration into either a spacious "American sublime"[3] or a serenely optical and acutely rational domain known as Color Field painting. Obviously, given the diverse nature of the images produced by these artists, it couldn't have been that simple, and none of the artists associated with the movement, especially not an artist whose sources and inspirations

were as complex as Guston's, fit comfortably into either scenario. Regarding the former, Guston was far too intrigued by the relationships between people and things and how those relationships might somehow be represented on a flat picture plane to be seduced into the metaphysical infinities of the sublime.

On the other hand, the latter proposition was too sterile for Guston. Throughout the 1950s and early 1960s, the influential American critic Clement Greenberg developed a rigorous concept of cleansing in which modernism would evolve to a radical formalist condition; an art of pure opticality. In order to maintain its distinction from other art forms, painting would focus exclusively on its inherent physical characteristics: color, shape, and support. Metaphysical qualities and underlying symbolic or allegorical themes associated with earlier phases of expressionism were to be eliminated in a rite of ascetic purity. The ultimate legacy of Greenberg's theory was the painter Frank Stella's laconic remark about his own influential abstract paintings: "What you see is what you see."[4]

Guston tended to see more than most, and certainly more than Greenberg would condone. Guston's rejoinder to Stella's remark was that ultimately a painting "is an illusion, a piece of magic, so what you see is not what you see. . . . I don't know what a painting is; who knows what sets off even the desire to paint? It might be things, thoughts, a memory, sensations, which have *nothing* to do directly with painting itself. They can come from anything and anywhere."[5] In Guston's case, they came from a

Figure 4
Review, 1949–50
Oil on canvas
39 3/8 × 59 inches
(100 × 149.9 cm)
National Gallery of Art,
Washington, D.C.

6 Thomas Albright, "Philip Guston: 'It's a Strange Thing to be Immersed in the Culture of Painting,'" *Art News* (September 1980): 114.

diverse range of inspirations, including music, books, philosophy, films, and history.

Guston made abstract paintings for approximately sixteen years, roughly one-third of his career, and he entered that realm understanding the complexities and impurities inherent in it. Unlike many artists working today, Guston didn't inherit abstraction as a foregone conclusion. His early skills developed out of an assiduous study of the Old Masters, and later Cézanne, de Chirico, Picasso, Léger, and Beckmann. For Guston, abstraction was still an experiment, involving a careful deconstruction in a search for the internal structure that gives an image its emotional resonance.

That deconstruction began in a transition that took place between two paintings: *Porch No. 2* of 1947 (plate 15) and *The Tormentors* of 1947–48 (plate 18). *Porch No. 2* depicts a carnivalesque troupe of children playing/fighting on a porch. At the time, Max Beckmann was a particularly important source of inspiration for Guston, who appreciated the German artist's skeptical view of society's appearances. The proscenium effect, enigmatic symbolism, and densely layered space of *Porch No. 2* suggest the uneasy, often incipiently violent mood of Beckmann's art. The strange distortions of Guston's figures, especially the enlarged heads and hands, also recall Beckmann's Gothic expressiveness. In Guston's painting, however, the figures are flattened and compressed into an even more cramped and claustrophobic space. Often simply

referred to as one of the artist's "children" pictures, *Porch No. 2* was partially inspired by photos the artist had seen of survivors of the Nazi death camps.[6]

In *The Tormentors*, the legs of the performers in *Porch No. 2* have been isolated and unraveled, their spectral presence establishing an oblique but mysterious reverberation in the image. The effect created is of something strangely there at the same time something is poignantly missing. A dark, funereal painting, *The Tormentors* carries only the ghosts of the victims alluded to in *Porch No. 2*. Fragile white lines seem stitched into a dark ground, hinting at the shoe soles, hoods, and mock battle regalia of his earlier figurative canvases. These are invaded by abstract red shapes rising up through the image like ominous stalagmites. Guston may have felt that these "tormentors" were best not literally described, but rather their evil and conflict projected through undefined forms and abstract presences. Measuring only forty by sixty inches, *The Tormentors* is unexpectedly powerful and disturbing; the opening scene in Guston's abstract drama.

The Tormentors was followed by *Review* of 1949–50 (figure 4), a semiabstract still life of flattened-out, shadowy objects situated on a table, the farthest edge of which creates a kind of horizon line between the table surface and a dark empty space. The resonance of the objects in *Review*—you can make out a hammer, cups, a book, possibly paint cans, paintbrushes, and a

Figure 5
Mark Rothko
No. 9, 1948
Oil and mixed media on canvas
53 × 46⅝ inches
(134.6 × 118.4 cm)
National Gallery of Art,
Washington, D.C.
Gift of The Mark Rothko
Foundation, Inc.

7 Maurice Merleau-Ponty,
   Phenomenology of Perception,
   trans. Colin Smith (London:
   Routledge and Kegan Paul, 1962):
   210.

8 Feldman in conversation with the
   author, May 20, 1986.

quill pen—suggest an elegy to the fact that Guston was not only leaving the world of figures, but of the objects that animated his daily existence. *The Tormentors* and *Review* were the beginning of an internalizing impulse in which objects are not necessarily eliminated, but are re-presented using a number of reductive strategies. In fact, the presence of things, the relationships between them, and the potential meanings those relationships could conjure never completely disappeared from Guston's art, and would play a central role in the way his abstraction developed. If his initial impulse was to deconstruct the things that anchored themselves in his imagination, his eventual desire would be to reconstruct them slowly. Two decades later *Review* would be reconstructed in monumental still lifes such as *Flatlands*, 1970 and *Painter's Table*, 1973 (plates 81 and 84).

Review and the even more abstract *Red Painting*, 1950 (plate 23) bear some relation to Rothko's early abstractions of 1948–49, often referred to as his "multiforms," in which hazy, Surrealist-inspired figures of a few years earlier became chromatically dissolved into eccentric shapes blended together (see figure 5). Both artists were evolving an abstract language, but they were moving in subtly different directions. By introducing generous amounts of white into his palette, as well as adopting a more improvisational paint application, Rothko created an ambiguous tonal blur in which light and lightness are central qualities. Unlike the ethereal shapes in Rothko's paintings, Guston's forms suggest gravity, something weighted in the abstract field. While Rothko's imagery evokes qualities of pure consciousness through an almost formless color experience,[7] Guston's paintings employ color—deep reds and blacks—to support the presence of form.

Guston would eventually test his innate attraction to the world of forms and objects, engaging in a further process of reduction that would allow him to question the very nature and construction of the pictorial image. In a series of gouaches from the late forties and early fifties, shapes become increasingly more oblique, and by the time he painted *White Painting I*, 1951 (plate 28), shapes have completely disappeared, and individual brushstrokes take center stage. The subsequent *To B. W. T.*, 1952 (plate 32)—which consists of red, orange, black, yellow, and pink brushstrokes woven into various levels of density—refers to Guston's friend Bradley Walker Tomlin, with whom he briefly shared a studio. As their mutual friend Morton Feldman remembered it, "He and Tomlin could talk for hours, I mean hours, on what a single brushstroke meant—what was its character and where was it going."[8]

The brushstroke had come to represent for Guston the essential building block of painting, the DNA of form. To focus on this fundamental act of marking,

9 Philip Guston, "Notes on the Artist," in John I. H. Baur, *Bradley Walker Tomlin* (New York: Whitney Museum of American Art in association with The MacMillan Company, 1957): 9.

10 Quoted in Sixten Ringbom, "Transcending the Visible: The Generation of the Abstract Pioneers," in *The Spiritual in Art: Abstract Painting 1890–1985* (Los Angeles and New York: Los Angeles County Museum of Art in association with Abbeville Press, 1986): 131.

11 Quoted in *Abstract Expressionism: Creators and Critics*, ed. Clifford Ross (New York: Harry N. Abrams, Inc., 1990): 139.

12 Quoted in *Abstract Expressionism: Creators and Critics*, 172.

13 Quoted in H. H. Arnason, *Philip Guston* (New York: Solomon R. Guggenheim Museum, 1962): 20.

however, could mean losing sight of those forms and objects that had always been the components of his compositions. Indeed, what was to become of composition and the tensions created by forms in space? Some years later, Guston would write a text for the catalogue documenting an exhibition of Tomlin's paintings at the Whitney Museum of American Art. One suspects that Guston was writing as much about himself as he was about Tomlin when he noted that Tomlin's work "possessed a tensile—and at times precarious—balance that covered an anguished sense of alternatives." He also wrote about how working through these alternatives resulted in a "reworked and scored painting surface," that "gradually exposed vein and nerve," ending the sentence by remarking that "this was the cost."[9] Guston was not apologizing for the surfaces of Tomlin's paintings, but offering a veiled concern over the potential loss of form.

The Abstract Expressionists understood that abstraction, in jettisoning the figure and the object, could be a slippery slope to nowhere. As early as 1913, Kandinsky, one of the pioneers of abstraction, described the dilemma: "A terrifying abyss of all kinds of questions, a wealth of responsibilities stretched before me. And most important of all: what is to replace the missing object?"[10] For Guston and many of his friends, the alternative to presenting the object was in "exposing the vein and nerve" of the object or figure. This involved an ambition to be inside the image and to provide the viewer with that same experience. Pollock's famous statement about his process is only a slight exaggeration of what many of the

Abstract Expressionists felt. "I prefer to tack the unstretched canvas to the hard wall or the floor," Pollock said in one of his rare and often quoted statements. "On the floor I am more at ease. I feel nearer, more a part of the painting, since this way I can walk around it, work from the four sides and literally be *in* the painting."[11] Rothko began increasing the size of his paintings for this very reason. "I paint very large pictures," Rothko acknowledged. "I realize that historically the function of painting large pictures is painting something very grandiose and pompous. The reason I paint them, however—I think it applies to other painters I know—is precisely because I want to be very intimate and human. To paint a small picture is to place yourself outside your experience, to look upon an experience as a stereopticon view or with a reducing glass. However you paint the larger picture, you are in it. It isn't something you command."[12]

Guston was also engaged in the challenge of getting "inside" the image, but his solution was unique. He didn't see a need to radically increase the size of his paintings, but rather to change his own proximity and relation to them. As Guston would later describe it, "The desire for direct expression finally became so strong that even the interval necessary to reach back to the palette beside me became too long. . . . I forced myself to paint the entire work without stepping back to look at it."[13] So at one end of the spectrum was Pollock, by this time standing over large unstretched canvases, slinging paint using a method in which the brush seldom touched the canvas. At the other end was Guston, scrutinizing

14 Quoted in Dorothy C. Miller, ed., *12 Americans* (New York: The Museum of Modern Art, 1956).

each stroke at such close proximity that he risked getting paint in his eyes.

In Guston's case, the result is a field of pictorial sub-particles in the form of relatively short, shimmering brushstrokes. Color and facture carry the impact of what many felt were some of the artist's most ravishing paintings to that point, *Zone*, 1953–54 (plate 36) and *Painting*, 1954 (plate 35). They also establish one of Guston's unique contributions to Abstract Expressionism. In contrast to Kline's gestural velocity, Pollock's spiraling webs, Newman's iconic "zip" form, or Rothko's ethereality, Guston laid claim to a special immediacy and intimacy related to "touch." The paintbrush was like a sacred tool to Guston. The nine-inch-long wooden shaft and the flattened horsehairs that protruded from its end were like an extension of his fingers. Guston had his pigments ground to create a particularly creamy consistency, and like thick butter applied to a hard surface, each stroke subtly squeezed out at its edges, creating a micro sculptural effect.

Unlike de Kooning or Kline's wider, housepainting-sized brushstrokes, Guston's brushstrokes throughout his period as an abstract painter remained at the scale of those used in representational easel painting. Guston envisioned the art of applying paint, whether employed in abstract or representational painting, as an innate and fundamental form of portraiture, like a fingerprint. One of the things Guston always remembered about the Phaidon art books he would study over and over as a young painter were the close-up details of works by the Old Masters, particularly Titian and Rembrandt. It was in these close-ups that

each artist's brushstroke would be fully revealed. From these, he could extrapolate an artist's identity, their uniqueness attributable to the way they applied paint, whether in depicting fabric, rendering hands, ears, or feet, or filling in backgrounds. In a time of abstraction, this signature quality could be reduced to the pressure of a brushstroke, which can declare itself as the artist's language, a function of the intuitive body as much as the rational mind, what Guston eloquently described as the "narrow passage from a diagramming to that other state—a corporeality." [14]

While a majority of his peers, then, chose to expand the field of action in which their images operated, Guston intuitively contracted, focusing on potent and condensed qualities of facture and tonalism. Like the works of Chardin, an artist he much admired, Guston's abstractions were large in scale if not size. Robert Irwin remembers seeing the Gustons of those years and the impact of their scale:

> I remember one time, for instance, seeing this small Philip Guston hanging next to a large James Brooks. Now the Brooks was a big painting on every scale: it had five major shapes in it—a black shape, a red, a green—big areas, big shapes, with strong major value changes, hue changes. Next to it was this small painting, with mute pinks and greys and greens, very subtle. . . . But anyway, my discovery was that from one hundred yards back—this was just one of those little breakthroughs—that from this distance of one hundred yards, I looked over, and . . . that goddamn Guston just blew the Brooks

Figure 6
Piet Mondrian, *Church Facade/Church at Domberg* (formerly *Cathedral*), 1914
Charcoal on chipboard
28¼ × 19⅛ inches
(71.8 × 48.6 cm)
San Francisco Museum of Modern Art
Purchase, 70.43

15 Quoted in Lawrence Weschler, *Seeing Is Forgetting the Name of the Thing One Sees: A Life of Contemporary Artist Robert Irwin* (Berkeley, Los Angeles, and London: University of California Press, 1982): 59–60.

off the wall. Now by all-over measures—size, contrast, color intensity—that shouldn't have happened. Everything was in favor of the Brooks. But the Guston just blew it right off the wall. Just wiped it out. . . . The Brooks fell into the background, and the Guston just took over. And I learned something about . . . some people call it "the inner life of the painting," all that romantic stuff, and I guess that's a way of talking about it. . . . A good painting has a gathering, interactive build-up in it. It's a psychic build-up, but it's also a pure energy build-up. And the good artists all knew it, too. That's what a good Vermeer has, or a raku cup, or Stonehenge."[15]

What Irwin intuitively perceived as an "energy build-up" was structural in nature. At the very moment Guston had broken down form to its fundamental pictorial components, he began to structure those painting units in a rebuilding process. The results were images that swelled with a tension between extemporaneous expression and organizational construction.

Structural memory was immensely important to Guston's abstractions. Throughout his career, he was attracted to artists whose works were built around solid structural lines and forms: Uccello, Piero della Francesca, Cézanne, Léger. The one abstract painter who would inspire him was Piet Mondrian. While some would see the late paintings of Monet in Guston's light-catching brushstrokes—temporarily labeling his work of the early fifties Abstract Impressionism—it was in fact the "plus-minus" paintings and drawings of Mondrian that inspired Guston's layered, slightly off-kilter crosshatch painting technique (see figure 6).

It seems ironic that while many of the Abstract Expressionists owed some debt to Monet for decentralizing the compositional format and spreading out the pictorial field, as he did in his water lily paintings, Guston's work would be the least affected. Cézanne was in fact the last modern French artist whose work Guston studied with great care. It was the "weight" of Cézanne that he appreciated and that he would address incrementally as his abstractions evolved further. His careful distortion of Mondrian's grid was a step toward the strange materiality of Cézanne's still lifes and figures.

It wasn't the geometry of Mondrian that interested Guston, but the scaffolding. In Guston's hands, however, that scaffolding would not sit as a static, ideal diagram, but would invariably shift and bend in search of a form in space. *Drawing Related to Zone*, 1954, for example (figure 8), predicts the choreography of layering, clustering, and density that takes place in the completed painting (figure 7). In this drawing,

Figure 7
Zone, 1953–54
Oil on canvas
46 × 48 inches
(116.8 × 121.9 cm)
The Edward R. Broida
Collection

16 Morton Feldman in conversation
with the author, May 20, 1986.

17 Quoted in *Abstract Expressionism:
Creators and Critics*, 75.

made with ink and a two-pronged bamboo quill pen, the pressure of the artist's hand determines the thickness and weight of each mark. In some cases, the quill head has been turned on its side, creating a slightly scratchy, staccato effect. When pressure has been applied with the prongs lying flat on the surface of the paper, the line is full and heavy. These different characters of line are combined to suggest that a form is about to "take hold." The structural suggestions in *Drawing Related to Zone* find their completion in the materiality of paint that becomes an ambiguous but assertive form in the painting *Zone*.

Mondrian's geometry is partially overridden by Guston's interest in Oriental calligraphy, particularly Chinese ink painting, which he appreciated "because it

appeared spontaneous but involved unbelievable deliberateness and patience.[16] While drawing is generally associated with spontaneity and speed, particularly in the latter half of the twentieth century, Guston often drew to slow himself down, to think carefully about each mark and its relevance to the surrounding space and the potentiality of form. "It is the bareness of drawing that I like," Guston once remarked. "The act of drawing is what locates, suggests, discovers. At times it seems enough to draw, without the distractions of color and mass."[17] Guston could often see the stark structures of his drawings in his completed paintings. He bemoaned the increased use of color in art books and magazines, preferring to see paintings, particularly his own, printed in good

18 Related by David McKee to the
author.

19 Wassily Kandinsky, *Concerning the
Spiritual in Art*, 10th ed., trans. by
Michael T. H. Sadler (accessed
through Project Gutenberg): part
1, chapter 4, "The Pyramid."

20 Quoted in Dore Ashton, *A Critical
Study of Philip Guston* (Berkeley,
Los Angeles, and Oxford:
University of California Press,
1990): 105; first published as
*Yes, But . . . : A Critical Study of
Philip Guston* (New York: Viking
Press, 1976).

21 Conversation with the author,
May 20, 1986.

22 Morton Feldman, "After
Modernism," *Art in America*
(November–December 1971):
71–72.

Figure 8
*Drawing Related to Zone
(Drawing No. 19)*, 1954
Ink on paper
17⁷/₈ × 24 inches
(45.4 × 61 cm)
Private Collection,
New York

black-and-white reproductions because those revealed
the works' "bareness," subtly emphasizing the
shadows of the built-up brushstrokes that make up the
structure of these pictures.[18] In the early 1950s, this
bareness of structure was not necessarily a grid nor an
identifiable form, but a subtle area, or *zone*, between
the two.

The gray area between presence and absence, form
and non-form, was a compelling subject for Guston,
as it was for his close friends the composers John Cage
and Morton Feldman. Cage and Feldman were both
attracted to Abstract Expressionism, relating it to their
own ideas about breaking away from traditional
forms, which eventually would radically redefine the
term *music*. The relationship between abstract
painting and music has been a recurring theme in the
art of the twentieth century. Kandinsky suggested that
painting should take the lead from music: "A painter,
who finds no satisfaction in mere representation,
however artistic, in his longing to express his inner
life, cannot but envy the ease with which music, the
most non-material of the arts today, achieves this end.
He naturally seeks to apply the methods of music to
his own art."[19]

Guston occasionally referred to music and sound
in describing the effects of a painting. "Look at any
inspired painting," he told a *Time* magazine reporter in
1952. "It's like a gong sounding; it puts you in a state
of reverberation."[20] Artists' statements are easy to
misuse, and it is also true that relating painting to
music can be the desperate resort of those incapable
of grasping abstract, pictorial thinking. In the case of
Cage, Feldman, and Guston, however, "influence"
undoubtedly found itself moving between all three
artists, often revolving around philosophical discussions about Zen Buddhism and "nothingness." As
Feldman remembered it, Guston's paintings were a
critical catalyst for discussion. "The thing about the
paintings was that they sat there in front of you,
flickering in and out of focus, taunting you to verbalize
what they were, what they meant. Guston's paintings
were very close, sometimes maybe even ahead of what
we were thinking. They were just there, compared
to music, which is here and gone. They were a very
physical evidence of what we were all thinking."[21]

Feldman, who had composed the music for the
famous Namuth-Falkenberg film on Pollock, compared
Guston's paintings of the early 1950s to Beethoven,
in the sense that "we don't know where the passage
begins, and where it ends; we don't know we are
in a passage. . . . The overall experience of the whole
composition becomes the passage."[22]

Feldman was a master of soft, sometimes radically
elongated compositions and a creator of shimmering

Guston and Morton Feldman
in Guston's studio, 1965

23 Ashton, 94.

24 Conversation with the author,
May 20, 1986.

25 Quoted in "Conversations: Philip
Guston and Harold Rosenberg:
Guston's Recent Paintings,"
Boston University Journal (Fall
1974): 44.

26 Baselitz in conversation with the
author, March 18, 1999.

pianissimo in twelve-tone music. It was undoubtedly the latter that attracted him to Guston's paintings. Feldman once told an audience, "I have always been interested in *touch* rather than musical forms."[23] He would later elaborate on Guston's paintings of the early 1950s: "There is this relationship—applying paint could be like touching the keys of a piano. You can strike softly and go long, or strike sharply and quick. Pollock and de Kooning were quick—Guston and Rothko soft, elegant, and long. My music is soft and long."[24] Also speaking of Guston's work of the early 1950s, Cage described that moment as being such "a beautiful land," and the regret he experienced when Guston felt a need to leave it.[25]

Feldman and Cage began to drift away from Guston's art in the mid-1950s, when stronger forms appeared in his art. For all their camaraderie, it could be argued that they misinterpreted Guston's overriding motivation for making images. Although they often talked about striking a gentle balance between presence and absence, that balance was difficult to maintain. Cage and Feldman gradually shifted to grayer areas of quietness, while Guston, according to Feldman, engaged a "louder and more forceful" process of rebuilding.

Rather than the subtly intoned shapes or forms of Guston's work in the early 1950s, by the mid-1950s strong gestural eruptions began to occur in localized areas of his crosshatched fields. The allure of *Beggar's Joys*, 1954–55 (plate 37) is a result of the dramatic way red, orange, pink, and blue clots of paint come together off center of a pinkish-gray field. In *The Room*, 1954–55 (plate 39), thick strokes of black and charcoal gray disturb an otherwise gentle painterly field. Tension is created in these mid-1950s paintings by the sense that something is pushing its way into the picture.

Like actors on a stage, even more congealed and suggestive forms would soon emerge and intersect in increasingly more dense pictorial dramas. Guston's drawings also began to reflect a greater determination to locate forms. The loose grid that had earlier helped locate a developing shape was replaced by scratchy curves that gather the space of the drawing into barely identifiable configurations—not quite a head, closer to a rock, maybe a hood? *Forms in Change*, 1958 (plate 44) becomes a telling title.

By the time a young German painter named Georg Baselitz would see Guston's work in Berlin in 1959, a new imagery was unfolding. Baselitz remembers that Guston's paintings were "not that abstract," but a "distortion of the abstract, full of concrete forms."[26] A European painter who appreciated the dynamics of traditional composition and who was

27 Harold Rosenberg, "The American Action Painters," *Art News* (December 1952): 22–23, 48–50.

28 Clement Greenberg, "'American-Type' Painting," in *Clement Greenberg: The Collected Essays and Criticism* (Chicago and London: The University of Chicago Press, 1993): 228.

29 Clyfford Still, "Letter to Gordon Smith, dated Jan. 1, 1959," in *Paintings by Clyfford Still* (Buffalo: Albright Art Gallery, 1959).

30 Leo Steinberg, "Fritz Glarner and Philip Guston at the Modern," in *Other Criteria: Confrontations with Twentieth-Century Art* (London, Oxford, and New York: Oxford University Press, 1972): 282.

skeptical of the sublimity of abstraction, Baselitz appreciated the dialogue between ambiguous but suggestive shapes in Guston's paintings. Baselitz would soon be inspired to create a series of canvases in which rich painterly gestures are punctuated by vaguely defined heads or facial parts, as in his *Rayski Heads* of the early 1960s.

Although Guston's gestures could be vaguely related to Harold Rosenberg's concept of "Action Painting,"[27] his development seemed to counter the evolutionary drift of Abstract Expressionism in general. Throughout the 1940s and 1950s, there was a sense of Abstract Expressionism opening up and sometimes subtly, sometimes radically dissolving form in the process. Rothko's imagery virtually dematerialized into mists of color, and Still's craggy formations gradually became dispersed, with less and less paint applied to more and more bare canvas. Clement Greenberg would see Still's imagery as the ultimate opening up and breaking out of the Cubist grid and the figures and still life objects it contained.[28] Still himself would describe the development of his imagery in a dramatic allegory that begins in the density of doubt and concludes in a glorious open landscape: "It was as a journey that one must make, walking straight and alone. No respite or shortcuts were permitted. And one's will had to hold against every challenge of triumph, or failure, or the praise of *Vanity Fair*. Until one had crossed the darkened and wasted valleys and come at last into clear air and could stand on a high and limitless plain."[29] Even de Kooning, whose attachment to the figure was perhaps

the most powerful of all the Abstract Expressionists, gradually dismantled his *Women* into abstract, light-filled panoramas.

Guston, on the other hand, was repopulating his painterly fields with new forms, gradually moving toward greater containment, compression, and density. His titles began to imply meaning inherent in his colors and forms. *For M*, 1955 (plate 38), an homage to his strawberry-blond-haired wife, Musa, is distinguished by strong bursts of orange and red that flower out of a pinkish-white field. Orange and red are colors that the artist would later identify with himself and his wife, and that would play an important role in such later figurative paintings as *Wharf*, 1976 and *Source*, 1976 (plates 100 and 98).

The familial gesture of *For M* notwithstanding, words such as *disturbing*, *conflict*, *anxious*, and *vexing* have been used to describe these works of the mid- to late 1950s, which do not contain recognizable forms, but also do not seem completely abstract. In 1956, Leo Steinberg could see a kind of surrogate figure and its attendant soul in Guston's abstractions, writing that they were "slowed and hauled up from unspeakable depths of privacy. . . . It is as if the hollow of man's body—scarred and stained with sin and hunger, pain and nicotine—were flattened like an unrolled cylinder and clothes-pinned to the sky."[30]

Steinberg's intense description reaches into the intriguing ambiguities between meaning and form in Guston's imagery. On a visit to the Albright Art Gallery in 1957, with Kline, Motherwell, and Rothko, Guston provoked a dinner discussion about the danger of

Philip Guston, Jimmy Ernst, Seymour H. Knox, Franz Kline, Robert Motherwell, and Mark Rothko at the Albright Art Gallery (now the Albright-Knox Art Gallery) in 1957

31 Seymour H. Knox in conversation with the author, September 27, 1987. Guston visited the Albright Art Gallery on the occasion of an exhibition of recent acquisitions that included his work and that of Kline, Motherwell, and Rothko, among others. Knox often asked visitors to the Gallery what their favorite painting in the Gallery's collection was, and why. In a later interview, Knox said that during a dinner discussion Guston compared Gorky's *The Liver is the Cock's Comb* with a 15th-century Italian panel painting in the Gallery's collection. Known as the *Cassone Panel*, it depicts a battle in the right foreground. For a more detailed account of a possible interpretation of *The Liver*, see Auping, *Arshile Gorky: The Breakthrough Years* (Fort Worth: Modern Art Museum of Fort Worth in association with Rizzoli International Publications, 1995).

32 Knox in conversation with the author, September 27, 1987.

33 Conversation with the author, May 20, 1986.

putting pictorial form into strict categories of realism or abstraction by proclaiming that Chaim Soutine's *Carcass of Beef*, 1925 was the most abstract painting in the Museum's collection, while Arshile Gorky's *The Liver is the Cock's Comb*, 1945 projected the "realism" of a 15th-century Italian battle painting.[31] Guston marveled at Soutine's plasticity and the extreme malleability of his figures. Soutine's images of beef carcasses, constructed of dripping red, blue, and whitish-yellow brushstrokes, are a classic example of the way the artist pushed at the edges of form and structure; through the process of painting, a literal image becomes an "abstraction." Gorky's *The Liver is the Cock's Comb*, on the other hand, which seems decidedly abstract, was for Guston a highly charged narrative. Guston is remembered as saying, "You always feel that a very specific action, often a figurative action, is taking place, even if you don't know the specifics of the figure or the action."[32]

In an article on the work of Piero della Francesca, Guston would ask the fundamental question "Where can everything be located and in what condition can everything exist?" This question, which he asked throughout his career and perhaps most earnestly during his years as an abstract painter, was answered by the history of painting, which Guston continually referred to. His inspiration would range from

Watteau's *Embarkation for the Island of Cythera*, 1717, which resulted in Guston's *Voyage*, 1956 and *Cythera*, 1957; to Léger's *The City*, 1919, which inspired Guston's *Painter's City*, 1956–57. In reacting to his appreciation of such paintings by making homages to them, he was looking for equivalencies—in these cases, to the theatrical color and delicate brushwork of Watteau and Léger's ability to anchor the space of a picture with bold interlocking forms.

For Guston, the picture plane was a cryptic theater of potential enigmatic scenes. *To Fellini*, 1958 (plate 46) is an example of a dense and shadowy drama in which twisting forms push their way from edge to edge. Like its companion, *Fable I*, 1956–57 (plate 42), *To Fellini* is an intense battle of growing and competing shapes. Feldman once remarked about Guston, "This was a guy who would have you look at an abstract painting and ask you if you could feel Uccello in it, and usually you could."[33] *Fable I* and *To Fellini* could be such paintings, abstract echoes of one of his favorite images, Uccello's *Battle of San Romano*, c. 1455, in which horsemen with lances crisscross, creating a dynamic yet silent and static drama.

Guston was an avid filmgoer in the 1950s. After spending eight to ten hours painting, he would often retreat to a movie theater, where he would unwind watching images move across the screen. Federico

34 Sidney Tillim, "Philip Guston's Restlessness," *Arts* (February 1960): 51.

35 John Canaday, "Two American Painters," *The New York Times* (January 3, 1960): B18.

36 Quoted in *Philip Guston* (San Francisco and New York: San Francisco Museum of Modern Art in association with George Braziller, 1980): 40.

Fellini was one of his favorite directors, whose use of itinerant performers and symbolic props found a parallel in Guston's earlier figurative paintings. More fundamentally, Guston appreciated the textures and unexpected forms that often found their way into Fellini's films. Fellini came of age as a filmmaker in reaction to the neorealist style of filmmaking, in which society was accurately observed and morally judged. In these films, meaning or content was arrived at prior to the construction of an image. For Fellini, however, the image always came first, carrying with it or implying a number of possible meanings. His screen was always filled with mysterious conflicts and startling passages. Although abstract, *To Fellini* is also packed with compressed and discordant dramas. In titling an image in homage to Fellini, who engaged modern society's psychological fragility, Guston was tacitly acknowledging his growing conviction that "subjectivity," so much discussed in relation to Abstract Expressionism, does not exist in a vacuum. It is a result of engaging the world at large and the strange, conflicting images it presents.

By the late 1950s and early 1960s, Guston's imagery was stretching beyond certain categorical boundaries of Abstract Expressionism, and the effect was unsettling for those trying to keep those boundaries intact, or at the very least trying to decide what those boundaries should be. In a review of Guston's 1960 exhibition at Sidney Janis Gallery, Sidney Tillim wrote, "The restlessness which has infected Guston's style in two previous exhibitions was even more painfully evident here because in attempting to expand within a scheme that logically called for greater anonymity on the part of the artist, he has lost the motivation for painting abstractly at all." The critic also questioned Guston's "effort to graft symbolic meaning upon a style which can't face its formal commitment and can't reject it either." He concluded by saying that the exhibition "reveals his [Guston's] need to communicate, and intensifies the conflict between the need to progress and the negational aspect of having to keep his image abstract."[34] In his Sunday review in *The New York Times* of the same exhibition, John Canaday, puzzled by Guston's increasingly cantankerous abstractions, wrote that, in the end, "his [Guston's] problem is the problem of abstract expressionism in general—where next, if this is the ultimate?"[35]

The problem was Abstract Expressionism, not Guston. Images and titles that challenged the abstract nature of Abstract Expressionism continued to emerge in Guston's search to locate a "recognition." Speaking about the phenomenon of recognizing a semiabstract image that is not planned, but simply emerges in the process of adjusting various shapes, Guston said, "It is an ironic encounter and more of a mirror than a picture."[36] *Mirror to S. K.*, 1960 (plate 49) presents a dark, headlike form staring out of a turbulent field of shapes and colors, all competing for attention on the picture plane. "S. K." refers to the philosopher Søren Kierkegaard, who addressed the mirror the way a painter confronts first the possibility of conjuring an image and then the challenge of discovering its identity. Guston's appreciation of Kierkegaard involved

37 Søren Kierkegaard, *The Sickness unto Death: A Christian Psychological Exposition for Edification and Awakening*, by Anti-Climacus, ed. by Søren Kierkegaard, 1849, trans. by Alastair Hannay, 1989 (London and New York: Penguin Books, 1989): 66–67.

38 Newman quoted in *Abstract Expressionism: Creators and Critics*, 127.

39 Philip Guston, "Faith, Hope, and Impossibility," *Art News Annual* XXXI, 1966 (October 1965): 103.

40 Ibid.

41 Quoted in Sam Hunter, *Philip Guston: Recent Paintings and Drawings* (New York: The Jewish Museum, 1966).

42 William Berkson, "Philip Guston: A New Emphasis," *Arts Magazine* (February 1966): 17.

43 Ashton, 127.

the search for the elusive recognition of self. As Kierkegaard put it, "Even to see oneself in a mirror one must recognize oneself, for unless one does that, one does not see oneself, only a human being. But the mirror of possibility is no ordinary mirror; it must be used with the utmost caution."[37]

In addressing the essential source of Abstract Expressionist imagery, Barnett Newman had declared, "We are making it out of ourselves."[38] The actuality of this self swelled up gradually and powerfully in Guston's imagery of the late 1950s and 1960s. A small gouache entitled *Actor*, 1958 suggests a darkly evolving apparition that soon becomes *The Painter*, 1959 (plate 48), which is the abstract equivalent of an early figurative work, *If This Be Not I* (plate 13), completed in 1945, just prior to *Porch No. 2* and his transition to abstraction. The titles *The Painter* and *If This Be Not I* both suggest the artist's need not just to depict or invent an image, but to identify himself within it.

With *The Painter*, Guston was in exceedingly impure territory, and it is clear from his comments that he knew this and in fact fed on the ambiguities he was engaging. On the one hand, it is relatively easy to see the scaffolding of a hooded figure, arm raised and brush in hand, working on a half-formed, crescentlike image—not only an echo of his figurative images of the 1940s, but a foreshadowing of the studio self-portraits that would emerge in the late sixties. On the other, it is tempting to avoid such a reading and see these seemingly discursive forms and gestures as a beguiling complex of shapes and marks. Apparently, Guston did both, suggesting that he had reached a

critical point where abstraction and representation meet. "A thing is recognized only as it comes into existence," Guston argued. "To will a new form is inacceptable, because will builds distortion. Desire, too, is incomplete and arbitrary."[39]

Titles such as *Close-Up*, 1959 and *Looking*, 1964 suggest an artist scrutinizing the abstract field in search of that recognition, anxious to engage what he called "the weight of the familiar."[40] The "contest" that Guston spoke of was now in full development, and he was testing the purity of abstraction from many directions. Guston believed in the open-ended nature of abstraction, because a recognizable image "excludes too much. I want my work to include more," the artist intoned. "I am therefore driven to scrape out the recognition, to efface it, to erase it. I am nowhere until I have reduced it to semi-recognition."[41] Yet he was equally fascinated by the seemingly innate impulse to create recognizable forms. In an attempt to describe the strange shapes emerging in his paintings and to articulate the ambiguous law embodied in these tenebrous entities, Guston said, finally, "Doubt itself . . . becomes a form."[42]

Throughout much of the 1960s, Guston would explore the implications of *The Painter*. In an almost cinematic evolution, more and more identifiable forms and the artist's relationship to them would be revealed. At the time, Guston spoke of "'the last mask' and of how close he was to tearing it away."[43] For much of the decade, he would produce a strange and moody body of work that would constitute his last abstractions. These predominantly gray and black

44 Rosenblum, "The Abstract Sublime," and Alloway, "The American Sublime."

45 Immanuel Kant, *The Critique of Judgement*, trans. by J. C. Meredith (London: Oxford University Press, 1952).

46 Quoted in K. E. Lokke, "The Role of Sublimity in the Development of Modernist Aesthetics," *Journal of Aesthetics and Art Criticism* (Summer 1982): 426.

47 Frank Stella, from a lecture delivered at the Pratt Institute, 1960. In *Frank Stella: The Black Paintings* (Baltimore: Baltimore Museum of Art, 1976): 78.

paintings, or "dark paintings," as they are often referred to, remain some of the artist's most intriguing and critically unexplored groups of works. It is tempting to compare them to Rothko's late dark paintings of 1969, which suggest we are peering over the edge of an empty horizon. These late Rothkos offer a rare moment of melancholic purity and a classic illustration of the void or Edmund Burke's concept of the sublime, and man's fear of having to come to terms with limitlessness. Evocations of this eighteenth-century aesthetic and philosophical concept have figured prominently in considerations of Abstract Expressionist painting[44] and the work of certain painters—Newman, Rothko, and Still, in particular—have especially been singled out as evoking Burke's concept and those of later writers who have helped form the fundamental characteristics of Burke's ideas. For Kant, who acknowledges his indebtedness to Burke in *The Critique of Judgement*, the sublime evokes the idea of boundless and infinite space, whereas beauty is associated with form and limitation.[45] Coleridge sees this preoccupation with space as distinctly modern: "The Greeks idolized the finite, and therefore were the masters of all grace, elegance, proportion, fancy, dignity, majesty—of whatever, in short, is capable of being definitely conceived by defined forms or thoughts. The moderns revere the infinite, and affect the indefinite as a vehicle of the infinite; hence their passions, their obscure hopes and fears, their wanderings through the unknown, their grander moral feelings, their more august conception of man as man, their future

rather than their past—in a word, their sublimity."[46]

Guston would have to side with the Greeks. Hence, his dark paintings evoke a different feeling and trajectory than Rothko's. In Guston's late abstractions, the stage is initially cleared, but then, in a Genesis-like sequence, the artist introduces atmosphere, light, and finally form: clumps of dark brushstrokes threaded together and resonating with potential recognition. These last abstractions recapitulate everything his abstract work had been about—the intuitive creation of structures and forms that activate meaning or presence in the pictorial field.

The drawings of this period also reflect his insistent search for form and a new reductive mode of finding it. The line is radically reduced and thickened. Each stroke carries with it an incredible weight and density. Two thick lines, one vertical and one horizontal, come together to suggest the edge of a table (*Edge*, 1967, plate 58), while three lines, one short horizontal held up by two meandering verticals, looks like a dog's leg (*Form*, 1967, plate 59). Conversely, a single vertical mark is boldly only itself (*Mark*, 1967, plate 61). These are drawings that operate at the very edge of description, a place where the abstract and the world meet, where the purity of the mark and the impure nature of recognition begin.

In these last abstractions, it is as if Guston was beginning all over again. Stella was compelled to ask, "Why did Guston leave the canvas bare at the edges?"[47] Perhaps because the artist needed to witness clearly the image rising out of the most fundamental conditions: willful marks on a canvas stretched over

Guston in his Woodstock studio, 1964

48 William Carlos Williams, "A Sort of a Song," in *Selected Poems of William Carlos Williams* (New York: Book-of-the-Month Club, 1991): 108.

49 Related by David McKee to the author.

50 Guston in a talk at Brandeis University, Waltham, Massachusetts, 1966.

wooden sticks. Yet he portrays this conjuring form in a magical fashion. The initial painted ground of grays, pinks, and blues is smoky, but eventually condenses to darker, solid forms. These paintings are not about sublime infiniteness; rather, they suggest the poet William Carlos Williams's statement "no ideas but in things."[48]

The period of Guston's abstractions in the late 1960s is similar to that crucial moment between *Porch No. 2* and *The Tormentors* in the late 1940s, except in reverse. As he had gradually deconstructed the representational image, without leaving the emotional underpinnings that had always been the source of his structures, he was now reconstructing it, identifying various shapes as *Head* and eventually *Portrait*. Could these images of dark, congealed brushstrokes against a flickering gray field be the silhouette of the solitary Guston in the ambient light of a dark movie theater?

Guston described the three headlike shapes in *The Three*, 1964 as a family (himself, his wife, and his daughter),[49] but similar kidneylike shapes could morph into other recognizable forms, such as the sole of a shoe, perhaps a punning reminder that the "soul" of any image is multivalent.

Guston's abstractions tended to refute narrow, modernist distinctions between abstraction and representation. Speaking to students in 1966, he said, "I'm puzzled all the time about what you're asking about. About representation and not. . . . I mean the literal image and the *not* non-objective. . . . I don't know what non-objective art is. There is no such thing as non-objective art. Everything has an object. Everything has a figure. The question is, what kind?"[50] De Kooning, who always seemed to understand and appreciate the many changes in Guston's paintings, understood the ironies of abstraction early on. When

51 De Kooning quoted in Thomas B. Hess, *De Kooning Recent Paintings* (New York: M. Knoedler & Co., 1967): 40.
52 Gorky died in 1948, Pollock in 1956, and Kline in 1962.
53 Sam Hunter, in a question to Guston at a talk at Brandeis University, 1966, wondered whether Abstract Expressionism was dead.

confronted with Greenberg's claim that by the late twentieth century it was impossible for a successful artist to paint a face, de Kooning announced, "That's right, and it's impossible not to."[51]

During the late 1950s and early 1960s, Guston's abstractions played a point/counterpoint role within Abstract Expressionism, at an uncertain time for that movement's future. Guston's generation, which throughout the previous decade had been the voice of American art, was now sharing the critical spotlight with a younger generation that would soon make up the Pop and Minimalist movements. Gorky, Pollock, and Kline had died,[52] and de Kooning was spending much of his time out of the city, working in relative isolation. There was talk that Abstract Expressionism itself was "dead."[53]

Guston and Pollock had literally grown up together as artists, and throughout their careers they were like the mythic tortoise and hare. Guston was the early talent, an accomplished draftsman and keen observer of structural composition, while Pollock struggled in his early years to find his way around the pictorial stage. Once Pollock found it, however, Guston witnessed his friend's meteoric entry into abstraction. De Kooning had boldly declared that it was Pollock who had "broken the ice" in regard to Abstract Expressionism. Guston worked his way through abstraction the way Cézanne worked his way through still life and landscape, one stroke at a time, coming to grips with structures and images that dirtied the water of pure abstraction. But those impurities are what the following generations would use in recreating the movement in their own vision. They had less need for purity than for the doubt that Guston cultivated. If Pollock pioneered the way into Abstract Expressionism, it was Guston who was most suited to lead the way out.

Michael Auping

A Maker of Worlds: The Later Paintings of Philip Guston

In 1970, after devoting the previous twenty years of his life to the creation of an impressive body of complicated, introverted, and often extremely beautiful abstract paintings, Philip Guston suddenly reinvented himself as a figurative artist. Unveiling his new work at the Marlborough Gallery in New York, the painter simultaneously unveiled a new world. He was fifty-seven years old and would spend the remaining ten years of his life charting its territory. "Old men ought to be explorers," T. S. Eliot had written in *Four Quartets*. Guston acted on the advice.

It is a strange and intriguing place, this late-created domain of a painter's fertile imagination: a dusty hinterland from which rises a city, as pink as a prawn, peopled by unsavory types doing all sorts of odd and unpredictable things. Wearing the ghoulish cowls of the Ku Klux Klan, white hoods with oblong slits for eyeholes, they cruise the city's streets, presumably on the lookout for victims. Cartoonish figures in a world that looks itself as though it might have been drawn by a child, they are armed with rudimentary planks of wood from which rusty nails protrude at harmful angles. They smoke fat cigars and drive cars with almost square wheels, reminiscent of the model favored by Fred and Wilma Flintstone. They are implicitly malevolent but also more than slightly pathetic. They bluster but seem ultimately no more threatening than plumped pillows, which they faintly resemble.

In such ways is their sinister aspect tempered with absurdity. They are representatives of man's inhumanity to man, but there is more (and less) to them than that. They do not engage in thuggery alone. They also play the part of creative individuals. One of them sits slumped in his chair, head crooked in his hand as if going through the motions of agonized, solitary inspiration. Another paints a picture. Another ponders it and hazards a critical remark. For Guston to work in this clunky, demotic style, after years of carrying the banner for serious, tasteful abstraction, was in itself an act of iconoclastic heresy. But in enlisting painters and people who write about painting into his cartoon goon squad, he may have meant to sharpen one of the messages behind his iconoclasm (as well as forestalling the criticism, the accusations of betrayal, that he suspected would come his way; getting his retaliation in first, so to speak). It was his way of reminding his audience that artists and critics can be members of the thought police too, sometimes without even knowing it.

The paintings with which Guston announced the onset of his late style are by turns funny and angry works of art, fueled by satiric wit and an intense dissatisfaction. The artist was dissatisfied with himself, for having reached what seemed like a terminal impasse in his work. But he was equally dissatisfied with his own generation of American

1 Quoted in Musa Mayer, *Night Studio: A Memoir of Philip Guston* (London: Thames & Hudson, 1991): 170.

2 Hilton Kramer, "A Mandarin Pretending to be a Stumblebum," *The New York Times* (October 25, 1970): B27.

Guston talking with Willem de Kooning at the opening of Guston's Marlborough exhibition, 1970

artists, art theorists, and critics—the generation responsible for, *inter alia*, the invention of Abstract Expressionism, Color Field painting, and the formalist aesthetics of Clement Greenberg—for having allowed what had once seemed a liberating faith in the expressive capacities of abstract art to petrify into dogma. Having become profoundly disenchanted with the idea that all serious painting was, by definition, abstract painting, Guston set out to demolish it. The fact that he had himself, for so long, been one of America's leading abstract painters seemed only to increase the relish and vigor with which he swung the wrecker's ball.

Guston was an eloquent speaker and a fluent writer who left ample, vivid testimony of the intentions that lay behind his startling late volte-face. "American Abstract art is a lie, a sham, a cover-up for a poverty of spirit," he scribbled angrily in his notebook at around the time of the 1970 exhibition. "A mask to mask the fear of revealing oneself. A lie to cover up how bad one can be. Unwilling to show this badness, this rawness. It is laughable, this lie. Anything but this! What a sham! Abstract art hides it, hides the lie, a *fake*! Don't!

Let it show! It is an escape from the true feelings we have, from the 'raw,' primitive feelings about the world—and us in it."[1]

It has become part of an established Guston mythology that his late pictures fell, initially at least, on stony ground. The critics universally hated the show at the Marlborough Gallery, it is usually said, while Guston's own contemporaries, including some of his most longstanding supporters, found his new style and subject matter puerile and offensive. The reality, however, was more complicated. The exhibition did receive one true stinker of a review, a dismissive piece by Hilton Kramer, published in *The New York Times* under the headline "A Mandarin Pretending to be a Stumblebum."[2] It certainly shocked or at least disconcerted many of those who were unprepared for the spectacle of a painter apparently jettisoning his entire oeuvre, so late in the day, to strike off into such peculiar terrain (Guston's daughter Musa Mayer, who attended the opening of the show and recalled the event in her touching memoir of her father, *Night Studio*, remembers a general atmosphere of awkwardness and relates that more than one visitor

3 Mayer, 157.

4 Ibid.

5 Harold Rosenberg, "Liberation from Detachment," *The New Yorker* (November 7, 1970): 136–41.

6 Ibid., 136.

7 Ibid., 141.

confessed to finding the work "embarrassing"[3]). But it was warmly received by at least one of Guston's fellow painters, Willem de Kooning, who saw the new pictures as a celebration of "freedom."[4] And it received a long, thoughtful, and overwhelmingly favorable review from one of the most sensitive and cant-free American art critics of the day, Harold Rosenberg, published in the pages of *The New Yorker*.[5]

Bad publicity is more readily remembered than good. But the fact remains that Guston's new pictures and the apparent U-turn they represented were instantly recognized in certain quarters as significant works of art, works that set out to redraw the map of American art, and to furnish not only Guston's own painting, but American painting itself, with a new sense of direction. In Rosenberg's review of the first Klansmen paintings, published in November 1970, the writer observed that "the 'scandal' of the Marlborough exhibition is not that this leading Abstract Expressionist has introduced narration and social comment but that he has done his utmost to make problems of painting seem secondary."[6]

Rosenberg understood the nature of the discontent that lay at the heart of Guston's pictures, and he admired the bravery and élan with which the artist had sought to break free from the straitjacket of formalized abstraction—a mode that, by the end of the 1960s, was in danger of subsiding into little more than a series of exercises in emptily self-referential pictorial gesture. The critic concluded his piece with these remarks:

The separation of art from social realities threatens the survival of painting as a serious activity. Painting has, of course, other interests than politics, but a too long immersion in itself has infected art with ennui. Painting needs to purge itself of all systems that place so-called interests of art above the interests of the artist's mind. Abstract Expressionism liberated painting from the social-consciousness dogma of the thirties; it is time now to liberate it from the ban on social consciousness. Guston has demonstrated that the apparent opposition between quality in painting and political statement is primarily a matter of doctrinaire aesthetics. He has managed to make social comment seem natural for the visual language of postwar painting. . . . Guston is the first to have risked a fully developed career on the possibility of engaging his art in the political reality. His current exhibition may have given the cue to the art of the nineteen-seventies.[7]

Rosenberg's intuitions were subsequently confirmed by several of Guston's remarks about the sources of his own dissatisfaction. The slowly unfolding catastrophe of the Vietnam War and the scenes of violence at the Democratic Convention in Chicago in 1968 had left him with an uncomfortable and, eventually, intolerable sense of the irrelevance of his own activities. While the world unraveled about him, there he was (or so he felt) in the ivory tower of his studio, painting abstract pictures, locked up within an idiom that he increasingly found incapable of expressing his true

Figure 9
From the Phlebitis Series, 1975
Ink on paper
24 × 19 inches (61 × 48.3 cm)
Private Collection

8 Mayer, 171.

9 See Debra Bricker Balken, *Philip Guston's Poor Richard* (Chicago: The University of Chicago Press, 2001).

feelings about life, and about the times in which he lived: "When the 1960s came along I was feeling split, schizophrenic. The war, what was happening in America, the brutality of the world. What kind of a man am I, sitting at home, reading magazines, going into a frustrated fury about everything—and then going into my studio *to adjust a red to a blue*. I thought there must be some way I could do something about it. I knew ahead of me a road was laying. A very crude, inchoate road. I wanted to be complete again, as I was when I was a kid. . . . I wanted to be whole between what I thought and what I felt."[8]

Guston was not to achieve the wholeness that he was looking for by addressing the ills of his time head-on. He had painted large didactic pictures during his formative years, long before he turned to abstraction. These included a vast and enthusiastically left-wing mural done during his trip to Mexico in 1934 on the subject of *The Struggle Against Terror*, as well as numerous frescoes created under the auspices of the WPA in America in the later thirties and early forties, on patriotic themes such as *Work the American Way* and *Maintaining America's Skills*. A return to the

fervent but thin pieties of such juvenilia, more than thirty years on, held little interest for him. He had acquired a distrust of overtly political art, realizing that it carried the threat of just another form of emptiness to substitute for the emptiness of "adjusting a red to a blue."

Guston gave vent to his suppressed political dissatisfactions by drawing numerous, barbed caricatures throughout the sixties and early seventies, a body of work that culminated in a brilliantly scabrous series of eighty drawings recounting the distinctly unheroic life and times of Richard Nixon (figure 9). Begun in 1971 but published only posthumously, under the collective title *Poor Richard*, Guston's drawings presciently caricatured the man soon to be known as the most famously corrupt president in modern American memory by transforming him into a weak, self-serving monster.[9] Like Gillray's Napoleon and Cruikshank's pear-shaped King George IV, Guston's Nixon is a man whose corruption has burst the confines of the mind and written itself all over his face and body. He has testicles for cheeks and a distended but limp phallus for a nose.

10 Mayer, 153.
11 See Dore Ashton, *A Critical Study of Philip Guston* (Berkeley, Los Angeles, and Oxford: University of California Press, 1990): 132; first published as *Yes, But . . . : A Critical Study of Philip Guston* (New York: Viking Press, 1976).

Interestingly, he and his henchmen frequently resort to wearing Ku Klux Klansmen's masks, in a futile attempt to hide their deformity. This suggests a point of contact between Guston's political caricatures and the paintings that marked the start of his adventurous old age. But the painter was careful to maintain a *cordon sanitaire* between his work as a caricaturist, which he appears to have regarded as a sideline, and the art for which he wished to be remembered.

There is an exception to this in the form of a picture painted in 1975 and entitled *San Clemente* (plate 95). Here the Nixon figure of the *Poor Richard* drawings is allowed by Guston to strut and fret upon the stage of a full-blown oil painting. A furtive, self-pitying grotesque in a frock-coat (a detail of costume ironically suggestive of his unfittedness for the Abe Lincoln role), teardrop trickling down one of his hairy, testicular cheeks, this luridly reimagined and none too presidential President is seen pathetically marooned on the beach of the so-called "summer White House" at San Clemente. He drags an enormously distended left leg behind him. Nixon suffered in real life from a circulatory disease that caused his limbs to swell, but in Guston's picture the illness symbolizes a more than merely personal malaise. Phlebitically distended, exploding with pustules, and crisscrossed with veins, elephantine foot bursting from an inadequate gray suspendered sock, this inflamed and evilly enlarged member stands for the diseased body politic of America as a whole.

San Clemente is the only picture of its kind, which suggests that Guston harbored doubts about it. It was more explicit than, in general, he liked to be. "I got sick and tired of all that purity!" he railed, during the years following his apostasy from abstraction. "I wanted to tell stories!"[10] But the question of just what those stories are about is, in the case of most of Guston's later pictures, open to question. He liked to quote the poet Paul Valéry's dictum that "a bad poem is one that disappears into meaning."[11] Enigmatic works of art, as he well knew, tend to be rather more durable than those which readily succumb to definitive explanation.

In the Klansmen paintings that inaugurated his rebirth as a figurative painter, there is often a sense of horror underlying the pervasive absurdity of Guston's puzzling narratives—a sense of atrocities being carried out as a form of routine, which is heightened by the repetition of scene, character, and action. The Klansmen, who play their political role in Guston's paintings not as stand-ins for the real Ku Klux Klan but as generalized mythical figures, emblems of human blindness, dishonesty, and malevolence, drive around with bodies spilling out of the boot of their car. They stand accused by lurid pointing hands, in rooms where the bodies spill, this time, from heaped trash cans. They loiter in interiors that might be interrogation chambers, under bare light bulbs, whiling away the time. There is perhaps an affinity between Guston's repetitiousness and that of the cartoons and funny papers he used to study as a child. Memories of the eternal sagas played out by Ignatz the mouse and Krazy Kat, in George Herriman's eponymous comic strip of the twenties and thirties, lurk behind the

12 Ibid., 177.
13 Mayer, 170.

structure of Guston's own parallel world. But the comedy, in Guston's case, is often dark; and it seems to get darker as the later work unfolds.

If his work resembles a cartoon, he seems to imply, that is because the same mistakes and the same atrocities are repeated throughout history with cartoon-like predictability. As sure as Tom will chase Jerry, man will kill man and genocide will be succeeded by holocaust. The laughable predictability of this process is one of the principal subjects of the late pictures. Guston's own bitter laughter is touched by disgust and a pathos that reveals itself most truly in the lines and surfaces of his paintings, which thoroughly belie their initial appearance of artlessness. The Klansmen disappear soon enough from the late work, having outlived their usefulness. But the accumulations of limbs remain, and they are often composed with surprising tenderness and delicacy. Arms and legs, or just boots and shoes, are stacked in recriminatory piles in the gradually darkening wasteland that becomes Guston's favored milieu. It often seems as if the painter has not merely arranged these forms, but laid them to rest. Touch and brushstroke are equally important (the pictures are not mere illustrations; the shapes within them are far from merely filled in). These mute, pathetic objects —still lifes composed from dead lives, so to speak— are painted with a weight of feeling, a gravity and a solemnity of touch, that lends them monumentality and softly implies an act of commemoration. *Monument*, aptly, was the title Guston chose for one of his several variations on this theme.

In a particularly black mood, he once wrote to his biographer Dore Ashton, "Our whole lives (since I can remember) are made up of the most extreme cruelties of holocausts. We are the witnesses of the hell. When I think of the victims, it is unbearable. To paint, to write, to teach in the most dedicated sincere way is the most intimate affirmation of creative life we possess in these despairing years."[12] *Pyramid and Shoe*, a painting from 1977 (plate 114), seems to encapsulate this brooding mixture of despair and resistance. The spectacle of a discarded human shoe next to a mighty pyramid is apt to recall Henry Fuseli's well-known and often reproduced eighteenth-century drawing *The Artist in Despair over the Magnitude of Antique Fragments*, c. 1778–80. But the implication of Guston's work is rather different. Fuseli's theme is awe in the face of the grandiose achievements of the past, while Guston's painting suggests a more truculent attitude toward antiquity. The shoe in his painting evokes Van Gogh's battered workboots. Against a symbol of power and the inhumanity that so often goes with it, he sets a counter-symbol of art, and life: an "intimate affirmation of creative life" and of ordinary humanity.

The characteristic obliqueness of Guston's later painting does not only stem from his aversion to crude didacticism. It is also a measure of the extent of his ambition. One of his principal aims was to find a way of reinserting himself back into history, to stop murmuring the "soothing lullaby" (his phrase[13]) of so-called "pure" painting, and to recover for himself a way of expressing what he felt about the subjects that seemed important to him. But the precise

Guston in Rome, 1960

14 Norbert Lynton, "An Obverse Decorum," in *Philip Guston: Paintings 1969–1980* (London: Whitechapel Art Gallery, 1982).

15 Mayer, 141.

relationship between Guston's late paintings and history is anything but straightforward. With delicacy, morbidity, irony, and absurdity they address political history, transmuting its atrocities into the forms of a strange and enigmatic mythical world. They also address his personal history, both as a man and a painter; and they contain within them, too, both Guston's attempt to reassess the history of art in his time and his struggle to find his own place in it.

In another time, Guston might have been reported to the Un-American Activities Committee, so sustained was his assault on postwar American painting (or at any rate the jewel in its crown, the work of the New York School). As the critic Norbert Lynton observed, in an essay written to mark the exhibition of Guston's late paintings at the Whitechapel Art Gallery in London in 1982, "All around him he saw colleagues locked in the idiom they had chosen in the name of freedom. . . . I see Guston's late paintings as monuments against Rothko, Still, and Newman, or at any rate against the easy piety and ready greed that they engender—sublime ripostes to their much vaunted sublimity."[14] Guston's attacks on the artists whom Lynton singles out sometimes seem aggressively specific. A painting of 1969, *Edge of Town* (plate 73), has a pair of Klansmen cruising along against a vertically divided abstract ground of blue

and white somewhat reminiscent of the bipartite structure of Barnett Newman's "zip" paintings; while the composition of numerous later paintings seems to mimic the horizontal divisions of Rothko's "abstract sublime." He parodies such pictorial formats, only to inhabit them with his own seething fancies. It is as if Rothko's abstract mode has been demeaned, made the mere backdrop for an increasingly wild theatre: a stage set for the tuber-like Cyclopean head that takes center stage in so much of the late work; for the heaped tangles of skinny legs; for the clashing trash-can lids (like shields in a battle scene by Paolo Uccello) wielded by sinewy, livid, disembodied arms and hands.

"There is something ridiculous and miserly in the myth we inherit from abstract art—that painting is autonomous, pure and for itself, and therefore we habitually defined its ingredients and define its limits. But painting is 'impure.' It is the adjustment of impurities which forces painting's continuity. We are image-makers and image-ridden."[15] Guston's sense of his own transgression in returning to the painting of images was sharpened by an awareness that in doing so he was not merely going against the grain of his generation, but playing with ancient and occult forces. There was a primitivist imperative to his change in style and approach. He was attempting to rediscover for himself the role of the painter as it had been before

Figure 10
Giorgio de Chirico
The Soothsayer's Recompense, 1913
Oil on canvas
53 3/8 × 70 7/8 inches
(135.6 × 180 cm)
Philadelphia Museum of Art
The Louise and Walter
Arensberg Collection

16 Ibid., 65.

art theory, art critics, and art galleries had redefined, intellectualized, and emasculated it. Long before images had been proscribed within the charmed circle of American formalist aesthetics, they had been outlawed—and for more compelling reasons—by religion, their dangerous magic recognized in the Second Commandment issued to Moses by the jealous God of the Old Testament: "Thou shalt not make unto thyself any graven image." Guston, whose Jewishness can only have sharpened his sense of his own temerity, wanted to make of himself a shaman and a conjuror. He spoke frequently, with relish, of creating "golems," in his later years. He wanted to be a maker of worlds, not merely an established practitioner of a certain type of late twentieth-century painting with an intellectually respectable label attached to it.

Morton Feldman once rather mean-spiritedly speculated that the true catalyst for Guston's late change of approach was the painter's realization that he had not been accepted into the canon of indisputably major American abstract painters. He had been long associated with Abstract Expressionism but ultimately excluded from the charmed circle of its principal practitioners. "The book was out," as Feldman put it, "and he wasn't included."[16] But it was Guston's audacity to suggest that "the book" of New York School painting was in fact just a footnote or excursus—a marginal text eccentrically fixated, in its later paragraphs, on such ideas as the notion that the essence of painting lay in "the assertion of the picture

plane," and other formalist shibboleths. The real book, as far as Guston was concerned, was that of world art.

In this sense, his late pictures—however "American" their style, subjects, and settings may be— amount to an attempt on Guston's part to step outside the history of American painting and onto a wider stage. It is hard to think of an American artist to whose work Guston's later pictures can usefully be compared. By contrast, the number of Western European painters on whose example he drew, and by whose art he was sustained, seems almost countless. In his late work, Guston gave himself the freedom to subsume his own considerable expressive and gestural gifts within a figurative idiom: an art of representation, and images. In doing so he was, as he himself explicitly remarked, reconnecting himself to the European tradition of art. His career runs counter to the All-American pattern of the artist-as-pioneer, someone whose destiny it is to shed the baggage of history, escape the onerous past, and emerge into the radiance of a New Vision. Guston went back to the past at the end of his life, picking up as much left luggage as he could.

Giorgio de Chirico, with whom Guston had been fascinated since his twenties, furnished him with usefully irrational principles of composition and juxtaposition, and set a compelling example of how to create a parallel world remote from and yet capable of commenting on the real one. The lonely arcaded piazzas of de Chirico's early work in particular conjure

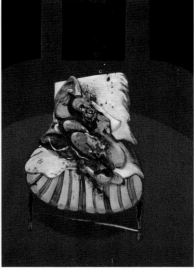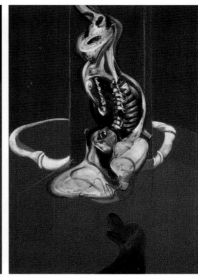

Figure 11
Francis Bacon
Three Studies for a Crucifixion,
March 1962
Oil with sand on canvas
Three panels,
each 78 × 57 inches
(198.2 × 144.8 cm)
Solomon R. Guggenheim
Museum, New York
64.1700.a–c

17 David Sylvester, *Interviews with Francis Bacon* (London: Thames & Hudson, 1980): 14.

18 Mayer, 142.

19 Guston's encounter with the Sicilian puppet tradition is recounted in Ashton, 171.

up a sense of melancholy that plainly moved and inspired the older Guston (see figure 10). The free, myth-making (and often unashamedly crude) spirit of Picasso lurks behind Guston's later pictures. So too does that of Francis Bacon. Like Bacon, Guston at the end of his life set out to describe the atrocities of his century without descending to the literal. He shares Bacon's manic wild hilarity and morbid disgust, and pervasive sense of the absurd. Bacon was a disenchanted mythological painter, an artist for whom transcendence was an impossibility, and who revisited the art of the past to confirm his own inability to believe in its sublime spiritual certainties. Painting his own version of Cimabue's famous *Crucifixion* (figure 11) he inverted the image, remarking that he wanted his Christ to seem to crawl down the cross "like a worm"[17]—a phrase that calls to mind Guston's own, later remark, that he felt as though he had metamorphosed "from something in flight into some kind of grub."[18] Like Bacon, Guston worried at the religious iconography of the past and found himself unable to invest it with much in the way of spiritual uplift. His *Ladder*, 1978 (plate 117) alludes perhaps to Jacob's ladder but leads nowhere, stranding a disembodied pair of spaghetti-like legs in mid-air. *Pit*, 1976 (plate 99) recalls many a Renaissance scene of the harrowing of hell (as well as, perhaps, the burial pits of genocide). A television set poised above Guston's abyss broadcasts the image of a red rain falling into a red sea. Flames scorch the land. Down in

the pit below bodies cluster, eyed anxiously by the disembodied head that is the painter's alter ego. Christ is nowhere to be seen.

Guston was also influenced by traditions of popular art in the West, going back to the Renaissance and beyond. In the Middle Ages, visual art had always been regarded as the most "vulgar" (in the sense of popular) art, because it could communicate so readily with people, regardless of their language, even reaching those who could not read or write. Guston's vulgarity is animated by a similar motive. He wanted to create pictures that would speak as vividly as possible to as many people as possible, and that no one would require a doctorate in art theory to appreciate. It seems interesting that in the last decade of his life, on a trip to Sicily, he became fascinated by the persistence there of an ancient puppet-show tradition, in which all kinds of grotesque or amusing brightly painted figures were used to animate stories from folk literature, or the legends of the Italian poets Ariosto and Tasso.[19] Guston's own late work has something of the raucous puppet theatre about it.

The painter's deepest and most frequently acknowledged debt was to the Old Masters of the Western European painting tradition—and at the heart of his love for their work, ultimately, lay his appreciation of the way in which it showed how image and the expressive capacities of paint could be so fruitfully combined. "In the old painting I love, early Renaissance painting," he remarked, "the 'information'

20 Mayer, 152.
21 Ibid., 62.
22 Letter to Dore Ashton, August 25, 1974, Archives of American Art, Smithsonian Institution. Quoted in Mayer, 12.

is fast, no? But the 'painting' is slow, dwelt upon."[20] Goya, Titian, and Rembrandt were also plainly important to him. Guston recognized or remembered—and those artists helped him to do so— that the painting of an image was by no means incompatible with the communication of feeling through paint itself. He realized, at the end, that there always had been scope for "abstract" painting within the figurative tradition. The fear of death could be put into the darkness and depth of a shadow (Goya had shown him this with especial force). Guston's own later paintings contain a good deal of "abstract" painting themselves: fields of glimmering black or red that are like rage given sensual form; marks that dance with exuberance or trail off into nothingness, dragged or scumbled, like visible premonitions of death.

In fact, the chasm between Guston's abstract paintings and his later work was never as wide as has sometimes been assumed. This cuts both ways. In creating even his most resolutely non-objective paintings, the works of the 1950s, produced from layer upon layer of brushstrokes and subtle erasures, he had always been reluctant to abandon the scale of the easel painting, with its implications of an image to be discerned. This may be one reason why the label "Abstract Impressionist"—with its interesting implication that his work had always represented some kind of hybrid between an "American" and a "European" sensibility—briefly affixed itself to Guston. Unlike his contemporary Jackson Pollock, for example, whose gestural paintings aspired to the condition of an all-encompassing field, intended to overwhelm the

viewer, to make from painting a sublime visual environment, Guston created abstractions that remained in this respect resolutely picture-like. His tendency to pile the paint into the middle of his abstract canvases seems similarly to speak of a certain iconic impulse. The exquisite record of an arduous process is *framed*, isolated, held up for inspection. Some of them can be seen as pictures, so to speak, of the artist's own mental anxiety; others, as he explained them, as equivalents for "the forces of nature . . . sky and earth, the inert and the moving, weights and gravities, the wind through the trees, resistances and flow."[21] But the viewer is always invited to stand before them, to look *into* them, as if they were pictures. In the scale and choreography, so to speak, of his work, Guston had always been "an image-maker, and image-ridden." So in this sense his work of the 1970s could be seen not as a turning away from his former self but as a form of belated self-recognition.

That Guston himself saw the process in something like these terms is clear from various writings. "Oh, it is all so *circular*, isn't it?" he wrote to Dore Ashton in the mid-1970s. "The recent work makes me free to use whatever formal and plastic imagery and capabilities I may possess. I mean from my own past too—all the memories."[22] Guston had encapsulated the sense of blockage and frustration he felt just before embarking on his late works in a painting entitled, simply, *Wall*, 1970. Cartoon bricks cover the canvas, edge to edge, in a bitter parody of "all-over" painting. The image of the cul-de-sac into which he felt he had painted

23 Mayer, 173.

himself, it is a grim dead end of an image, the emblem of a walled-up sensibility. Six years later he revisited the motif in a work entitled *The Painter*, 1976 (plate 103). This time the wall only occupies the bottom half of the painting. Peeping over the top of it, dark sky behind him, we find the artist himself, trademark cigarette in hand: Guston's way of painting his sense that he had finally allowed himself—all of himself— into his own art.

The soul of Guston's later work is, as he remarked, "impurity." Just as the motives that lie behind its creation are mixed, so too are the meanings that can be attributed to its iconography. His masked Klansmen-painters could be Guston's enemies and opponents—the image of the painter he is determined not to become—or they could be his image of the painter that he feels himself to be, in his more self-hating moods. The ubiquitous tangle of legs could stand for the victims of war but also has a potential personal meaning for the painter, whose much loved brother Nat had died of gangrene many years before, after having his legs crushed in an automobile accident. Guston's attachment to piles of junk may conceal melancholy memories of his Russian émigré father, a reluctant junkman who had hung himself from shame and disappointment—and had been discovered by Guston himself as a boy, aged ten. Guston's wife, Musa, is present too in the late work, rendered, perhaps in a pun on her name, as an oceanic muse, in the form of an anthropomorphized sun setting (or rising?) over a vast blue sea.

"There is nothing to do now but paint my life," the artist wrote in a note dated 1972. "My dreams, surroundings, predicament, desperation, Musa—love, need. Keep destroying any attempt to paint pictures, or think about art. If someone bursts out laughing in front of my painting, that is exactly what I want and expect."[23] Following his own advice, Guston painted the things that surrounded him: his brushes, the irons he used to smooth out the wrinkles in his canvases, his books. He also painted himself, ceaselessly, in the form of that huge, potato-shaped disembodied head with its great staring expressive eye, which looks like a painter's equivalent to the writer Samuel Beckett's disembodied talking mouth in *Not I* but could also be a sly backward reference to Cézanne's famous remark about Monet: "He was only an eye, but my God what an eye!" The bruised Cyclops head confronts loneliness; bends over the bottle of his drink addiction, eye to eye with his own weakness; smokes while eating a plate of thick-cut potato fries, lying in bed while his incorrigibly strange art—in the form of a painting within a painting—takes shape behind him.

As the late work unfolds, in all its raucous, battered majesty, it creates the strong impression that there was really nothing that Guston, at the last, was not prepared to try and incorporate in his work. He had finally found a way of depicting his thoughts, dreams, and aspirations, his anger, his morbidity, and his love. Late, but not too late, he had achieved the wholeness that he sought. He had found a way to create paintings that leapt the boundary of "painting," and entered life.

Andrew Graham-Dixon

Figure 12
Detail from George Herriman's
Krazy Kat, September 10, 1922

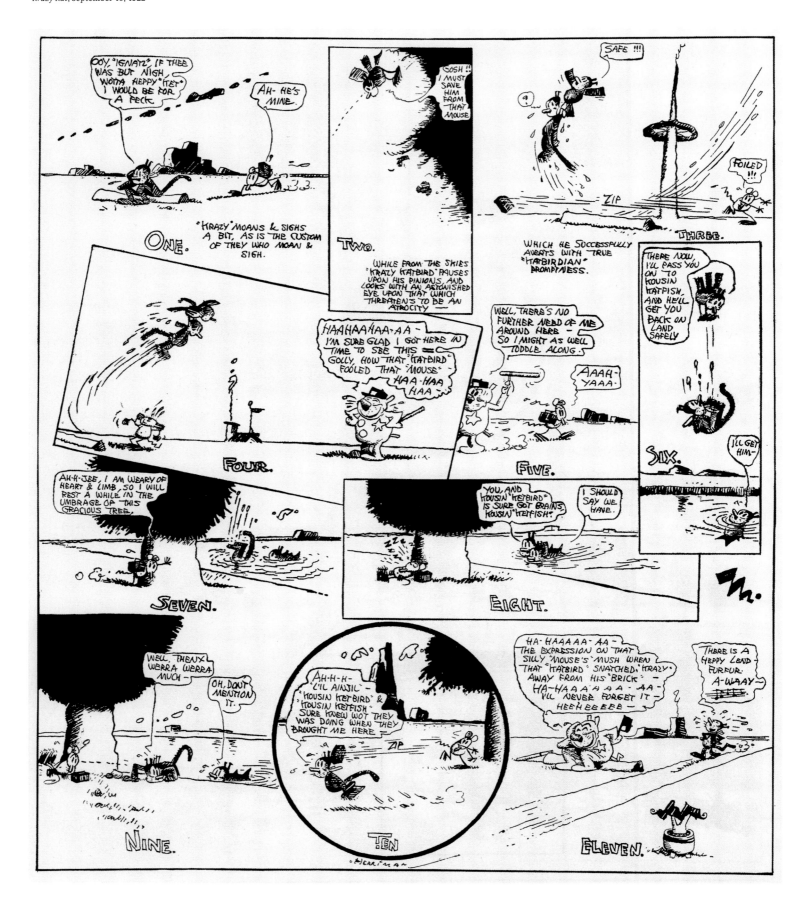

Pyramid and Shoe: Philip Guston and the Funnies

Sometimes when my painting is getting too artistic, I'll say to myself, "What if the shoe salesman asked you to paint a shoe on his window?" Suddenly everything lightens. I feel not so responsible and paint directly what the thing is, including the necessary distortions.[1]

PHILIP GUSTON

1 Quoted in Mark Stevens, "A Talk with Philip Guston," *The New Republic* (March 15, 1980): 28.

2 Stuart Davis, *Stuart Davis*, American Artists Group Monograph Number 6 (New York: American Artists Group, 1945): unpaginated.

Philip Guston belonged to the generation of American painters who made large-scale abstraction the dominant mid-20th-century fine-arts genre. By no small coincidence, Guston and his contemporaries were also the first to grow up with movies, widespread advertising, and comics—"the funnies," as young readers in the early 1900s began calling them— as prime cultural facts. Such relatively new urban phenomena were more formative, if only because more plainly visible, than other types of visual art. Pictorial culture, for artists of Guston's age and circumstances, existed primarily in commercial graphics: on the street, art meant ads, magazine illustration and single-frame cartoons, and more pervasively, comic strips, as they appeared in daily newspapers. Fine art, the art of the museums, if anyone knew about it, was remote— as was fine-arts training, especially in methods not guaranteed to be stultifying—while stylish, dazzlingly reproduced commercial images were everywhere. It's likely that most American artists born between 1900 and 1950 began (and, as often as not, ended) their formal art educations with correspondence courses in cartooning or other methods of popular illustration. The import of the young Willem de Kooning's schooling in applied art at the Rotterdam Academy is well-documented, while Guston's, Franz Kline's, and David Smith's early starts as teenage cartoonists are usually treated as biographical oddments of little consequence.

More should be said for the relation of graphic art, and design generally, to the domain of serious American painting. Stuart Davis, whom Guston knew during their days on the WPA, achieved his first fame as an illustrator for *The Masses*. In the 1890s, when Davis was born, his cartoonist father was art editor of the Philadelphia *Press* with a staff that included John Sloan, George Luks, William Glackens, and Everett Shinn. Sloan and Luks went on to join the likes of George Grosz and Bill Steig as contributors to the Los Angeles–based *Americana*, a journal that Guston saw regularly during its run in the early 1930s. And so it went. What Stuart Davis called "broad generalization of form," his way of bringing out the basics of an image in abrupt scale and definition, was normal for comics and crucial for Davis's ultramodern type of abstract painting.[2] Neighbors during the thirties in New York, Willem de Kooning and Rudy Burckhardt gleefully showed one another the *Krazy Kat* installments they clipped from the daily papers (see figure 12). (Burckhardt mounted his in scrapbooks, which still exist.) It's said that Kline preferred the *Daily News* to the *Times* because the *News* had a comics page. Guston recalled that whenever his mentors among the Mexican muralists, David Alfaro Siqueiros and José Clemente Orozco, came north of the border, they immediately sought out the latest in Hollywood-produced animated cartoons. As Magdalena Dabrowski has pointed out, the preternaturally outsized chains and feet Orozco used in the 1930s as symbols of political oppression anticipate similar details in late Guston. When Larry Rivers writes of the "dipsy-doodle energy" in de Kooning "that kept pestering you long after looking" and of an Arshile Gorky as "a Romantic animated cartoon with the

3 Larry Rivers, "A Discussion of the Work of Larry Rivers," *Art News* (March 1961): 54.

4 Guston in *Philip Guston: A Life Lived, 1913–1980* (New York, Michael Blackwood Productions, 1980). Color film, 58 minutes.

5 Quoted in Jan Butterfield, "Philip Guston—A Very Anxious Fix," *Images and Issues* (Summer 1980): 31.

6 Frank O'Hara, *Standing Still and Walking in New York* (San Francisco: Grey Fox Press, 1975): 110.

7 Coulton Waugh, *The Comics* (New York: Luna Press, 1947): 32.

8 Ron Padgett, "Mad Scientist," in Jena Osman and Juliana Spahr, eds., *Chain* #8 (Summer 2001).

digestive tract as the still-life he painted from," he is indicating facets of cultural bedrock.[3] The grand, expansive force lines in Action Painting may be said to have burst from finely wrought Cubist daubs, but locally they read as enlargements of a set of speed zips behind A. Mutt's brogues or some later application of the same graphic shorthand.

Style, said Guston, is "all circular."[4] Artistic style circulates among an artist's intentions, his varied needs, and his abilities at different times. (Guston, one might say, became a great cartoonist, incidentally, in his late style.) The route to an authentic style is rarely, if ever, direct. Nor is there a high road, free of commercial constraint. "High" and "low" persist as fuzzy terms for gauging aesthetic hierarchy; over time they come out in the wash, like lint. Guston spoke of guarding his art against becoming too artlike, and presumably George Herriman, about whose comics Guston liked to hold forth at length, had to monitor closely any inclination he had to take his highbrow admirers too literally. Herriman is but one of several instances of a patently serious artist who enjoyed great popular appeal. On the other hand, only the most canonically insular of modern artists would deny being, as Guston put it, "a student of all art," whether pictorial or graphic, demotic or pure.[5] "After all, only Whitman and Crane, of the American poets, are better than the movies," remarks Frank O'Hara, allowing that those who have no need of poetry might sensibly find gratification in another major form.[6] In other words, beyond matters of need or taste (which probably amount to the same thing), there is no

legitimizing one above the other. In the early 1990s, when I described to Bill Blackbeard, director of the San Francisco Academy of Comic Art, the guidelines of a show I was in the process of curating on Herriman and the extent of his crosscutting influence, he said, "Oh, you're including those display artists"—artists, he meant, who, unlike those who make work for reproduction in the print media, normally show theirs on the walls of commercial galleries. The distinction, even if delivered with a dash of rancor by one who prefers images designed for print, is of a useful, practicable kind.

See you in the funny papers.

Valediction, Anonymous, 20th-century U.S.

Their [Mutt and Jeff's] heads are both "doodles," simple forms happily arrived at without any worry about anatomy, although each character has a separate "doodle" of his own. Fisher's "doodle" for feet, however, extends to all his characters. It is one of the funniest points about his technique; these feet, so unreal, are curiously human. Mr. A. Mutt is a mean man, just what his name implies; but his feet save him for us. They are ironic, and—a supreme quality in cartooning—touching, pathetic.[7]

Coulton Waugh, *The Comics*

because anything cartoon is immortal in its own funny little way.[8]

Ron Padgett, "Mad Scientist"

Wall hung with Guston's small panels painted in 1968–70

9 For "cartoon-like," see Robert Storr, *Philip Guston* (New York: Abbeville Press, 1986): 49; Paul Brach, "Looking at Guston," *Art in America* (November 1980): 96. For "cartoon-type figures," see Debra Bricker Balken, *Philip Guston's Poor Richard* (Chicago: The University of Chicago Press, 2001): 95.

10 Musa Mayer, *Night Studio: A Memoir of Philip Guston* (New York: Alfred A. Knopf, 1988): 12.

Comic-strip panels are miniature sites for simplified—ergo readily apprehensible—images, usually humorous or fantastic or both. In the efficient hands of a genius like George Herriman, the comic strip's modest, economical, quick-read form takes on a riveting frame-by-frame intensity and an unanticipated staying power ("immortal," as Padgett's apt line of verse would have it) overall, in its momentum. In the Guston literature, formulas such as "cartoon-like" and "cartoon-type figures" persist somewhat abashedly as ways of generalizing about the recognizable, at once funny and appalling imagery his canvases began blurting forth at the end of the sixties.[9] Guston's complex images were worked up on large sheets of drawing paper and considerably larger canvases. His "miniatures" are the roughly foot-wide Masonite panels, snapshot renderings of single objects—an easel, clock, cup, head, shoe, brick, or book—or of compound objects: a couple of cigar-smoking miscreants in a 1930s-vintage automobile with the top down, like a wind-up toy.

As a boy, we learn, Guston "always had a pencil in his hand." For his thirteenth birthday, after a year of particularly intense drawing (his father had committed suicide a year or two before), his mother enrolled him in a correspondence course from the Cleveland School of Cartooning, which he quit after three lessons.[10] His interest in cross-hatching exercises may have slackened, but he continued to hone his skills well enough to win a cartooning contest in the Los Angeles *Times* a couple of years later. During the 1950s Guston called those skills, in the meantime taken up some notches, into service when he performed a series of caricatures of his artist friends; the portrait heads, by turns rambunctious and exquisite, show John Cage stretched and lumpy like a fibrillating golf bag (figure 13); Harold Rosenberg barricaded behind thatches of facial hair; Frank O'Hara adrift in reverie, a Duccio angel; a workaday de Kooning in his cap; Landes Lewitin envisioned as a distraught yam.

In 1929 Guston and his friend Jackson Pollock got themselves expelled from Manual Arts High School partly for drawings lampooning the English department and the administration's prioritizing of athletic pursuits over academics. At loose ends, however, after a few disappointing months at Otis Art Institute, Guston dismissed a relative's suggestion that he find work either in advertising or the Disney Studios. He was intent on becoming a serious artist. During the remainder of the thirties and well into the 1940s the beaux-arts leanings of his early maturity favored wispy, carefully shaded contours, in the subtle flowings of which his childhood taste for the

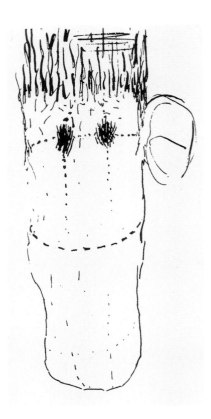

11 Statement in John I. H. Baur,
Nature in Abstraction
(New York: Whitney Museum
of American Art, 1958): 69.
12 Letter to the author, March 2,
1969.
13 Elizabeth Murray in Michael
Kimmelman, "The 20th Century
in Art: Just How American Was
It?" *The New York Times* (April 18,
1999): 37.

vernacular was selectively repressed. Guston exploited this soft drawing style to the greatest advantage in portraying women's hair, especially the long tresses of his wife, the poet Musa McKim, which reappear in more tensile guises in pictures of the late seventies such as *Source*, 1976 (plate 98) and *Tears*, 1977. The one surviving instance of Guston as an illustrator is the set of drawings he did for O. Henry's short story "The Gift of the Magi"—the "gift," of course, being a watch the heroine buys as a Christmas present for her husband with money gotten by cutting off her knee-length hair and selling it.

Among his Abstract Expressionist peers, Guston was acknowledged as being possessed of the most refined touch. In the 1950s the typical Guston brushstroke—a smooth, amply ridged index finger's length and width of fat pink, black, or green pigment—was seized upon as an adaptable stylistic device by younger artists as distinct from one another as Joan Mitchell and Jasper Johns. By 1968, when his late manner took off, Guston had his touch, his palette, forms, and a flexible enough space to accommodate the tangible, sometimes brutal things he felt it necessary to depict. Retrieving his feeling for comics at an advanced stage of accomplishment, Guston wasn't quoting or taking a secondary genre as subject matter; he was releasing, and in strictly

painterly terms enlarging upon, a way of realizing images that had long before been made second nature. As early as 1958, Guston had complained that "the loss of faith in the known image and symbol for our time" was "a loss from which we suffer," thereby acknowledging the default factor in abstract art's run for freedom.[11] "I choose to veil the image," said Jackson Pollock. Like Pollock, Guston was ill at ease with abstraction as an operative principle. Rather than veiled, Guston's imagery was at first scraped away, then caked over until the accumulated layers pronounced themselves as the nameable substances they had perhaps stood for all along. The surrogate world of such forms as accrued had to be recognizable yet rendered in other than perceptual (i.e. "realist") terms. "I cannot make a dot or line which doesn't represent a known thing," Guston said.[12]

To call the products of Guston's late manner "sad, nutty songs," as Elizabeth Murray has done, is to imply deeper links to the doings in Herriman's cosmos, for one, than mere looks would let on.[13] For Guston, comparisons of his new pictures to the funnies registered as shuttling edgily between embarrassing and irrelevant, if not entirely odious. "I don't see much relationship between my images and cartoons," he told me, but at once went on to specify the relevant coordinates as he remembered them:

Of course since youth I've loved *Mutt and Jeff*—
Bud Fisher was the best draftsman—*The Gumps*—
Polly and Her Pals, Cliff Sterrett did the best
furniture. Also Frank King's *Gasoline Alley*—

Figure 14
Detail from Bud Fisher's
Mutt and Jeff, March 6, 1918

14 Letter to the author, August 16,
   1970.
15 Waugh, 32.

the backyards, porches, screen doors, litter on
the steps, dogs, old cars being fixed, dismantled.
Of course I've loved that color—I used to dream
of having my own strip one day.[14]

Guston's birth coincided with the transformation of
American comics into the classic phase represented by
most of the artists he lists, and then some. (It's notable
that Herriman, who occupied a special niche in
Guston's pantheon, was omitted from this one-time
roster—perhaps as a way of placing him in a class by
himself, above the rest.) Nineteen thirteen proper saw
Krazy Kat rise to independent-feature status after its
humble beginnings as an add-on strip below
Herriman's first daily venture, *The Dingbats*; it was also
the year that Fontaine Fox's *Toonerville Folks* achieved
syndication and Cliff Sterrett decided on *Polly and Her
Pals* as a replacement name (it was *Positive Polly*, to
begin with) for his cast of walleyed characters and
their "futuristic" surroundings. Over the next twenty
years or more, Herriman, Fox, Sterrett, and their
colleagues built on innovations dating from the 1890s
and after. Some of the old masters of the funnies' long,
frothy first wave were Richard Fenton Outcault,
Rudolph Dirks (whose paintings were in the Armory
Show), Winsor McCay, James Swinnerton, Lyonel
Feininger, the sports cartoonist known as Tad,
Frederick "Happy Hooligan" Opper, and Bud Fisher,
whose *Mutt and Jeff* premiered in 1907 (figure 14). In
1917 Sidney Smith initiated *The Gumps*; Rube Goldberg
began *Boob McNutt* in 1918; and in 1919 came Billy
DeBeck's *Barney Google* and Frank King's *Gasoline Alley*,

the first comic centered on car culture. Along the same
timeline, the movies developed in tandem with the
comic strip, two graphic art forms establishing fateful
cross-pollinating patterns. (Guston's favorite movie
director was Federico Fellini, who had been a
cartoonist in his youth. The titles of late Gustons often
resemble the intertitles of silent films: *Bad Habits*;
Edge of Town; *Painting, Smoking, Eating*.)

How cartoon-like are Guston's images? Dagwood's
Inferno, one thinks. In his history of the comics,
Coulton Waugh writes of "the hard life of Mr. A.
Mutt, the dweller, as of old, in the garbage cans of
America."[15] Not a place of high rhetorical pomp at all,
which is much to the point. The bricks in Guston's
troubled paradise arrive courtesy of Herriman's
Ignatz; the beefy, thick-soled shoes from Fisher,
Sterrett, Disney, and a host of others similarly inclined.
To Disney's Mickey Mouse, too, may be traced the
origins of the recurring, accusatorily pointing,
red-gloved hand. But a drawing by Herriman, Fisher,
or Disney is designed for reproduction, whereas
the gleaming matrix of Guston's paint—its painted
light—is silenced in color plates. Comics are
narratives developed over multiple panels. (A
Herriman strip is comparable in its parts to the
three-minute theme-and-variations recording form
Jelly Roll Morton uniquely mastered in the 1920s.)
For Guston, the luxury of painting was that it could
condense onto a single canvas every element of a
three-act play. Ultimately, of course, it is the fulmi-
nating physicality of Guston's paint that separates
his imagery from more succinctly two-dimensional

Figure 15
Bricks, 1970
Oil on canvas
32$^1/_2$ × 76$^1/_2$ inches
(82.6 × 194.3 cm)
Collection of Alan and Dorothy
Press, Chicago

16 Letter to the author, January 19, 1976.
17 R. Crumb, *The R. Crumb Coffee Table Art Book*, Peter Polanski, ed. (Boston and New York: Little, Brown and Company, 1997): 77.
18 Quoted in "R. Crumb," by Steve Burgess, salon.com (http://archive.salon.com/people/bc/2000/05/02/crumb/index.html), accessed July 26, 2002.
19 Crumb, 109.
20 *Weirdo* Number 7 (San Francisco: Last Gasp Eco Funnies, 1983).

graphic work, and from comics in particular. But Guston also saw how the narrative possibilities in grouping his paintings could be tremendous and fairly limitless. He mused over "the linkage of images, when they are together in a certain way and then how all changes, when in another combination on the wall. . . . I shifted pictures around for days and nights, *reeling* from the diverse possible *meanings*. . . ."[16]

Herriman runs his stylized characters through infinite permutations of the same routine; although vantage point and setting vary, the flying brick connects with Krazy's noggin every time. Herriman's slapstick ménage speaks an idiom of its own devising; Guston's is glaringly speechless. His pantomime forms are snagged one by one between metamorphic shuffles. And his bricks don't fly, they levitate and hover (figure 15). Like everything else in Guston's physics, they stay put for their inglorious moment of form. From painting to painting, there's no continuity as such, no singularity of character repeated the same way twice, no force lines, beads of sweat, or other action-y accoutrements. The provisional versions of figure or thing are many, without template. Things represent "thingness" agitating in separate chunks of uncertain space. Guston endows his figures with the deliberate stubbiness and raggedy elongations common to classic comic-strip characters—traits that keep them close to the ground. But he also exacerbates this essential gravitas (a rumbling presence all its own, multivalent and raucous, like Thelonious Monk chords knuckled out on piano keys while the sustain pedal thumps): we see remnants strewn about the horizon, and men and women plunged up to their eyeballs, clogging cadmium seas.

Cartoons were just these dumb drawings of dumb guys with big shoes. . . . Cartoons were very working class, cheap amusement for the masses, like vaudeville, early movies, pulp magazines, and so on.[17]

R. Crumb

The critic Robert Hughes, who for a time held Guston's work in contempt, called R. Crumb "the Brueghel of the last half of the 20th century."[18] What Crumb calls "the art thing" seems to have become a sore point when he himself became alert to the coexistence of Guston's images with his own.[19] The front and back covers of *Weirdo* Number 7, dated 1983 (figure 16), feature, among other, more typical Crumb creations, rows of shoes (upended, in the Guston mode); a pathetically twisted version of Guston's tragic one-eyed, disembodied, bean-shaped head (to which Crumb has added torso, arms, and legs); and the subtitle "A Fine Art Piece of Business." Next to his signature Crumb wrote, "Yes, I did it . . . "—possibly mimicking Guston's painterly self-reflexive finger-pointing. The comic book includes a single Crumb narrative, "Uncle Bob's Mid-Life Crisis," in which the artist's self-image is seen musing about taking up "a fine art career, oil painting maybe. . . ."[20]

Well before *Weirdo* Number 7 appeared, a rumor was put into circulation that Crumb had been an influence on Guston's late paintings. In fact, both

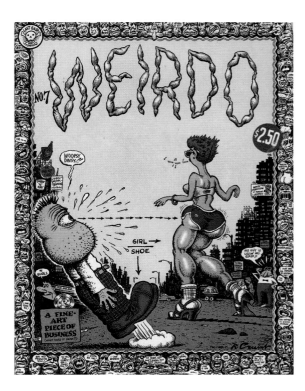

Figure 16
R. Crumb, *Weirdo* No. 7, front
and back covers

21 Coolidge in a letter to Tom Clark,
   June 8th, 1969.
22 Storr, 52.
23 Crumb, 247.
24 Guston in Blackwood, *Philip
   Guston: A Life Lived.*
25 Guston in conversation with the
   author and Clark Coolidge, 1969.

artists had arrived at their distinctive iconographies simultaneously: Guston's outright images of clocks, shoes, and hooded figures began appearing in drawings done in Woodstock during 1967–68; Crumb produced his first unique "comix" in 1967 in San Francisco, but publication was delayed until 1968. In 1969, in the course of a visit to Guston's studio, Clark Coolidge and I were struck at once by resemblances in the new work to some of Crumb's more melancholy creations. Soon after, Coolidge recalled a motif "where shoes are sticking out, sole-forward, with the legs/socks extending back like the guy's body is shoved back through the wall somehow: Looks a lot like Crumb World."[21] Guston, for his part, expressed curiosity—he hadn't heard of Crumb nor indeed had any underground comics crossed his desk. At some point one of us may have shown him a copy of *Zap Comix* or *Head*; if so, the coincidence would have been duly noted. But the affinity of both men separately was with the older, longer lineage of comics artists— from Herriman and Fisher to Disney and Ernie Bushmiller, on down. Then, too, each for his own purposes had come up with a spontaneous graphic manner that functioned, as Robert Storr says apropos Guston, "at a pace commensurate with the rush of images through his mind."[22]

Born in 1943, Crumb grew up in the 1940s and fifties heyday of comic books (the genre had begun in 1933). In his adolescence, he liked the inheritors of the classic mode: Ernie Bushmiller's *Nancy*, John Stanley's *Little Lulu*, Walt Kelly's *Pogo Possum*, *Donald Duck* and other Disney items. While in high school, Crumb discovered the political cartoons of Thomas Nast, taught himself cross-hatching, and found kindred spirits in Basil Wolverton, Harvey Kurtzman, and others associated with *Mad Magazine*. A self-described "wiseas [*sic*] who wanted to use traditional comic book techniques to do shocking things," Crumb writes, "As far as visual art goes, it has to reveal something about reality that you can't really put into words."[23] As Guston would say, "There isn't a blueprint for it."[24] What Crumb and Guston have in common are elements within their separate worlds of forms. The bodies of Crumb's buxom hippie girls triangulate as readily as Guston's "hoods"; in general, both artists share a fascination with the hirsute and knobby.

The "pure" artist takes shelter from anything that would compromise a putatively unalloyed authenticity. During 1967–68, "sick of all that purity," Guston sought to leave the rarefied precincts where his art had flourished and to "tell stories" that somehow engaged with the world he felt to be about him.[25] Crumb considers his comics pure as compared to the "commercial art" employment (greeting-card illustrations, for example) from the clutches of which the commercial success of his comics keeps him free.

26 Quoted in Bill Berkson, "Dialogue with Philip Guston, November 1, 1964," *Art and Literature: An International Review* (Winter 1965): 67.

27 Quoted in Jerry Tallmer, "Creation Is for Beauty Parlors," *New York Post* (April 9, 1977).

28 R. Crumb, Introduction in Gary Groth and Robert Boyd, eds., *The Complete Crumb*, vol. 7 (Seattle: Fantagraphic Books, 1991): viii.

29 Philip Guston, "Faith, Hope, and Impossibility" *Art News Annual* XXXI, 1966 (October 1965): 153.

30 Herman Melville, "Journal Up the Straits 1856–57," in Jay Leyda, ed., *The Portable Herman Melville* (New York: Penguin Books, 1976): 568. This passage was read by Clark Coolidge at the memorial held for Guston at St. Mark's Church in New York in December 1980.

Both Crumb and Guston eschewed formal art training. Their individual careers are marked throughout by a restlessness verging on implacability. Where Guston's fabled doubt self-sublimated into a working principle, Crumb's festers as one more pathological tic. Each artist is an exemplar in his way of the late throes of 20th-century duress, but Crumb is a tormented satirist and Guston an allegorical poet of the Absurd. Crumb's "underground" grotesqueries tend toward the erotic and gross, Guston's toward the bloody and arcane. Crumb's Rapidograph line quivers with vexation; where its paroxysms breed perpetual unrest ("Keep on truckin"), Guston's objects are quasi-static repositories of fear and trembling ("I really just want to nail something down so that it will stay still for a while.").[26] Guston touches upon metaphysics in ways that would never occur to Crumb, although Crumb's Mr. Natural might con us in that direction. As occurs with most satire, the force of Crumb's sixties and seventies drawings by now has tended to dwindle into a period look. Crumb evokes topicality with a zeal Guston approached only in passing, however sincere the fury they shared when it came to current events, which to Guston was "the war, what was happening in America, the brutality of the world."[27] Crumb would later write of 1970 as "the peak, the high-water mark" of his youth-rebellion constituency.[28] Nineteen seventy was also the year of Guston's revelatory Marlborough show; the following year he would produce his personal variant of counterculture burlesque, the mock-sympathetic suite of eighty-some-odd caricatures savaging Richard Nixon and his cabinet, *Poor Richard*.

Human consciousness moves, but it is not a leap: it is one inch. One inch is a small jump, but that jump is everything. You go way out and then you have to come back—to see if you can move that inch.[29]

Philip Guston

They must needs have been terrible inventors, those Egyptian wise men. And one seems to see that as out of the crude forms of the natural earth they evoke by art the transcendent mass & symetry [*sic*] & voids of the pyramid so out of the rude elements of the insignificant thoughts that are in all men, they could rear the transcendent conception of a God. But for no holy purpose was the pyramid founded.[30]

Herman Melville, "Journal Up the Straits 1856–57"

Classic comic-strip figures inhabit reductive anatomies to flesh out their parcels of designated space. Large heads and heavily shod feet bracket abbreviated, if otherwise impressively robust, torsos and legs. Or else the coinage is reversed: the head shrinks to gumdrop proportions; the body swells, elephantine. A third option is an assembly of slender tubes and pegs upon which a few squiggles are hung for facial features and hair.

How many features will suffice to make a face? Guston gave his otherwise blank hoods two black strokes for eye slits. The few embellishments consist of dotted seams of patchwork and contour shading. Shadows in Guston are expressive of objects grounded in unblinking light. Each black stroke takes a slight

31 Robert Storr, *Philip Guston* (New York: Abbeville Press, 1986): 52.

curve upward, like a parenthesis, following the contours of the white hood. Words in (or on) a book are similar marks, but short and straighter. (Under the book is a slab or tablet—you can easily imagine another text hidden there.) The book is entitled *Matter*, 1969. Another drawing, called *Water*, 1967, is twenty-four squiggles, all of them vertical as well, and, although longer, only marginally distinct from the inscriptions in *Matter*. In what Robert Storr calls Guston's "Narrative Action Painting," numbers assume key roles: the parts in a drama often deploy themselves by twos, threes, and fives, their divisions as exact as the coordinates of a ground-plan elevation in a quattrocento panel or the stresses in a line of blank verse.[31] By the numbers, so to speak, is a good way to read Guston.

In the nearly ten-foot-wide *Pyramid and Shoe*, 1977 (plate 114), the "inch" in question is a square patch of proportionally exact, scumbled blue-gray atmosphere as resistant to traversal as the butt-end of a two-by-four. The painting is built of three large elements against a background, a shambles of air and sky that takes up half the picture. On a low, wide stretch of uneven, bloodshot ground, pyramid meets shoe, the latter seemingly having arrived at a slow skid. The ground takes a dip where the monument has settled. Shoe is a triple-decker affair, a grisly, grubby loaf, with two-tiered sole and uppers threaded with a beautifully highlighted shoelace. The scenario would seem to be one of shuddering contingency meeting eternal order—it is neatly Homeric in that way. But is one personage staring down, or are they each of them sizing up, the other? The pyramid, bearing two distinct black marks for eyes, doubles as a bricked-up head. The shoe (despite the nice lace—a rarity in Guston footwear) keeps resembling a set of three raw, standard-Guston-issue scalps in a heap. The effect of this nearly preposterous extravagance is to give solid matter its due, a catastrophic dignity. The urgent, indelible image, in its momentary pause, amounts to a fulsome sight gag of cosmic scale: a panoramic gauge of actuality at its root.

Bill Berkson

My thanks to Steve Anker for his guidance in writing this essay. B. B.

Figure 17
Pantheon, 1973
Oil on panel
45 × 48 inches (114.3 × 121.9 cm)
The Estate of Philip Guston
Courtesy of McKee Gallery,
New York

The Culture of Painting: Guston and History

It's a strange thing to be immersed in the culture of painting and to wish to be the first painter.[1]

PHILIP GUSTON

1 Guston to Harold Rosenberg in "Philip Guston's Object: A Dialogue with Harold Rosenberg," *Philip Guston: Recent Paintings and Drawings* (New York, The Jewish Museum, 1966). Quoted from Henry T. Hopkins, "Selected Works for the Exhibition," *Philip Guston* (New York and San Francisco: George Braziller in association with the San Francisco Museum of Modern Art, 1980): 44.

2 Musa Mayer, *Night Studio: A Memoir of Philip Guston* (Alfred A. Knopf, New York, 1988): 204.

3 "Piero della Francesca: The Impossibility of Painting" *Art News* (May 1965): 38–39.

4 "A Conversation between Philip Guston and Joseph Ablow," reprinted in Kim Sichel and Mary Drach McInnes, *Philip Guston 1975–1980: Private and Public Battles* (Seattle, University of Washington Press, 1994): 35.

There is abundant evidence, from his own words and above all in the works themselves, to assure us of the depth of Philip Guston's immersion in the culture of painting. The famous high school dropout was, perhaps, the most cultivated painter of his generation. His knowledge of past and present art was formidable. The pleasure he took in it was immense and complex, as was the use he made of it through his art and, occasionally but deliciously, in words.

He was constantly using this knowledge to test and define his own position in the artistic food chain, both for the making of his own art in the hugely varied way it played out, but also for his own definition of his place in posterity. This dialogue between the past and present is a (often, the) central issue in Guston scholarship. The problems arise simply from the abundance of artistic references brought into play and how to balance these with the still more powerful internal forces that drove Guston's art.

In a view of his studio painted in 1973 called *Pantheon* there appear the names Masaccio, Piero, Giotto, Tiepolo, and de Chirico (figure 17).[2] This (with the addition of Michelangelo) is completely consistent with those figures who guided him through his first artistic explorations beginning in the late 1920s. As a young student he did drawings (as had Michelangelo before him) after several of Masaccio's heads from the Brancacci Chapel, in this case at the Los Angeles Public Library, not in Florence. The 1930 *Mother and Child*, the earliest painting in this exhibition (plate 2), might take for her origins a sibyl in the Sistine Chapel, while *Bombardment*, 1937–38 (plate 4) would seem, in part,

to be a reference to Michelangelo's Doni tondo in the Uffizi. Guston is later photographed under Giorgio de Chirico's copy of this work while visiting the artist's studio in 1948. Soaring figures in Giambattista Tiepolo's ceiling frescoes may play a role here too, the purpose now turned from exaltation to death.

A critical insight into Guston's concern and absorption with art of the past is his 1965 *Art News* article on Piero della Francesca:

> He is so remote from others masters; without their "completeness" of personality. A different fervor, grave and delicate, moves in the daylight of his pictures. Without familiar passions, he seems like a visitor to the earth, reflecting on distances, gravity, and positions of essential form.[3]

His loyalty to Piero as an artist is absolute. In a 1966 conversation with Joseph Ablow at Boston University he says, "I don't mean to be perverse, but I certainly would rather look at Piero's *Flagellation* painting in Urbino or his *Baptism* picture in the National Gallery than I would at any modern painting. It seems so complete, so total, so balanced/unbalanced. All I can tell you is that I've had a reproduction on my wall of these two paintings for about twenty-five years in the kitchen where you really look at things. I not only never get tired of them, but I see new things all the time."[4] The Denise Hare photographs taken in Woodstock in 1975 that illustrate Dore Ashton's 1976 book proved him true to his word. These two post-cards share the kitchen wall with Dürer's *Melencolia I*,

Gerard Tempest, Philip Guston, and an unidentified man at a reception held at Giorgio de Chirico's apartment near the Spanish Steps, Rome, 1948. De Chirico's copy of Michelangelo's Doni tondo, made in 1920, hangs on the wall behind them.

5 Dore Ashton, *Yes, But . . . : A Critical Study of Philip Guston* (New York, Viking Press, 1976): 21. Michael Taylor, to whom I'm indebted for the studio photograph and several productive discussions, is presently working on Guston's relationship with de Chirico in connection with the exhibition *Giorgio de Chirico and the Myth of Ariadne*, Philadelphia Museum of Art, Autumn 2002.

de Chirico's 1912 *The Anguishing Morning* from Cologne, and a monumental twenties Picasso nude.

These pleasures taken in 15th-century Tuscan painting (adding Uccello and Signorelli to the list early on, which helps explain a painting like the 1938 *The Gladiators*, plate 6), coincide with his youthful encounter with the Mexican muralists. First (in company with his classmate Jackson Pollock) Guston met José Clemente Orozco, who was executing a monumental fresco at Pomona College (1930) in Claremont, California; then in 1934 Guston traveled to Mexico to assist David Alfaro Siqueiros with a still more ambitious mural project in Morelia. To this mix was soon added, through his friendship with the "post-Surrealist" Lorser Feitelson—who brought to Los Angeles his contacts and his appreciation of Italian Metaphysical painting—an enthusiasm for de Chirico (who placed himself firmly in the Italian Renaissance tradition), two paintings by whom he would have seen on his visits to the collection of Louise and Walter Arensberg (see figures 10 and 18).[5]

With Guston's move to New York in the winter of 1935–36 a broader world opened, both in terms of live contacts and contacts with the past. Of particular impact was his visit to Albert E. Gallatin's Museum of Living Art in a study hall at New York University. He saw there Léger's *The City*, 1919 (figure 19) and Picasso's *Three Musicians*, 1921. These two works go far in allowing us entry into his three most ambitious easel paintings of the 1940s: *Martial Memory*, 1941, *If This Be Not I*, 1945, and *Porch No. 2*, 1947, with their complex integration of silhouetted figures into a stage-flat background (plates 7, 13, and 15). This said, the haunting isolation of the figures in a cityscape is more akin to de Chirico, while it's certainly Piero beneath the mute, emotional distance of these works.

During the war Guston left New York for the relative isolation of the Midwest, where his contemplative side—the artist as interested in talk and ideas and criticism and art history as in the making of art, so vividly characterized by Ashton—had more time to be exercised. This was always the case: as a youth he read Lionel Venturi, both on the Renaissance and on Cézanne. At the University of Iowa, Iowa City, from 1941–45, he was on the faculty with Horst Janson (one of many preeminent émigré art historians to come to America from Europe), with whom he was also on the staff at Washington University in St. Louis, where Guston was Artist in Residence from 1945–47. Particularly in those isolated war years in Iowa, it doesn't take much imagination to realize how these two men must have reveled in each

6 H. W. Janson, "Philip Guston,"
Magazine of Art (February 1947):
55.

7 *Philip Guston: Paintings 1969–1980*
(London: Whitechapel Art Gallery,
1982): 55.

8 Michael Auping, "A Disturbance
in the Field," *Philip Guston
Tableaux/Paintings 1947–1979*
(Bonn: Kunstmuseum Bonn in
association with Hatje Cantz,
2000): 29.

Figure 18
Giorgio de Chirico
The Poet and His Muse, c. 1925
Oil and tempera on canvas
35⅞ × 29 inches (91.1 × 73.7 cm)
Philadelphia Museum of Art
The Louise and Walter
Arensberg Collection, 1950

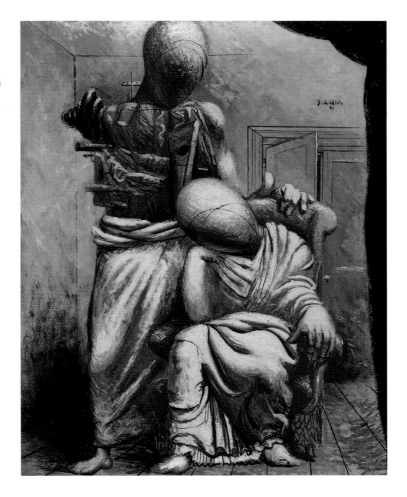

other's company. Ashton reports that Janson put Guston on to Heinrich Wöfflin and, more current, Henri Focillon. The depth of their friendship is recorded in a 1947 article by Janson in which he fervently argues for a new cosmopolitan spirit to lift American art out of its provincial isolation and declares Guston to be the best equipped American painter of his generation to "command an international audience."[6]

In 1948 Guston received a fellowship to the American Academy in Rome and, for the first time, had the chance to see firsthand those works that had so absorbed him since his high school days. The 1948 award stands, in many ways, as a kind of coming-of-age, particularly in the way he uses art from the past to guide and stimulate him. Before then, the references are very much in the spirit of feeding and exploration; thereafter the dialogues seem more between equals. And with this maturity his interest in the past ranged more freely. Trips to Arezzo and

Orvieto, Sienna and Florence, reinforced his love of the Tuscan Renaissance, but he also discovered firsthand Titian and Tintoretto in Venice, Goya and El Greco in Spain, and Poussin in France. Rembrandt, Watteau, Chardin, Manet, and Cézanne drew his attention over the next few years. Essentially the appetite for the past and its regenerative allure keeps pace with the quickening range and velocity of his own artistic output. The explorations never let up, with many new departures. He states in a 1978 lecture at the University of Minnesota: "I think in my studies and broodings about the art of the past my greatest ideal is Chinese painting, especially Sung painting dating from about the 10th or 11th century."[7]

This is reflected in his ink drawings of the 1960s. The year before he died he declared, "I'm finished with Italy; I want to go to Spain and Egypt."[8] Add to this a deep passion and knowledge of the movies (he was a Hollywood extra in his youth, and his profound interest in Fellini goes far to help our understanding

Figure 19
Fernand Léger
The City, 1919
Oil on canvas
91 × 117¹/₂ inches
(231.1 × 298.5 cm)
Philadelphia Museum of Art
A. E. Gallatin Collection

of the later works) as well as literature (particularly Kafka and Beckett, with Philip Roth as a close Woodstock friend) and music (Morton Feldman and John Cage), and one is well within a creative milieu equal to the 19th-century Paris of Delacroix and Manet or, for that matter, the Florence of Alberti.

This cultural density means, of course, that the attempt to second-guess Guston's artistic intentions becomes more difficult over time, even while the dialogue between the past and present persists as one of the best ways to come at the growing enigma of his work.

The painting that declares this new sophistication and ease with the past is *The Tormentors* from 1947–48 (plate 18), done just at the moment when Guston is about to test his friend Janson's faith in him by confronting Europe head on. In its sinister majesty, suggested figures still static in paneled fields of cityscapes, it carries with it all the suggestion of Léger's *The City* and Picasso's *Three Musicians* so

evident in the major paintings done over the previous five years. The persistent hobnails and hooded cloaks arch back to the Los Angeles protest paintings of his youth, but within all this disturbing spirit of admonition and menace, there is also a new quality of almost imperial authority, which signals insights into de Chirico and, most important, Piero, into whose work he'd never plummeted before. The surface, canvas that it is, has all the layered complexity of a plaster wall, deeply marked with the suggestions of sinopie beneath. The nervous white drawing animates the space and gives a completely new energy to the work, quite literally opening it up and back in ways. The effect of this is equal, as different as is the means, to Piero's *Flagellation*. The fluidity of this drawing in paint also establishes a plane from which he can depart, beginning in the early 1950s.

Many of the initial reactions to Guston's first showing of his abstract paintings in 1951 found their voice by reflections on the past. It was just at the

9 See Katsunori Fukaya and Hiroo Yasui et al., *Monet Later Works: Homage to Katia Granoff* (Nagoya, Japan: Entwistle Japan, 2002).

10 For a review of the critical state at the moment see Ashton, chapter VIII, and Auping, 34–35.

11 See *Claude Monet . . . up to Digital Impressionism* (Munich: Prestel, 2002), exhibition organized by the Beyeler Foundation held in Munich and Basel in 2002, which reexamines in depth Monet's legacy and his influence on abstract painting. Pollock, Rothko, and Newman are included; Guston is markedly absent, as he would have had it.

12 William Seitz, introduction to the exhibition catalogue at the Rose Art Museum, Brandeis University, 1966; quoted in Ashton, 103.

13 Martin Wilson, ed., *The Hydrogen Jukebox: The Selected Writings of Peter Schjeldahl, 1978–90* (Berkeley: University of California Press, 1991): 227.

14 It is pleasingly ironic to find that by 1990, in his introduction to the by-then historical show of Guston, *1961–1965*, at the McKee Gallery, Bill Berkson feels it necessary to defend these works, which are in danger of getting lost in the shuffle.

moment when the late work of Claude Monet was being reconsidered, or rather seriously considered for the first time, and it seems inevitable that Monet should be called forth as a precedent for Guston's delicately woven fields of color that gained density and mass near their centers.[9] This latter aspect also suggested the late works, particularly the unfinished paintings and watercolors, of Cézanne to some, also for good reason.[10] "Abstract Impressionism" entered the critical language.[11] However, Guston seems never to have taken much interest in Monet and objected to this comparison. William Seitz, whose exhibition at The Museum of Modern Art did much to declare the legitimacy of Monet's late works, with a particular interest in his connections with abstraction, should perhaps be given the last word when he says in 1966, "It is these pictures which were once said, quite wrongly, to derive from Monet. The illumination and pulsation that radiates through a fog of muted tones is more akin to the mystical light of Rembrandt than to the sunlight of Impressionism."[12] This rings true and underscores the essential feeling of these paintings which, even at their most vaporous and elusive, seem not to refer to any landscape tradition, but rather carry with them (Piero again, perhaps now supported by Mondrian) a quality of theatrical structure— literally interleafed planes of stage drops and translucent curtains. Even the most charged and worked-up canvases maintain a great, formal elevation, like Racine, like Poussin, with or without actual narrative.

These critical thoughts about past sources of

Guston's departure into abstraction were rarely negative, as if the strength of his exploration invited, if didn't actually need, the support of historical comparison, which, in some magical way, held him comfortably within the canon of his generation of abstract painters, just as they were being challenged by another generation.

The first showing in 1970 of his return to figurative painting blew this cover. While they were ominously predicted by the thundercloud abstractions of the mid-1960s, nothing could quite prepare viewers for the new works' level of energy and emotional stridency. In a confessional note written in 1984, Peter Schjeldahl vividly remembers that moment: "When in 1968 Philip Guston abruptly abandoned the most restrained and elegant of all abstract expression painting styles for a mode of raucous figuration, I hated it. It seemed a rank indecency, profanation, a joke in the worst conceivable taste."[13] Hilton Kramer's famous review declared that a Mandarin was pretending to be a stumblebum; a primitive force had triumphed over civilization. Guston had broken the faith of the high art of New York Abstraction, and had leaped from high to low, from (for some) Monet to the Katzenjammer Kids.

The rage and disbelief was almost universal, and these works were slow to find a receptive audience, but as they did, in part the process depended on historical referencing.[14] What is striking about this remarkable (and remarkably varied) production over the last decade of Guston's life is how deeply, and knowingly, steeped they are within his culture of painting.

15 Robert Storr in *Philip Guston: Retrospectiva de Pintura* (Madrid: Centro de Arte Reina Sofia, 1989): 155.

The joy, as grizzly as the subject may sometimes be, of painting flesh tones—delicate pinks against sunburn scarlets—links back to his early abstractions of the sixties and from here to his excitement in discovering Titian. The blunt outlining of figures in black against a light background has its parallels in Tintoretto. And above all, the memory of a nightmare world where Reason sleeps leads back to his own lynching images of the 1930s, and swiftly from there to Goya's *Disasters of War*. Probing further, it is interesting to reflect on how many of these late images sit firmly within the tradition of still life as a genre. Guston spoke fondly of Chardin: the piles of shoes, and legs and heads, are not so foreign, in their intrinsic formality and palpable authority, to a dead rabbit tossed on a stone shelf, just as *Cherries II*, 1976 (plate 106) seems like a wink and a bow to Chardin's more steeply pyramided painting of strawberries in a basket. While Goya's most political and horrible images certainly provide release from, if not actual precedent for, many of the late painting of the seventies, what have been overlooked perhaps, in this reflection on the still life tradition, are those ten still lifes by Goya that he kept for himself all his life (figure 20), which are not unlike Guston's more compressed images, such as *Monument*, 1976, in their deeply muted terror and—and this may be the most telling key—their mordent wit.

To this list could be added the horses' asses of Delacroix or the cadaver still lives of Géricault or the inflated heads of Redon. And is it too corny to recall Van Gogh's worn boot soles in reference to the single image that haunted Guston the most? Finally, the even, high-noon lighting of these works and their very formal balance, no matter how unhinged the subject, take one back to de Chirico, and Poussin and before him, Piero: "A different fervor . . . moves in the daylight of his pictures."

As understandable as the shock of his return to the figure was in the late sixties, the works from the last decade of his life now rest comfortably with those that preceded them. Which is not to rob or diminish the power and novelty of his creations and their wondrous reflection of a titanic sensibility. The enigma of the artist (like his definition of Piero) who wants to stand completely alone while, at the same time, to find his place in history, should never be undercut, at the cost of missing the dynamic of Guston's work. Philip Guston's career, for all of its expansive stylistic and emotional range, is (within the power now of historical hindsight) remarkably consistent and constant, both in terms of his loyalty to himself and the renewing freshness of his relationship to art of the past. This is not a new thought: Rob Storr early on gently reminds us of just this with his apt quote from T. S. Eliot: "In my beginning is my end."[15]—and yet on reflection the dynamics of the stylistic and emotional shifts of fifty years are still absorbing elements in the critical reception of the artist. Why, one now can so comfortably question, was this move from narrative/figurative representation into abstraction and back again so very shocking for a 1960s audience who knew Picasso's career perfectly well? The still-redefining evaluation of a figure of such canonical

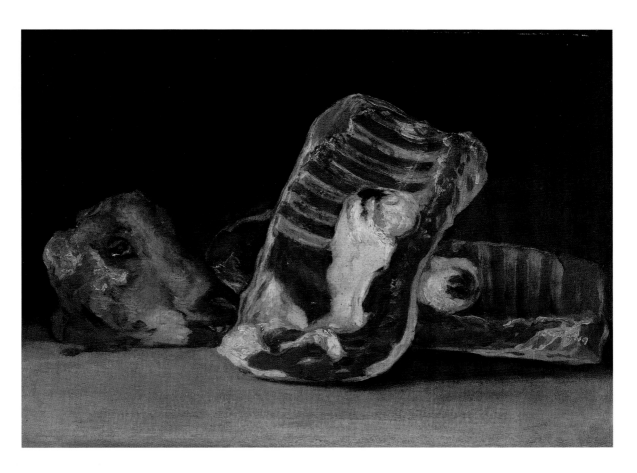

16 Ashton, 6.
17 "On Cave Art, Church Art, Ethnic Art and Art." *Art News* (December 1974): 38.

greatness as Cézanne can perhaps shed some light on this subject. In Cézanne's case (reversing the Guston bell curves) the hard-to-take rough stuff happens early (the edgy and Dionysian, as it were), with the elevated poetical/classic Apollonian to follow and triumph. This early, "adolescent" "coularde" phase of Cézanne's was long isolated as a kind of embarassing preface to his "real" modern career, even as one now understands how completely unified that career was, early to late.

Guston seems to have never relinquished his devotion to the past, even as the work went more deeply into his own psychic and physical world (the cigarettes! the drink!). Dore Ashton's observation in 1963 certainly holds true for the next thirteen years: "Unlike many contemporary artists who create themselves deliberately into the confined space of the present, Guston has kept alive his faculty of memory: 'It thrills me to think of the enormous Past.'"[16] And what we sometimes miss in this often deadly pursuit of historical references and associations is a process that fulfills Harold Rosenberg's prescient caveat, mentioned in his 1974 New York Studio School public conversation with Guston, "Another way of putting it is that modern culture consists of two things: grave robbery and esthetics. Our appetites turn all art into modern art."[17] Unsettling, if apt, in that for Guston, more than nearly any other of that moment, the urge to move back and forth was irresistible, with Piero and de Chirico as his fixed stars.

Joseph Rishel

Figure 21
Talking, 1979
Oil on canvas
68 $^1/_2$ × 78 inches (174 × 198.1 cm)
The Edward R. Broida Collection

Parallel Worlds: Guston as Reader

1 *Philip Guston Talking*. Lecture at the University of Minnesota, 1978, edited by Renee McKee.
2 Ibid.

There is scarcely a painter who has not heard the demeaning French simile *bête comme un peintre*, dumb like a painter, and who has not bridled at the judgment. Guston, who so often reiterated Leonardo's thought, saying "a painting moves in the mind,"[1] spent rich hours engaging his mind both at the easel and in the act of reading. Perhaps he would not have wholly embraced the ancient formula *ut pictura poesis*—as is painting so is poetry—but he firmly believed that the poet and the painter drew from the same sources. He was always after what quickens the mind and emotions, and took it wherever he found it: in daily life, travels, conversations, books. Late in his life he told his audience at the University of Minnesota:

There are people who think that painters should not talk. I know many people who feel that way, but that makes the painter into some kind of painting monkey.[2]

That painting monkey was despised by one of Guston's undeniable precursors, Goya. I have no doubt that Guston, whose knowledge of art history was vast, and who carried about a great cache of images, had taken Goya's meaning in several of his drawings. There is one, for instance, that indicates Goya's scorn for the "naturalist's" approach, which he referred to as "aping." He depicts a monkey-musician, stupidly playing the back of a guitar. Goya's preparatory drawing for the etching *Ni Mas Ni Menos*, 1796–97 is more specific: He portrays a monkey painting a portrait of an ass whose ears support a dandy's wig. Goya's contempt for the servility and collusion of the monkey is given in the caption: *No moriras de hambre*—you will not starve. In the announcement for the *Caprichos*, published in 1799, Goya cautiously put forward his aesthetic:

Painting (like poetry) chooses from the universal what it considers suitable to its own ends: it reunites in a single fantastic personage circumstances and characteristics that nature has divided among many. From such a combination, ingeniously arranged, results the kind of successful imitation for which a good artificer deserves the title of inventor and not that of servile copyist.

And, in his commentary, Goya states more directly his position:

Imagination deserted by reason begets impossible monsters. United with reason, she is the mother of all arts and the source of their wonders.

Goya's reverence for the imagination united with reason inhabits the minds of many intelligent painters. If you read "reason" as the governing power of skill, craft, memory, knowledge, there is no good painter without it. Guston was superbly endowed in that respect. He desired to know, as Aristotle said all

3 William Corbett, *Philip Guston's Late Work: A Memoir* (Cambridge, Mass.: Zoland Books, 1994): 13.

4 Boris Pasternak, *Safe Conduct* (New York: New Directions, 1958): 28.

5 Philip Guston, *It Is* (Spring 1960).

men do. In his quest, he often had recourse to books. His desultory reading habits were known to all his friends who shared their own reading passions with him. His lifelong conversation with writers, living and dead, had great variety, and no doubt each of his friends saw different patterns in his relationship to reading. I eventually came to believe that the very first writers he and I discussed, who were Russians, may have had the most sustained grip on his thoughts. He always came back to them. Two months before his death in 1980, Guston wrote to one of his poet friends, William Corbett, "Could it be that Odessa is not a fantasy at all—in my blood somehow?"[3] Odessa was where his immigrant parents came from; where Isaac Babel, one of Guston's most sustained reading passions, came from; and was the site of many of Babel's most precisely observed, yet fantastic stories.

It is possible that Guston became acquainted with Babel early in his artistic life. By the age of seventeen he had found his way to radical sources such as the *New Masses*, which was advertising Babel's *Red Cavalry Stories* throughout 1930. Since Guston's reading habits were based on two fundamental needs—the need to think about art and its magnetic hold on him, and the need to be seized by images—it is not surprising that he gravitated to the Russians, specialists in both realms. As Gaston Bachelard used to point out, we read that which concerns us.

My first intensive conversation with Guston about reading centered on a book he lent me with great excitement, Boris Pasternak's *Safe Conduct*, published in English in 1958. In this first version of his autobiography (later, in the second version, *I Remember: Sketch for an Autobiography*, published in English in 1959, Pasternak renounced the earlier manuscript as "spoiled by unnecessary mannerisms"), Pasternak offers both speculation on the nature of creating art and scores of eccentric images that patently excited Guston. There was plenty for us to talk about and we did so for more than a year. When I saw one of Guston's most brilliant late paintings, *Talking*, 1979 (figure 21), I thought immediately of that year in the mid-1950s in which Guston and I feasted upon Pasternak's words. An illuminated year. It is impossible to render the tenor of that year, and the "for instance" approach seems less than efficient. Yet, in Pasternak's short book, many of the ideas and feelings described remained close to Guston's heart for the rest of his life. Reading Pasternak again, I could find many passages that directed me to certain of Guston's late works:

> *The poet gives his whole life such a voluntarily steep incline that it is impossible for it to exist in the vertical line of autobiography where we expect to meet it. . . .*[4]

That incline is vivid to me in the disturbing painting *Ravine*, 1979, which, when I first saw it, directed my thoughts to Goya, who so often used inclining low hills for menacing effects.

As for images, there are many that forcibly direct us back to Guston's paintings, always remembering that he himself, as early as 1960, broadcast his fundamental belief that "we are image-makers and image-ridden."[5] This:

6 Pasternak, 22.

7 Ibid., 18.

8 Ibid., 59.

9 Ibid., 60.

10 Ibid., 142.

11 Corbett, 45.

12 Dore Ashton, *Yes, But . . . :
A Critical Study of Philip Guston*
(New York: Viking Press, 1976):
145.

13 Isaac Babel, "Guy de
Maupassant," *Collected Stories*
(New York: Meridian, 1960);
cited in Ashton, 145.

14 Konstantin Paustovsky,
"Reminiscences of Babel,"
Partisan Review 28, nos. 3–4
(1960).

*The smoke of a stump of a cigar, wavy like a tortoise
shell comb, pulled its way from the ashtray to the
light, on reaching which it crawled repletely along it
sideways as though it were a piece of felt.* [6]

Or:

*The music slapped its paw from there upon the
wooden front of the organ. . . .* [7]

How much Pasternak, like Guston, was "image-ridden"
can be felt throughout the book. When he speaks of
art, he says:

*It is concerned not with man but with the image
of man. The image of man, as becomes apparent,
is greater than man.* [8]

And:

In art the man is silent and the image speaks. [9]

Finally, I think that Pasternak's ambivalent feelings,
both strong attraction and considerable repulsion,
toward the ebullient young poet Mayakovsky very
closely match Guston's quivering ambivalence about
so many aspects of modern art and poetry. Pasternak
writes movingly of Mayakovsky's death and recalls the
celebrated line in *The Cloud in Trousers* that so nearly
characterizes Guston himself, particularly in the late
years with their deluge of images:

I feel that my "I" is too small for me. [10]

Reading Pasternak led naturally to reading Rilke,
whom Pasternak had known since childhood and

referred to with reverence. And it rekindled Guston's
interest in Babel. I first talked with him about Babel in
the mid-1950s, and in each decade thereafter other
friends, such as the poets Bill Berkson, Clark Coolidge,
and William Corbett, recalled Guston's devotion to
Babel. The phrases that Guston remembered, as all his
friends attest, were indices of his own attitudes
toward his work. As Corbett wrote, "In Babel Guston
found a soul brother and inspiration." [11] Babel's way of
piling up details, with "the precision of a bank check
or a military communiqué," [12] and his memorable
remark that "no iron can stab the heart with such
force as a period put in just the right place" [13] seemed
addressed to Guston, who, during the 1960s, was
about to cast off all but the most explicit allusions
to the real. Guston had not missed Konstantin
Paustovsky's "Reminiscences of Babel" in the *Partisan
Review*, in which the writer of one of the most genial
memoirs quoted Babel:

*What I do is to get hold of some trifle, some little
anecdote, a piece of market gossip, and turn it
into something I cannot tear myself away from.
It's alive, it plays. It's round like a pebble on
the seashore. . . . Its fusion is so strong that even
lightning can't split it.* [14]

When Guston was quoting Paustovsky to me in the
1960s, I think he was initiating his own revolution
within—revolution in its sense of a radical turning
away, around, and into—and was experiencing a deep
need for "something I cannot tear myself away from."
      Babel, in a way, superseded a writer whom Guston

15 Letter to Bill Berkson,
September 15, 1970; cited by
Debra Bricker Balken in *Philip
Guston's Poor Richard* (Chicago:
The University of Chicago Press,
2001): 94.
16 Pasternak, 73.
17 Ashton, 125.

had read while still in his teens, Nathanael West. We had a conversation about West in the fall of 1960, the year Guston declared himself image-ridden, and I remember that we discussed West's strong identification with the French Surrealists. Later, when I saw, and was shocked by, *Painter's Forms*, 1972 (figure 22), in which Guston painted himself spitting out, or vomiting, shoes, bottles, and butts, I remembered that the epigraph for West's first novel, *The Dream Life of Balso Snell*, 1931, was to have been a quotation from Kurt Schwitters: "Everything the artist spits out is art."

Guston's frequent citations of Babel were matched by his citations of Kafka. Kafka's first English translation was *The Castle*, published like Babel's in 1930. By 1937, when *The Trial* appeared, there was already a Kafka vogue that annoyed Edmund Wilson, who remarked many years later that the literati had built him up as a saint. Kafka, however, was not a saintly but a practical source for Guston, who understood Kafka's stylistic methods better than Wilson. Kafka, like Babel, would become even more charismatic for Guston as he himself embarked on his story-telling phase (that's what he called it, but of course, it was not to be taken literally, for he was a painter first, using what he did not hesitate to call "the language of painting," and was uneasy when so many commentators took him at his word). By the time he admitted identifiable objects into his works, Guston had defined for himself what it was in Kafka that held him and goaded him. It was, as he told me in the mid-1960s, Kafka's ability to create a world

parallel to our own, "parallel, but not this world." By 1970, in a letter to Bill Berkson, he could announce with elation, "I have *never* been so close to what I've painted, not pictures—but a substitute world which comes *from* the world."[15] Guston's process of introjection was spurred by Kafka's process. He was discovering what Pasternak called "the direct speech of feeling," which, as the Russian qualified, is "allegorical and cannot be replaced by anything."[16] Guston's entire oeuvre, in my view, is allegorical, and most especially the works of his last years. If you quite simply take the Greek root, *allos*, other, it is easy to understand that words and strokes of the brush are exactly that—not the thing, but its other. The images of books in the later works were other; were, in fact, what Guston quoted Kafka as saying:

> The books we need are of the kind that act upon us like a misfortune, that make us suffer like the death of someone we loved more than ourselves, that make us feel as if we were on the verge of suicide or lost in a forest remote from all human adaptation. A book should serve as an axe for the frozen sea within us.[17]

William Corbett, who became Guston's friend only during the last eight years, confirms the importance of Kafka's thought, noting that Guston "loved" to quote Kafka when the subject of the books in his paintings came up.

Guston was a desultory reader who, with his gimlet eye, fell upon words here and there that seemed explicitly addressed to him. I don't want to stress too much his dependence on Kafka and Babel, since there

Figure 22
Painter's Forms, 1972
Oil on panel
48 × 60 inches (121.9 × 152.4 cm)
Private Collection

18 Dore Ashton, *Philip Guston* (New York: Grove Press, 1960): 58.

19 Paul Valéry, *Cahiers* VII (Paris: Centre National de la Recherche Scientifique, 1957–61): 855.

20 Wallace Stevens, *The Necessary Angel* (New York: Knopf, 1951): 161.

21 *Letters of Wallace Stevens*, ed. Holly Stevens (New York: Knopf, 1966): 636.

were many other Europeans, Russians, Britons, and Americans he read and re-read. On various occasions I talked with him about Balzac, Flaubert, Sartre, and Camus, whose preoccupation with the absurd rang true to Guston, and whose interest in both Dostoyevsky and Shestov sent Guston back to the Russians yet again. Then there was Samuel Beckett. Guston had probably already discussed Beckett with the writer Robert Phelps during the late 1940s, but was stimulated by his young friend the poet Clark Coolidge, during the late 1960s, to delve into him again. All those talking heads in Guston's drawings after 1970 (usually his own head) can't help but remind us of Beckett, whose monologist's poetry is so like Guston's.

A constant in Guston's long dialogue with writers was Paul Valéry. Valéry was one of my own passions, so it was natural enough for us to discuss specific works from time to time. But undoubtedly Guston had shared his insights drawn from Valéry with other painters, since many painters of the New York School deeply respected him. I think that Guston's mind was trained on Valéry's unremitting thought about the creative act, and was probably stimulated by discussions with his friend Harold Rosenberg, who held Valéry in the highest esteem and was one of the fabulous talkers who kept Guston's mind racing for more than thirty years. While I was preparing my first small book on Guston I remember quoting from Valéry's *L'Idée Fixe* and his enthusiastic response to one thought in particular: "There is mysticism every time we do something other than repeat ourselves."[18]

(In his last years Valéry reiterated in his journals, "I think as an archi-pure rationalist and I feel as a mystic."[19])

Guston had many other literary experiences at various moments in his life. For a time he was engrossed in the poetry and essays of Wallace Stevens, who himself had been influenced by painters. Stevens often referred to "the pressure of reality" and, in his essays gathered and published in 1951, *The Necessary Angel* (another book Guston lent me and said had to be read), Stevens honored painters who experience that pressure. His bow to painters was appreciated by painters, many of whom had flocked to The Museum of Modern Art to hear his 1951 lecture "The Relations Between Poetry and Painting."[20] There they heard him affirm, "Just as poets can be affected by the sayings of painters, so can painters be affected by the sayings of poets and so can both be affected by sayings addressed to neither." Guston's unending, sometimes ferocious dialogues with Harold Rosenberg, another profound admirer of Stevens, were nourished by Stevens, whose views on his own later poems came close to Guston's on his own later works. Stevens, commenting on his poem "An Ordinary Evening in New Haven," wrote:

Here my interest is to get as close as possible to the ordinary, the commonplace, and the ugly as it is possible for a poet to get. It is not a question of grim reality but plain reality. The object is, of course, to purge myself of anything false.[21]

Guston and Philip Roth, 1972

22 Corbett, 102.
23 Ashton, interview with Clark Coolidge, May 1975.

Perhaps, also, Guston rallied to Stevens's more pessimistic thoughts, as when Stevens referred to the mind as a "catastrophic room." For the contents of that catastrophic room, Guston, at the end of his life, turned back to one of his earliest poets, T. S. Eliot, as did one of his intellectual painting companions, Robert Motherwell. The objects that appear in Guston's last works often seem to be the objects that are most starkly stated in *Four Quartets*. William Corbett easily slips into Eliot's world when he describes Guston's last works. He says "their slag heaps could be both a memory of Eliot's wasteland and a prophecy of the ecological hell we are determined to bring upon ourselves."[22] Eliot's intoning "In my beginning is my end" struck a resounding note in Guston, whose own beginning, as was the beginning of almost all American creators of his generation, was deeply marked by Eliot. Not only the grim portents in the *The Waste Land*, and *The Hollow Men*, but also the giddiness of certain of Eliot's forays into the vernacular and vulgar.

Throughout his adult life, Guston had always been in touch with men and women of letters, and poets.

For instance, from the mid-1950s until his death, Guston had shared with an important friend, the poet Stanley Kunitz, his enthusiasm for Gerard Manley Hopkins and William Butler Yeats, as well as his thoughts on the complicated subject of creativity. (In addition to their kindred aesthetics, Kunitz and Guston found an occult connection in the fact that both had fathers who had committed suicide.) Kunitz was Guston's elder sage, but, during his last decade, Guston had actively sought out younger poets, invited them to his studio, and occasionally illustrated their works. One of the first was Clark Coolidge, who reported that what attracted him to Guston was "Philip's feeling for structures, and his doubt . . . things that go together and things that don't."[23] They talked about Kafka and Beckett, but also Melville. I like to think that Melville's mysterious Bartleby, who "preferred not," was a silent partner in their conversations. The last chapter of Guston's life among poets has been documented by the poets themselves, as has his friendship with the novelist Philip Roth in a recent book by Debra Balken. But there is one relationship with a poet that Guston maintained despite the

24 Louis Aragon, *Paris Peasant*,
   trans. Simon Watson Taylor
   (Boston: Exact Change, 1994): 9.
25 Ibid., 186.
26 Ibid.

fact that he had never met him: the Surrealist poet Louis Aragon.

Aragon spoke to Guston's allegiance to the idea of subversion, but *not*, as he told me, the subversion of art. Aragon's youthful project—to undermine the Western tradition of logic in order to bring forward a culture of images, even images of profound disorder—or, as he put it, to tear himself away from the habit of analysis "so as to think simply, naturally, in terms of what I see and touch"[24] was almost identical to Guston's final project. With Aragon it was a matter of likeness. That kind of reading—for confirmation, for self-identity, for consolation—can be immensely stimulating. There is nothing so exhilarating as finding your own tangled thoughts lodged in someone else's imagination. Communion is essential in creative life. Guston was as excitable as a raw nerve, and when he discovered a kindred imagination he would often exclaim, as he once did to me in a letter, "I nearly jumped out of my skin!" Although Guston's predilections among modern painters included one of Surrealism's heroes, Giorgio de Chirico, I always felt his passion for Beckmann and Picasso was more intense. Yet, at some point in the 1970s, he quoted Aragon to me: "The vice called surrealism is the immoderate and passionate use of the drug which is the image." After Guston died I donated his letters to the Archives of American Art, but somehow had missed the single sheet of paper on which Guston had written that phrase from memory in a slightly different version from the original. That sheet of paper turned up a few years ago and inspired me to re-read

Aragon's *Paris Peasant*. I found the quotation. Guston's friends, both epistolary and in the studio, have all noticed that certain memorized quotations had accompanied him for years, and were often brandished to emphasize a point. I remember how often he used to quote Valéry's observation that a bad poem "vanishes into meaning." So it was with Aragon's phrases from *Paris Peasant*, written in the early 1920s, published in 1926, and translated into English only in 1971. When I re-read it long after Guston's death I was astounded at how much Guston might have mined from it, or conversely, how much Guston had paralleled Aragon's world, and words, in his last drawings and paintings. A few instances: In Chapter 18 of *Paris Peasant*, a delirious rant, a dream full of paths to Guston's last delirious (he called it that himself) cascade of images:

> *Beneath a wave on the point of breaking up, in this hollow like an eye socket, there is scarcely a breath left in me. . . .*[25]

So many of Guston's late drawings and paintings catch the artist, and most especially the symbol standing for him—his own eye—nearly drowning beneath the wave in Aragon's "cluster of foam."

> *Since the days of the caveman, no ground, not a single fold has been gained against mystery. . . . My heart beneath this rock bridge and adorned by it with plumes—of smoke? is full of the drift ice from the collision of great dead suns.*[26]

27 Ibid, 187.

28 Ibid, 188.

29 Philip Guston, "Piero della Francesca: The Impossibility of Painting," *Art News* (May 1965): 38–39.

Aragon imagines that he is not alone, that

there is a great mass of beings, quickened by this movement of the waters. . . . And I am dreaming and off goes my head. . . .[27]

No need to choose from the welter of Guston's drawings and late paintings in which his own head, sometimes just his eye, is pictured with the others, about to sink.

Drop, drop again my head, played at cup-and-ball enough, dreamed enough, lived enough. Enough, let the smoke return toward the flame.[28]

Smoke and flames. For Guston, a memory of Signorelli's Hell. I think of *Pit*, 1976 (plate 99), a travesty of Renaissance painting, the flames forming theatrical coulisses for the drama of murdered victims; the surface, a bloody sea that itself teeters on the brink of extinction. Aragon's head bounces off the sides of mountains, descends, makes for deep valleys, and then rolls toward the sea:

He who had finally parted company with his thought when far away the first waves had started licking the wounds of the spurned head stirred from his immobility like an inverted question mark. In the pure air, above the charred sierras, at those altitudes where the earth, scraped to the bone, bathes in the diamond sun's implacable glare, where each stone seemed marked with the hoofprint of an ironshod stellar horse . . .

That, too: The metamorphosis of the foot, symbolized by the ubiquitous shoes in Guston's later work, into ironshod heels, or, as they so often seemed to me, horseshoes—old, rusty horseshoes Guston redeemed from the heaps of "crappola" in the junkyards of Woodstock. Aragon tells us that the blood formed "monstrous ferns in the sparkling blue of space"— sparkling blue that appears again and again in Guston's late paintings, rendering the nightmare images all the more horrifying. And the head as stone that Aragon posits, as it rolls in Hell and in the firmament, is also Sisyphus's stone that Guston, having read Camus avidly, would never forget.

Guston's retrieval of the "story" was certainly abetted by his wide reading. But his late works are also a retrieval of a vast art history tradition with an emphasis on the mysterious. His deep appreciation of Piero's immensely mysterious story of *The Flagellation* was articulated: He saw in it "a certain graveness, a wisdom of forms, sweet to my eye and mind."[29] Neither he nor anyone else has ever been able to unravel the mystery of Piero's "story." Guston's prime question—*Where* is the painting?—could never be finally answered, nor could its "literary" sources ever be pure. Guston knew that there is no such thing as an empty mirror.

Dore Ashton

Guston talking with students at
Boston University, 1978

Faith, Hope, and Impossibility by Philip Guston

There are so many things in the world—in the cities—so much to see. Does art need to represent this variety and contribute to its proliferation? Can art be that free? The difficulties begin when you understand what it is that the soul will not permit the hand to make.

To paint is always to start at the beginning again, yet being unable to avoid the familiar arguments about what you see yourself painting. The canvas you are working on modifies the previous ones in an unending, baffling chain which never seems to finish. (What a sympathy is demanded of the viewer! He is asked to "see" the future links.)

For me the most relevant question and perhaps the only one is, "When are you finished?" When do you stop? Or rather, why stop at all? But you have to rest somewhere. Of course you can stay on one surface all your life, like Balzac's Frenhofer. And all of your life's work can be seen as one picture—but that is merely "true." There *are* places where you pause.

Thus it might be argued that when a painting is "finished," it is a compromise. But the conditions under which the compromise is made are what matters. Decisions to settle anywhere are intolerable. But you begin to feel as you go on working that unless painting proves its right to exist by being critical and self-judging, it has no reason to exist at all—or is not even possible.

The canvas is a court where the artist is prosecutor, defendant, jury, and judge. Art without a trial disappears at a glance: it is too primitive or hopeful, or mere notions, or simply startling, or just another means to make life bearable.

You cannot settle out of court. You are faced with what seems like an impossibility—fixing an image which you can tolerate. What can be Where? Erasures and destructions, criticisms and judgments of one's acts, even as they force change in oneself, are still preparations merely reflecting the mind's will and movement. There is a burden here, and it is the weight of the familiar. Yet this is the material of a working which from time to time needs to see itself; even though it is reluctant to appear.

To will a new form is inacceptable, because will builds distortion. Desire, too, is incomplete and arbitrary. These strategies, however intimate they might become, must especially be removed to clear the way for something else—a condition somewhat unclear, but which in retrospect becomes a very precise act. This "thing" is recognized only as it comes into existence. It resists analysis—and probably this is as it should be. Possibly the moral is that art cannot and should not be made.

All these troubles revolve around the irritable mutual dependence of life and art—with their need and contempt for one another. Of necessity, to create is a temporary state and cannot be possessed, because you learn and relearn that it is the lie and mask of Art and, too, its mortification, which promise a continuity.

There are twenty crucial minutes in the evolution of each of my paintings. The closer I get to that time—those twenty minutes—the more intensely subjective I become—but the more objective, too. Your eye gets sharper; you become continuously more and more critical.

There is no measure I can hold on to except this scant half-hour of making.

One of the great mysteries about the past is that such masters as Mantegna were able to sustain this emotion for a year.

The problem, of course, is more complex than mere duration of "inspiration." There were pre-images in the fifteenth century, foreknowledge of what was going to be brought into existence. Maybe my pre-image is unknown to me, but today it is impossible to act as if pre-imaging is possible.

Many works of the past (and of the present) complete what they announce they are going to do, to our increasing boredom. Certain others plague me because I cannot follow their intentions. I can tell at a glance what Fabritius is doing, but I am spending my life trying to find out what Rembrandt was up to.

I have a studio in the country—in the woods—but my paintings look more real to me than what is outdoors. You walk outside; the rocks are inert; even the clouds are inert. It makes me feel a little better. But I do have a faith that it is possible to make a living thing, not a diagram of what I have been thinking: to posit with paint something living, something that changes each day.

Everyone destroys marvelous paintings. Five years ago you wiped out what you are about to start tomorrow.

Where do you put a form? It will move all around, bellow out and shrink, and sometimes it winds up where it was in the first place. But at the end it feels different, and it had to make the voyage. I am a moralist and cannot accept what has not been paid for, or a form that has not been lived through.

Frustration is one of the great things in art; satisfaction is nothing.

Two artists always fascinate me—Piero della Francesca and Rembrandt. I am fixed on those two and their insoluble opposition. Piero is the ideal painter: he pursued abstraction, some kind of fantastic, metaphysical, perfect organism. In Rembrandt the plane of art is removed. It is not a painting, but a real person—a substitute, a golem. He is really the only painter in the world!

Certain artists do something and a new emotion is brought into the world; its real meaning lies outside of history and the chains of causality.

Human consciousness moves, but it is not a leap: it is one inch. One inch is a small jump, but that jump is everything. You go way out and then you have to come back—to see if you can move that inch.

I do not think of modern art as Modern Art. The problem started long ago, and the question is: Can there be any art at all?

Maybe this is the content of modern art.

This article originally appeared in Art News Annual *XXXI, 1966 (October 1965), and was based on notes for a lecture the artist gave at the New York Studio School in May 1965.*

1 **Drawing for Conspirators** 1930 Graphite, ink, colored pencil, and crayon on paper 22 1/2 × 14 1/2 inches (57.2 × 36.8 cm)

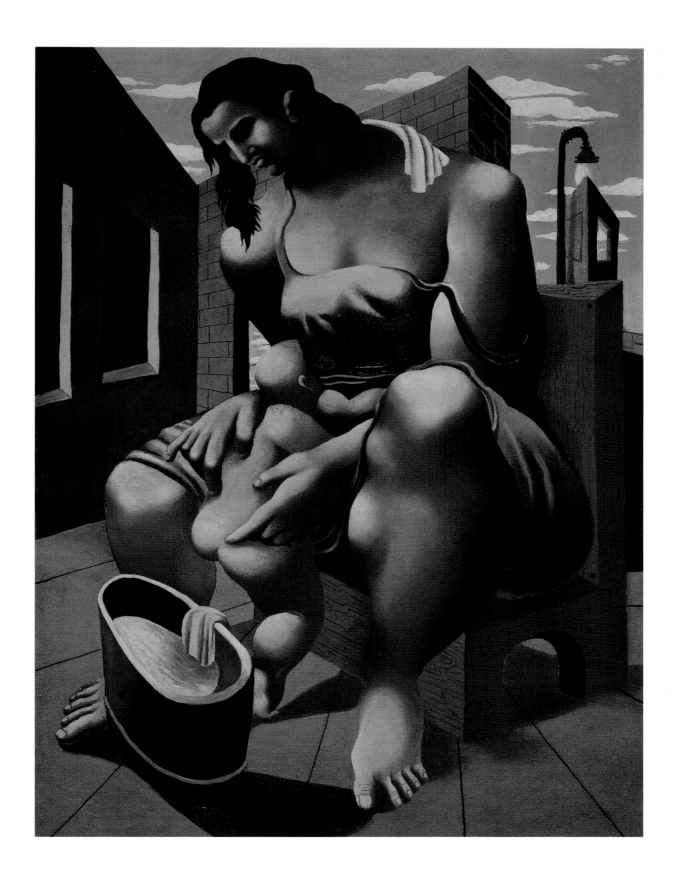

2 **Mother and Child** 1930 Oil on canvas 40 × 30 inches (101.6 × 76.2 cm)

3 **Drawing for Bombardment** 1936 Colored pencil on paper 17³/₄ × 23³/₄ inches (45 × 60.3 cm)

4 **Bombardment** 1937–38 Oil on Masonite 46 inches (116.8 cm) diameter

5 **Boys Fighting (Study for Queensbridge Housing Project Mural)** 1938 Colored pencil and pencil on paper 15 5/16 × 13 inches (38.9 × 33 cm)

6 **The Gladiators** 1938 Oil on canvas 24 ¹/₂ × 28 inches (62.2 × 71.1 cm)

7 **Martial Memory** 1941 Oil on canvas 40 1/8 × 32 1/4 inches (101.9 × 81.9 cm)

8 **The Air Training Program (Illustration for Fortune Magazine)** 1943 Gouache on paper 30 × 23 ³/₄ inches (76.2 × 60.3 cm)

9 **Clothes Inflation Drill (For Navy Pre-Flight Training)** 1943 Pencil and crayon on paper 22 $^1/_2$ × 29 inches (57.2 × 73.7 cm)

10 **The Glider Has Its Heart in Its Mouth** 1943 Watercolor and gouache on paper mounted on board 11^1/$_2$ × 9^1/$_2$ inches (29.2 × 24.1 cm)

11 **Oxygen Test Chamber** 1943 Watercolor and ink on board 16 $\frac{1}{4}$ × 25 $\frac{3}{4}$ inches (41.3 × 65.4 cm)

12 **Parachutes Hung Out to Dry** 1943 Watercolor and ink on paper 13 × 9 1/2 inches (33 × 24.1 cm)

13 **If This Be Not I** 1945 Oil on canvas 42 $^{1}/_{4}$ × 55 $^{1}/_{4}$ inches (107.3 × 140.3 cm)

14 **Untitled** 1946 Ink, pencil, and crayon on paper 11³/₄ × 9 inches (29.8 × 22.8 cm)

15 **Porch No. 2** 1947 Oil on canvas 62 ^{1}/$_2$ × 43 ^{1}/$_8$ inches (158.7 × 109.5 cm)

16 **Untitled** 1947 Ink, pencil, and gouache on paper 10⁵/₈ × 13⁵/₈ inches (26.9 × 34.6 cm)

17 **Drawing for Tormentors (Drawing No. 1)** 1947–48 Ink on paper 14 $^7/_8$ × 20 $^7/_8$ inches (37.8 × 53.1 cm)

18 **The Tormentors** 1947–48 Oil on canvas $40^7/_8 \times 60^1/_2$ inches (103.8 × 153.7 cm)

19 **Untitled** 1947–48 Ink wash, ink, and pencil on paper 10³/₄ × 13³/₄ inches (27.3 × 34.9 cm)

20 Drawing No. 2, Ischia 1949 Ink on paper 11 × 15 inches (27.9 × 38.1 cm)

21 **Ischia** 1949 Ink on paper 10³/₄ × 13³/₄ inches (27.3 × 34.9 cm)

22 **Composition in Greys, Whites, and Pinks** c. 1950 Gouache on paper 15 $^1/_8$ × 22 $^1/_2$ inches (38.4 × 57.1 cm)

23 **Red Painting** 1950 Oil on canvas 34$^1/_8$ × 62$^1/_4$ inches (86.4 × 158.1 cm)

24 Small Quill Drawing 1950 Ink on paper 12 $\frac{1}{8}$ × 16 $\frac{1}{8}$ inches (30.8 × 41 cm)

25 **Untitled** 1950 Ink on paper 18 ⁵/₈ × 23 ¹/₂ inches (47.3 × 59.7 cm)

26 **Drawing** 1951 Ink on paper 9^1/$_8$ × 11^3/$_8$ inches (23.2 × 28.9 cm)

27 **Untitled** 1951 Ink on paper 18³/₄ × 23³/₄ inches (47.6 × 60.3 cm)

28 **White Painting I** 1951 Oil on canvas $57\,^7/_8 \times 61\,^7/_8$ inches (147×157.2 cm)

29 **The Bell** 1952 Oil on canvas 46 × 40 inches (116.8 × 101.6 cm)

30 **Painting No. 5** 1952 Oil on canvas 46 × 40 inches (116.8 × 101.6 cm)

31 **Painting No. 9** 1952 Oil on canvas 48 $^{1}/_{4}$ × 60 $^{1}/_{4}$ inches (122.5 × 153 cm)

32 **To B. W. T.** 1952 Oil on canvas 48 $^1/_2$ × 51 $^1/_2$ inches (123.2 × 130.8 cm)

33 **Untitled** 1952 Ink on paper 18 × 23 inches (45.7 × 58.5 cm)

34 Drawing Related to Zone (Drawing No. 19) 1954 Ink on paper $17^{7}/_{8} \times 24$ inches (45.4×61 cm)

35 **Painting** 1954 Oil on canvas 63 $\frac{1}{4}$ × 60 $\frac{1}{8}$ inches (160.6 × 152.7 cm)

36 **Zone** 1953–54 Oil on canvas 46 × 48 inches (116.8 × 121.9 cm)

37 **Beggar's Joys** 1954–55 Oil on canvas 72 × 68 inches (182.9 × 172.7 cm)

38 **For M** 1955 Oil on canvas 76³/₈ × 72¹/₄ inches (194 × 183.5 cm)

39 **The Room** 1954–55 Oil on canvas 71^{7}/$_{8}$ × 60 inches (182.6 × 152.4 cm)

40 **Dial** 1956 Oil on canvas 72 × 76 inches (182.9 × 193 cm)

41 **The Evidence** 1957 Oil on canvas 65 × 68 inches (165.1 × 172.7 cm)

42　**Fable I** 1956–57 Oil on canvas 65 × 75 inches (165.1 × 190.5 cm)

43 **The Mirror** 1957 Oil on canvas 68⁷/₈ × 61 inches (174.9 × 154.9 cm)

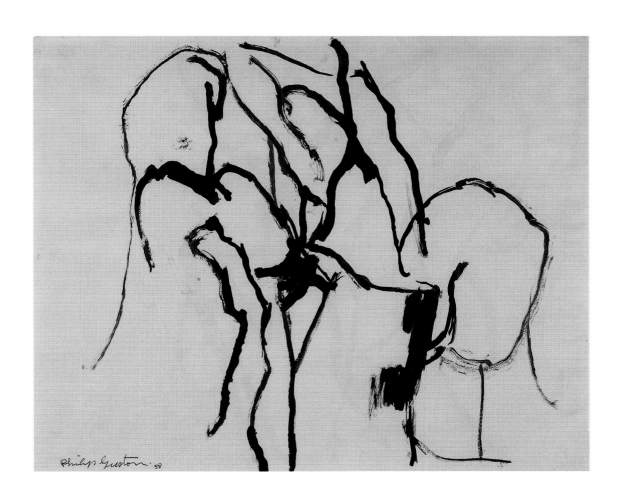

44 **Forms in Change** 1958 Ink on paper 18 × 23³/₄ inches (45.7 × 60.3 cm)

45 **Head—Double View** 1958 Ink on paper 20 × 24⁷/₈ inches (50.7 × 63.2 cm)

46 **To Fellini** 1958 Oil on canvas 69 × 74 inches (175.3 × 188 cm)

47 **Untitled** 1958 Oil on canvas 64 × 75 ¹/₈ inches (162.6 × 190.8 cm)

48 **The Painter** 1959 Oil on canvas 65 × 69 inches (165.1 × 175.3 cm)

49 **Mirror to S. K.** 1960 Oil on canvas 63 1/2 × 75 inches (161.3 × 190.5 cm)

50 **Celebration** 1961 Ink on paper 25^3/$_4$ × 30^1/$_2$ inches (65.4 × 77.5 cm)

51 **Close-Up III** 1961 Oil on canvas 70 × 72 inches (177.8 × 182.9 cm)

52 Untitled 1962 Ink on paper 26 × 39 1/2 inches (66 × 100.3 cm)

53 **The Light** 1964 Oil on canvas 69 × 78 inches (175.3 × 198.1 cm)

54 **New Place** 1964 Oil on canvas 75 3/4 × 80 1/4 inches (192.4 × 203.8 cm)

55 **The Scale** 1965 Ink on paper 18 × 24 inches (45.7 × 61 cm)

56 **Full Brush** 1966 Ink on paper 17 1/2 × 22 3/4 inches (44.5 × 57.8 cm)

57 **Chair** 1967 Ink on paper 14 × 16 1/2 inches (35.6 × 41.9 cm)

58 **Edge** 1967 Ink on paper 13 $^{1}/_{2}$ × 16 $^{3}/_{4}$ inches (34.3 × 42.5 cm)

59 **Form** 1967 Ink on paper 19 × 23 inches (48.3 × 58.4 cm)

60 **Horizon** 1967 Ink on paper 18 × 21 1/2 inches (45.7 × 54.6 cm)

61 **Mark** 1967 Ink on paper 14 × 16 1/2 inches (35.6 × 41.9 cm)

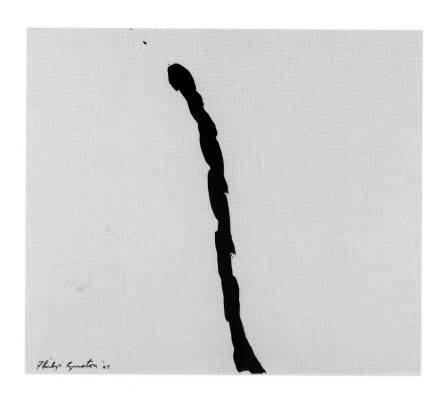

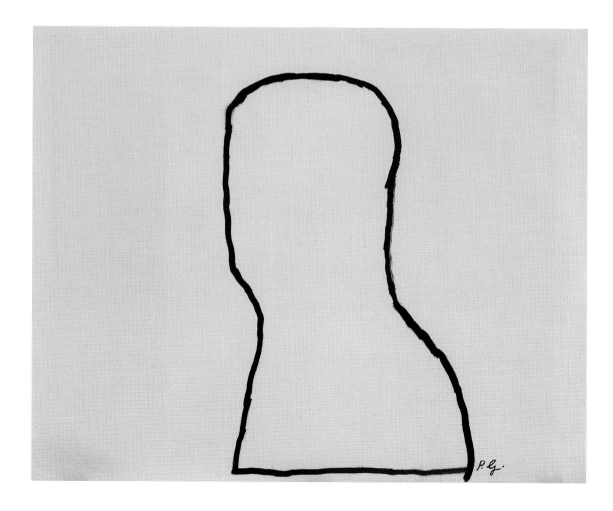

62 **Wave II** 1967 Ink on paper 14 × 16 ¹/₄ inches (35.6 × 41.3 cm)

63 **Head** 1968 Ink on paper 18 × 22 ¹/₂ inches (45.7 × 57.2 cm)

64 **Paw** 1968 Acrylic on panel 30 × 32 inches (76.2 × 81.3 cm)

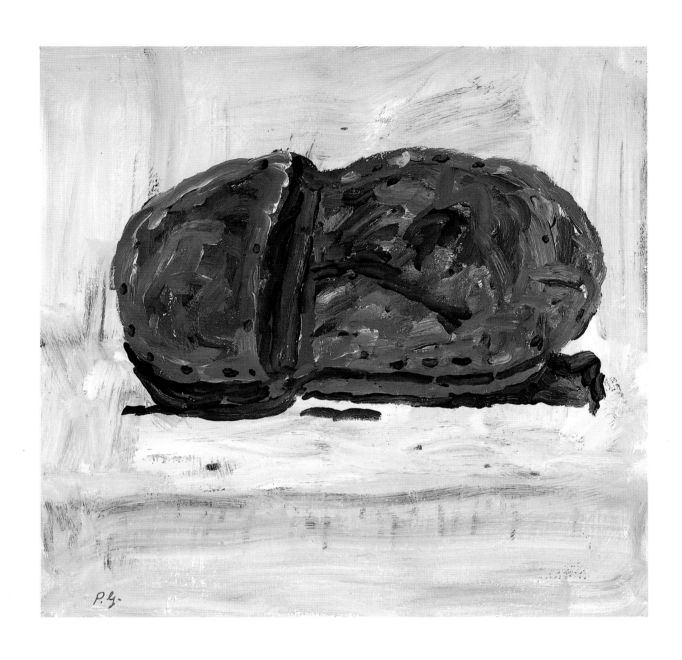

65 **Shoe** 1968 Acrylic on panel 30 × 32 inches (76.2 × 81.3 cm)

66 **Untitled** 1968 Acrylic on panel 18 × 20 inches (45.7 × 50.7 cm)

67 **Untitled** 1968 Acrylic on panel 18 × 20 inches (45.7 × 50.7 cm)

68 **Untitled** 1968 Acrylic on panel 18 × 20 inches (45.7 × 50.7 cm)

philip Guston

69 **Boot** 1968 Acrylic on panel 16 $^1/_2$ × 19 $^1/_2$ inches (41.9 × 49.5 cm)

70 **Blackboard** 1969 Oil on canvas 79$^{1}/_{2}$ × 112 inches (201.9 × 284.5 cm)

71 **By the Window** 1969 Oil on canvas 78 × 81 1/4 inches (198.1 × 206.4 cm)

72 **City** 1969 Oil on canvas 72 × 67¹/₂ inches (182.9 × 171.4 cm)

73 **Edge of Town** 1969 Oil on canvas 77 × 110 ¹/₄ inches (196.2 × 280 cm)

74 **Group** 1969 Ink on paper 23 1/4 × 26 1/2 inches (59.1 × 67.3 cm)

75 **The Law** 1969 Charcoal on paper 17⁷/₈ × 14⁵/₈ inches (45.4 × 37.1 cm)

76 **The Studio** 1969 Oil on canvas 48 × 42 inches (121.9 × 106.7 cm)

77 **Untitled** 1969 Acrylic on panel 18 × 20 inches (45.7 × 50.7 cm)

78 **Bad Habits** 1970 Oil on canvas 73 × 78 inches (185.5 × 198.2 cm)

79 **Courtroom** 1970 Oil on canvas 67 × 129 inches (170.2 × 327.7 cm)

80 **Dawn** 1970 Oil on canvas 67$^{1}/_{4}$ × 108 inches (170.8 × 274.3 cm)

81 **Flatlands** 1970 Oil on canvas 70 × 114 1/2 inches (177.8 × 290.8 cm)

82 **Scared Stiff** 1970 Oil on canvas 57 × 81 inches (144.8 × 205.7 cm)

83 **Window** 1970 Graphite on paper 18 × 21 inches (45.7 × 53.3 cm)

84 **Painter's Table** 1973 Oil on canvas 77^1/$_4$ × 90 inches (196.2 × 228.6 cm)

85 **Painting, Smoking, Eating** 1973 Oil on canvas 77 1/2 × 103 1/2 inches (196.8 × 262.9 cm)

86 **Pantheon** 1973 Oil on panel 45 × 48 inches (114.3 × 121.9 cm)

87 **Four Heads** 1974 Ink on paper 18 × 24 inches (45.7 × 61 cm)

88 **Lamp and Chair** 1974 Ink on paper 19 × 25 ¼ inches (48.3 × 64.1 cm)

89 **Self-Portrait** 1974 Ink on paper 13³/₄ × 16³/₄ inches (34.9 × 42.5 cm)

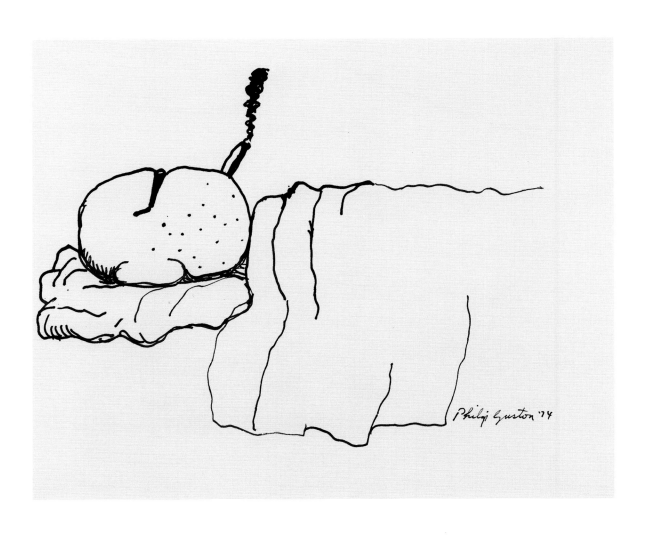

90 **Smoking in Bed** 1974 Ink on paper 19 × 24 inches (48.3 × 61 cm)

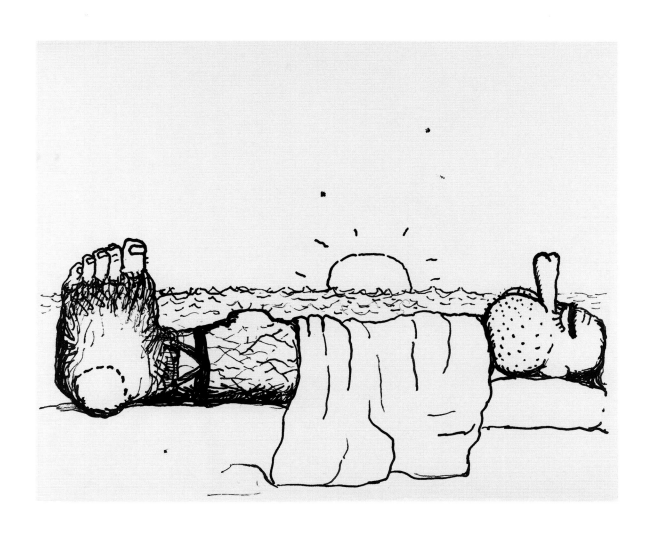

91 **From the Phlebitis Series** 1975 Ink on paper 19 × 24 inches (48.3 × 61 cm)

92 **From the Phlebitis Series** 1975 Ink on paper 24 × 19 inches (61 × 48.3 cm)

93 **From the Phlebitis Series** 1975 Ink on paper 24 × 19 inches (61 × 48.3 cm)

94 **Head** 1975 Oil on canvas 69 ¹/₄ × 74 ¹/₂ inches (175.9 × 189.2 cm)

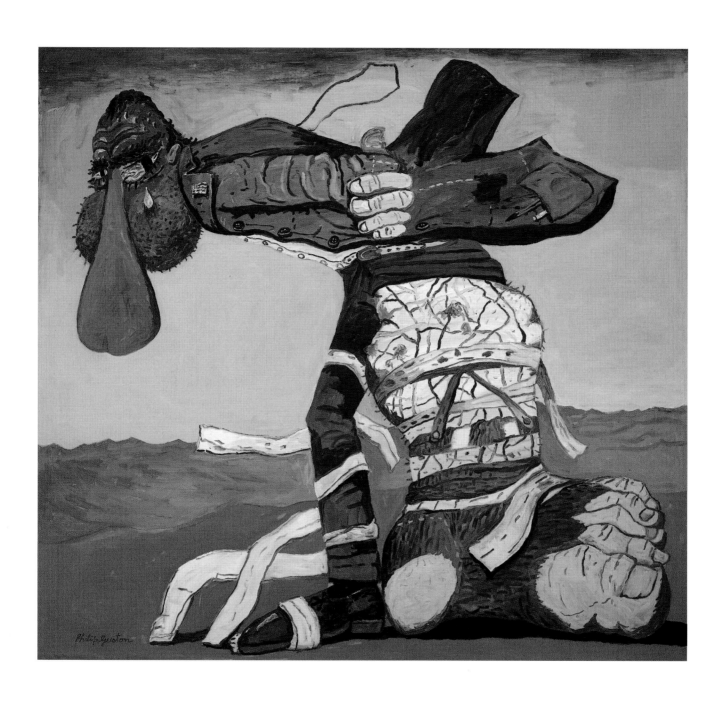

95 **San Clemente** 1975 Oil on canvas 68 × 73 ¹/₄ inches (172.7 × 186.1 cm)

96 **Web** 1975 Oil on canvas $67 \times 97^{1}/_{4}$ inches (170.2×247 cm)

97 **Web** 1975 Ink on paper 19 × 24 inches (48.3 × 61 cm)

98 **Source** 1976 Oil on canvas 76 × 117 inches (193 × 297.2 cm)

99 **Pit** 1976 Oil on canvas 74¹/₂ × 116 inches (189.2 × 294.8 cm)

100 **Wharf** 1976 Oil on canvas 80 × 116 inches (203.2 × 294.6 cm)

101 **Green Rug** 1976 Oil on canvas 94 × 68 ¹/₂ inches (238.8 × 174 cm)

102 **Ancient Wall** 1976 Oil on linen 80 × 93⁵/₈ inches (203.2 × 237.8 cm)

103 **The Painter** 1976 Oil on canvas 74 × 116 inches (188 × 294.6 cm)

104 Cherries 1976 Oil on canvas 69 × 116 inches (175.3 × 294.6 cm)

105 **Frame** 1976 Oil on canvas 74 × 116 inches (188 × 294.6 cm)

106 **Cherries II** 1976 Oil on canvas 78 × 115 inches (198.1 × 292.1 cm)

107 **Sleeping** 1977 Oil on canvas 85 × 70 inches (215.9 × 177.8 cm)

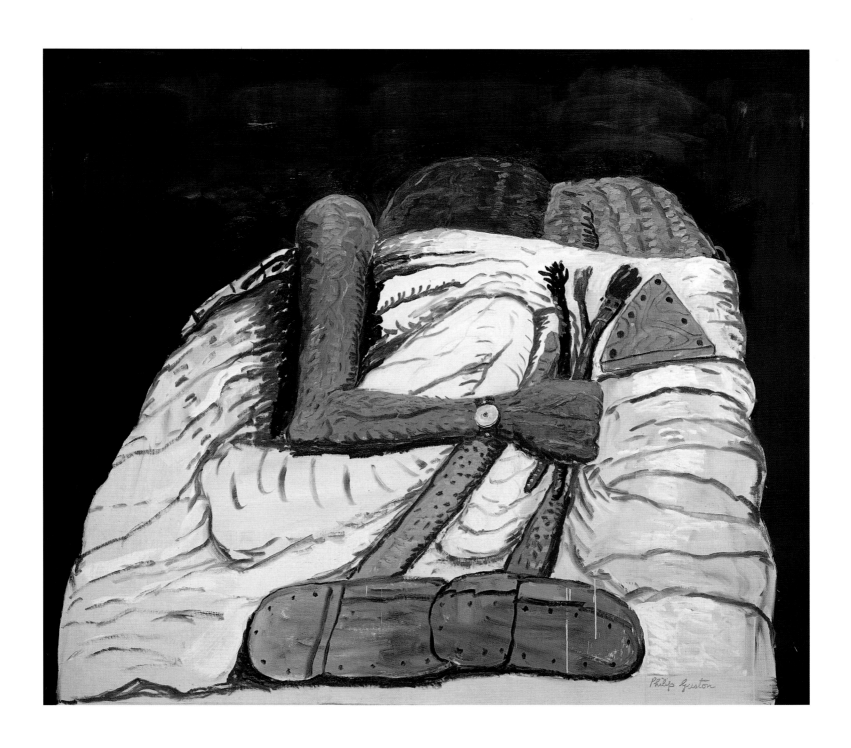

108 **Couple in Bed** 1977 Oil on canvas 81^1/$_8$ × 94^5/$_8$ inches (206.2 × 240.3 cm)

109 **The Night** 1977 Oil on canvas 68 × 120 ¼ inches (172.7 × 305.4 cm)

110 **Back View** 1977 Oil on canvas 69 × 94 inches (175.3 × 238.8 cm)

111 **To I. B.** 1977 Oil on canvas 67$\frac{1}{4}$ × 80 inches (170.8 × 203.2 cm)

112 **Cabal** 1977 Oil on canvas 68 × 116 inches (172.7 × 294.6 cm)

113 **The Street** 1977 Oil on canvas 69 × 110³/₄ inches (175.3 × 281.3 cm)

114 **Pyramid and Shoe** 1977 Oil on canvas 68 × 116 inches (172.7 × 294.6 cm)

115 **Curtain** 1977 Oil on canvas 69 × 106 inches (175.3 × 269.2 cm)

116 **Street II** 1977 Oil on canvas 67^1/$_2$ × 72^1/$_2$ inches (171.4 × 184.1 cm)

117 **Ladder** 1978 Oil on canvas 70 × 108 inches (177.8 × 274.3 cm)

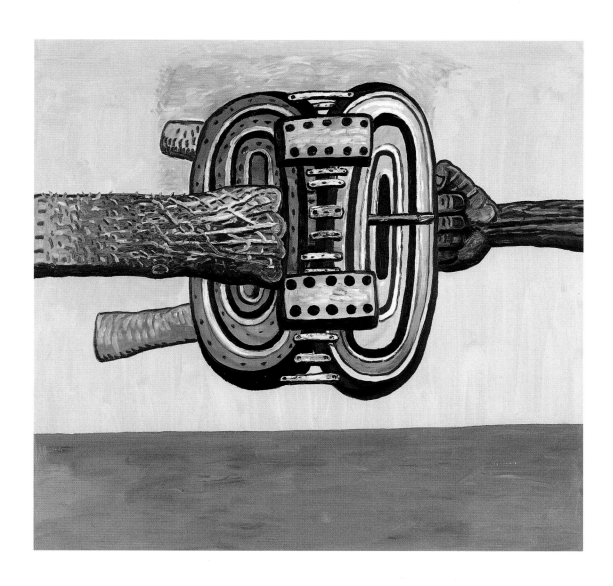

118 **Hinged** 1978 Oil on canvas 68 $^1/_2$ × 73 $^1/_2$ inches (174 × 187 cm)

119 **Feet on Rug** 1978 Oil on canvas 80 × 104 inches (203.2 × 264.2 cm)

120 **Red Sky** 1978 Oil on canvas 82 × 105 ¹/₂ inches (208.3 × 268 cm)

121 **Painter's Forms II** 1978 Oil on canvas 75 × 108 inches (190.5 × 274.3 cm)

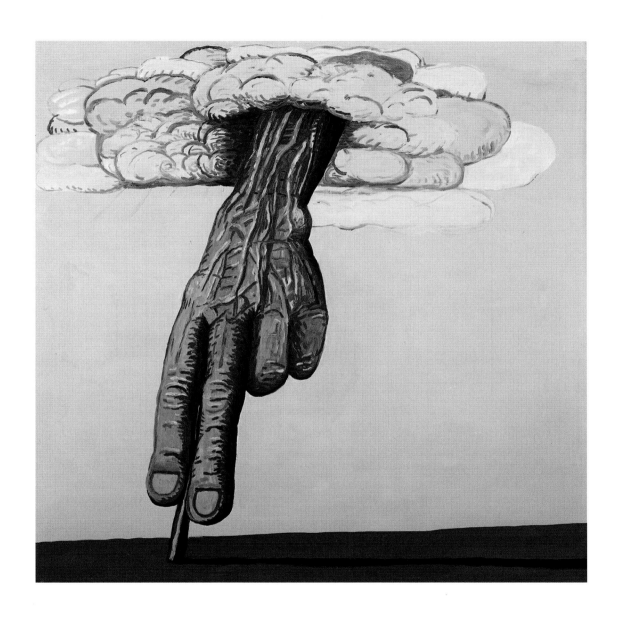

122 **The Line** 1978 Oil on canvas 71 × 73 ¹/₄ inches (180.3 × 186.1 cm)

123 **Friend—To M. F.** 1978 Oil on canvas 68 × 88 inches (172.7 × 223.5 cm)

124 **Aegean** 1978 Oil on canvas 68 × 126 inches (172.7 × 320 cm)

125 **Plain** 1979 Oil on canvas 69 × 93 inches (175.3 × 236.2 cm)

126 **Group in Sea** 1979 Oil on canvas 68 × 88 ¹/₂ inches (172.7 × 224.8 cm)

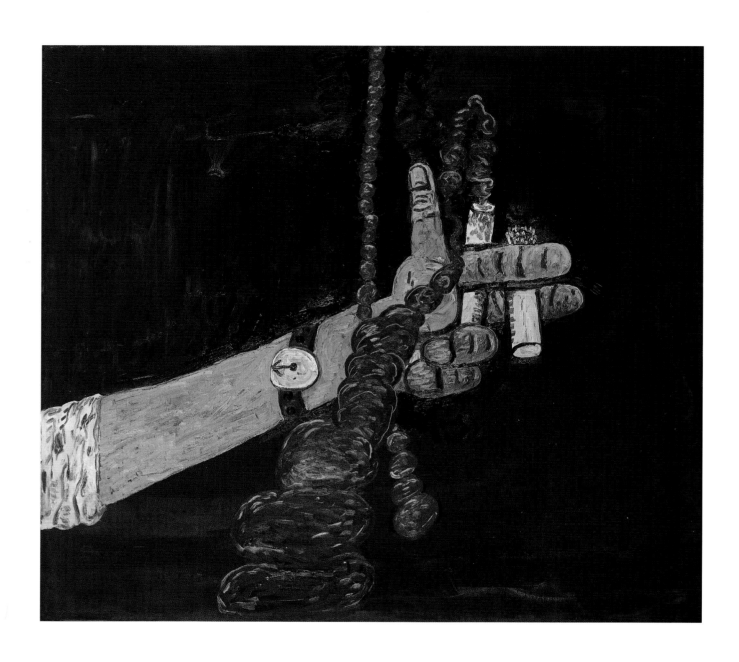

127 **Talking** 1979 Oil on canvas 68 $^1/_2$ × 78 inches (174 × 198.1 cm)

128 **Flame** 1979 Oil on canvas 48 × 60 inches (121.9 × 152.4 cm)

129 **Wheel** 1979 Oil on canvas 48 × 60 inches (121.9 × 152.4 cm)

130 **Large Brush** 1979 Oil on canvas 32 × 36 inches (81.3 × 91.4 cm)

131 **The Hand** 1979 Oil on linen 32 × 36 inches (81 × 91.5 cm)

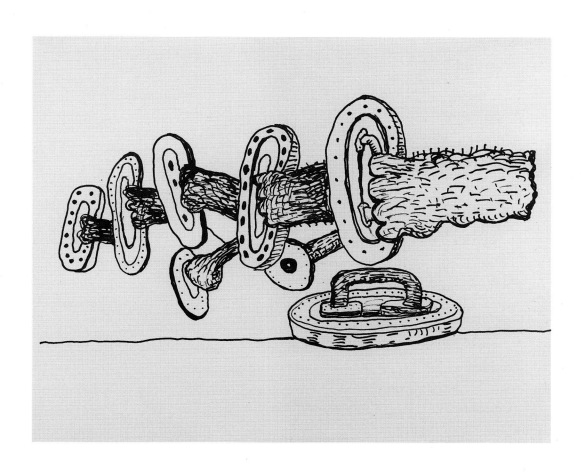

132 **Untitled** 1980 Ink on paper 23 × 29 inches (58.4 × 73.7 cm)

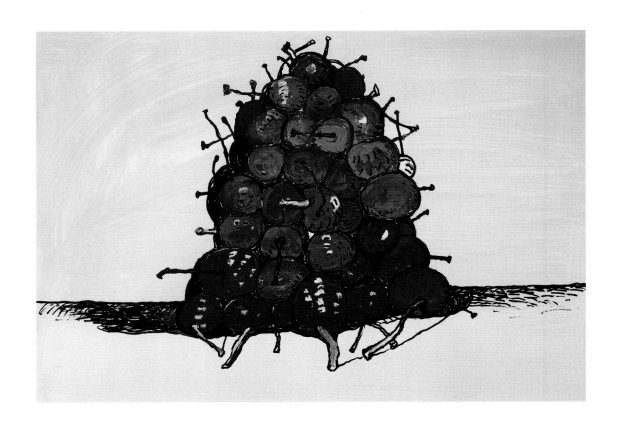

133 **Untitled (Cherries)** 1980 Acrylic and ink on paper 20 × 30 inches (50.8 × 76.2 cm)

134 **Untitled (Head)** 1980 Acrylic and ink on paper 20 × 30 inches (50.8 × 76.2 cm)

135 **Untitled (Hillside)** 1980 Acrylic and ink on paper 23 × 29 inches (58.4 × 73.7 cm)

136 **Untitled (Kettle)** 1980 Acrylic and ink on paper 20 × 30 inches (50.8 × 76.2 cm)

137 **Untitled (Ladder)** 1980 Acrylic and ink on paper 20 × 30 inches (50.8 × 76.2 cm)

138 **Untitled (Sandwich)** 1980 Acrylic and ink on paper 20 × 30 inches (50.8 × 76.2 cm)

Checklist of the Exhibition

1 **Drawing for Conspirators** 1930
Graphite, ink, colored pencil,
and crayon on paper
22 $^1/_2$ × 14 $^1/_2$ inches (57.2 × 36.8 cm)
Whitney Museum of American Art,
New York
Purchase, with funds from The Hearst
Corporation and The Norman and Rosita
Winston Foundation, Inc., 82.20

2 **Mother and Child** 1930
Oil on canvas
40 × 30 inches (101.6 × 76.2 cm)
Private Collection

3 **Drawing for Bombardment** 1936
Colored pencil on paper
17 $^3/_4$ × 23 $^3/_4$ inches (45 × 60.3 cm)
Private Collection

4 **Bombardment** 1937–38
Oil on Masonite
46 inches (116.8 cm) diameter
Private Collection

5 **Boys Fighting (Study for Queensbridge
Housing Project Mural)** 1938
Colored pencil and pencil on paper
15 $^5/_{16}$ × 13 inches (38.9 × 33 cm)
Private Collection

6 **The Gladiators** 1938
Oil on canvas
24 $^1/_2$ × 28 inches (62.2 × 71.1 cm)
The Edward R. Broida Collection

7 **Martial Memory** 1941
Oil on canvas
40 $^1/_8$ × 32 $^1/_4$ inches (101.9 × 81.9 cm)
The Saint Louis Art Museum,
Eliza McMillan Fund

8 **The Air Training Program
(Illustration for Fortune Magazine)** 1943
Gouache on paper
30 × 23 $^3/_4$ inches (76.2 × 60.3 cm)
Private Collection

9 **Clothes Inflation Drill
(For Navy Pre-Flight Training)** 1943
Pencil and crayon on paper
22 $^1/_2$ × 29 inches (57.2 × 73.7 cm)
Private Collection

10 **The Glider Has Its Heart in Its Mouth**
1943
Watercolor and gouache on paper
mounted on board
11 $^1/_2$ × 9 $^1/_2$ inches (29.2 × 24.1 cm)
Private Collection

11 **Oxygen Test Chamber** 1943
Watercolor and ink on board
16 $^1/_4$ × 25 $^3/_4$ inches (41.3 × 65.4 cm)
Private Collection

12 **Parachutes Hung Out to Dry** 1943
Watercolor and ink on paper
13 × 9 $^1/_2$ inches (33 × 24.1 cm)
Private Collection

13 **If This Be Not I** 1945
Oil on canvas
42 $^1/_4$ × 55 $^1/_4$ inches (107.3 × 140.3 cm)
Washington University Gallery of Art,
St. Louis
University Purchase, Kende Sale Fund,
1945

14 **Untitled** 1946
Ink, pencil, and crayon on paper
11 $^3/_4$ × 9 inches (29.8 × 22.8 cm)
Private Collection

15 **Porch No. 2** 1947
Oil on canvas
62 $^1/_2$ × 43 $^1/_8$ inches (158.7 × 109.5 cm)
Munson-Williams-Proctor Arts Institute,
Museum of Art, Utica, New York, 48.26

16 **Untitled** 1947
Ink, pencil, and gouache on paper
10 $^5/_8$ × 13 $^5/_8$ inches (26.9 × 34.6 cm)
Private Collection

17 **Drawing for Tormentors (Drawing No. 1)**
1947–48
Ink on paper
14 $^7/_8$ × 20 $^7/_8$ inches (37.8 × 53.1 cm)
Private Collection

18 **The Tormentors** 1947–48
Oil on canvas
40 $^7/_8$ × 60 $^1/_2$ inches (103.8 × 153.7 cm)
San Francisco Museum of Modern Art
Gift of the artist
© Estate of Philip Guston

19 **Untitled** 1947–48
Ink wash, ink, and pencil on paper
10 $^3/_4$ × 13 $^3/_4$ inches (27.3 × 34.9 cm)
Private Collection

20 **Drawing No. 2, Ischia** 1949
Ink on paper
11 × 15 inches (27.9 × 38.1 cm)
Private Collection

21 **Ischia** 1949
Ink on paper
10 $^3/_4$ × 13 $^3/_4$ inches (27.3 × 34.9 cm)
The Edward R. Broida Collection

22 **Composition in Greys, Whites, and Pinks** c.1950
Gouache on paper
15 $^1/_8$ × 22 $^1/_2$ inches (38.4 × 57.1 cm)
From the collection of the
Mulvane Art Museum
Washburn University, Topeka, Kansas
Donation of E.J.Erp

23 **Red Painting** 1950
Oil on canvas
34 $^1/_8$ × 62 $^1/_4$ inches (86.4 × 158.1 cm)
The Museum of Modern Art, New York
Bequest of the artist, 1981

24 **Small Quill Drawing** 1950
Ink on paper
12 $^1/_8$ × 16 $^1/_8$ inches (30.8 × 41 cm)
Private Collection

25 **Untitled** 1950
Ink on paper
18 $^5/_8$ × 23 $^1/_2$ inches (47.3 × 59.7 cm)
Private Collection, New York

26 **Drawing** 1951
Ink on paper
9 $^1/_8$ × 11 $^3/_8$ inches (23.2 × 28.9 cm)
Dore Ashton

27 **Untitled** 1951
Ink on paper
18 $^3/_4$ × 23 $^3/_4$ inches (47.6 × 60.3 cm)
The Estate of Philip Guston
Courtesy of McKee Gallery, New York

28 **White Painting I** 1951
Oil on canvas
57 $^7/_8$ × 61 $^7/_8$ inches (147 × 157.2 cm)
San Francisco Museum of Modern Art
T. B. Walker Foundation Fund Purchase
© Estate of Philip Guston

29 **The Bell** 1952
Oil on canvas
46 × 40 inches (116.8 × 101.6 cm)
Aaron I. Fleischman

30 **Painting No. 5** 1952
Oil on canvas
46 × 40 inches (116.8 × 101.6 cm)
The Metropolitan Museum
of Art, New York
Gift of Mrs. Lawrence Sophian, 1990
(1990.340)

31 **Painting No. 9** 1952
Oil on canvas
48 $^1/_4$ × 60 $^1/_4$ inches (122.5 × 153 cm)
Private Collection

32 **To B. W. T.** 1952
Oil on canvas
48 $^1/_2$ × 51 $^1/_2$ inches (123.2 × 130.8 cm)
Jane Lang Davis

33 **Untitled** 1952
Ink on paper
18 × 23 inches (45.7 × 58.5 cm)
Collection of the Modern Art Museum
of Fort Worth
Gift of Musa and Tom Mayer

34 **Drawing Related to Zone (Drawing No. 19)** 1954
Ink on paper
17 $^7/_8$ × 24 inches (45.4 × 61 cm)
Private Collection, New York

35 **Painting** 1954
Oil on canvas
63 $^1/_4$ × 60 $^1/_8$ inches (160.6 × 152.7 cm)
The Museum of Modern Art, New York
Philip Johnson Fund, 1956

36 **Zone** 1953–54
Oil on canvas
46 × 48 inches (116.8 × 121.9 cm)
The Edward R. Broida Collection

37 **Beggar's Joys** 1954–55
Oil on canvas
72 × 68 inches (182.9 × 172.7 cm)
Donald L. Bryant, Jr. Family Trust

38 **For M** 1955
Oil on canvas
76 $^3/_8$ × 72 $^1/_4$ inches (194 × 183.5 cm)
San Francisco Museum of Modern Art
Anonymous Gift
© Estate of Philip Guston

39 **The Room** 1954–55
Oil on canvas
71 $^7/_8$ × 60 inches (182.6 × 152.4 cm)
Los Angeles County Museum of Art
Museum Purchase, Contemporary
Art Council Fund

40 **Dial** 1956
Oil on canvas
72 × 76 inches (182.9 × 193 cm)
Whitney Museum of American Art,
New York, Purchase, 56.44

41 **The Evidence** 1957
Oil on canvas
65 × 68 inches (165.1 × 172.7 cm)
Collection of Phyllis C. Wattis,
San Francisco, California

42 **Fable I** 1956–57
Oil on canvas
65 × 75 inches (165.1 × 190.5 cm)
Washington University Gallery of Art,
St. Louis
University Purchase, Bixby Fund, 1957

43 **The Mirror** 1957
Oil on canvas
68 $^7/_8$ × 61 inches (174.9 × 154.9 cm)
The Edward R. Broida Collection

44 **Forms in Change** 1958
Ink on paper
18 × 23 $^3/_4$ inches (45.7 × 60.3 cm)
Roselyne Chroman Swig

45 **Head—Double View** 1958
Ink on paper
20 × 24⁷/₈ inches (50.7 × 63.2 cm)
The Museum of Modern Art,
New York, Purchase

46 **To Fellini** 1958
Oil on canvas
69 × 74 inches (175.3 × 188 cm)
Lyn and George Ross

47 **Untitled** 1958
Oil on canvas
64 × 75¹/₈ inches (162.6 × 190.8 cm)
Private Collection

48 **The Painter** 1959
Oil on canvas
65 × 69 inches (165.1 × 175.3 cm)
The High Museum of Art,
Atlanta, Georgia
Museum Purchase with Funds from the
National Endowment for the Arts, 1974

49 **Mirror to S. K.** 1960
Oil on canvas
63¹/₂ × 75 inches (161.3 × 190.5 cm)
Private Collection

50 **Celebration** 1961
Ink on paper
25³/₄ × 30¹/₂ inches (65.4 × 77.5 cm)
Private Collection, New York
Courtesy of McKee Gallery, New York

51 **Close-Up III** 1961
Oil on canvas
70 × 72 inches (177.8 × 182.9 cm)
The Metropolitan Museum of Art,
New York
Gift of Lee V. Eastman, 1972 (1972.281)

52 **Untitled** 1962
Ink on paper
26 × 39¹/₂ inches (66 × 100.3 cm)
Private Collection

53 **The Light** 1964
Oil on canvas
69 × 78 inches (175.3 × 198.1 cm)
Collection of the Modern Art Museum
of Fort Worth
Museum Purchase, The Friends of Art
Endowment Fund

54 **New Place** 1964
Oil on canvas
75³/₄ × 80¹/₄ inches (192.4 × 203.8 cm)
San Francisco Museum of Modern Art
Gift of the artist
© Estate of Philip Guston

55 **The Scale** 1965
Ink on paper
18 × 24 inches (45.7 × 61 cm)
Private Collection

56 **Full Brush** 1966
Ink on paper
17¹/₂ × 22³/₄ inches (44.5 × 57.8 cm)
Collection of the Modern Art Museum
of Fort Worth
Gift of Musa and Tom Mayer

57 **Chair** 1967
Ink on paper
14 × 16¹/₂ inches (35.6 × 41.9 cm)
Private Collection

58 **Edge** 1967
Ink on paper
13¹/₂ × 16³/₄ inches (34.3 × 42.5 cm)
Private Collection

59 **Form** 1967
Ink on paper
19 × 23 inches (48.3 × 58.4 cm)
The Estate of Philip Guston
Courtesy of McKee Gallery, New York

60 **Horizon** 1967
Ink on paper
18 × 21¹/₂ inches (45.7 × 54.6 cm)
The Estate of Philip Guston
Courtesy of McKee Gallery, New York

61 **Mark** 1967
Ink on paper
14 × 16¹/₂ inches (35.6 × 41.9 cm)
Private Collection

62 **Wave II** 1967
Ink on paper
14 × 16¹/₄ inches (35.6 × 41.3 cm)
Private Collection

63 **Head** 1968
Ink on paper
18 × 22¹/₂ inches (45.7 × 57.2 cm)
Janie C. Lee, Houston

64 **Paw** 1968
Acrylic on panel
30 × 32 inches (76.2 × 81.3 cm)
Private Collection

65 **Shoe** 1968
Acrylic on panel
30 × 32 inches (76.2 × 81.3 cm)
Collection of the Modern Art Museum
of Fort Worth
Gift of Musa and Tom Mayer

66 **Untitled** 1968
Acrylic on panel
18 × 20 inches (45.7 × 50.7 cm)
Private Collection, New York

67 **Untitled** 1968
Acrylic on panel
18 × 20 inches (45.7 × 50.7 cm)
Herbert and Annette Kopp, Munich

68 **Untitled** 1968
Acrylic on panel
18 × 20 inches (45.7 × 50.7 cm)
Private Collection

69 **Boot** 1968
Acrylic on panel
16 $\frac{1}{2}$ × 19 $\frac{1}{2}$ inches (41.9 × 49.5 cm)
Private Collection

70 **Blackboard** 1969
Oil on canvas
79 $\frac{1}{2}$ × 112 inches (201.9 × 284.5 cm)
Private Collection

71 **By the Window** 1969
Oil on canvas
78 × 81 $\frac{1}{4}$ inches (198.1 × 206.4 cm)
Private Collection

72 **City** 1969
Oil on canvas
72 × 67 $\frac{1}{2}$ inches (182.9 × 171.4 cm)
Private Collection

73 **Edge of Town** 1969
Oil on canvas
77 × 110 $\frac{1}{4}$ inches (196.2 × 280 cm)
The Edward R. Broida Collection

74 **Group** 1969
Ink on paper
23 $\frac{1}{4}$ × 26 $\frac{1}{2}$ inches (59.1 × 67.3 cm)
San Francisco Museum of Modern Art
In memory of Philip Guston's friendship,
gift of the Turnbull Foundation, Paule
Anglim, and William D. Turnbull
© Estate of Philip Guston

75 **The Law** 1969
Charcoal on paper
17 $\frac{7}{8}$ × 14 $\frac{5}{8}$ inches (45.4 × 37.1 cm)
Private Collection

76 **The Studio** 1969
Oil on canvas
48 × 42 inches (121.9 × 106.7 cm)
Private Collection

77 **Untitled** 1969
Acrylic on panel
18 × 20 inches (45.7 × 50.7 cm)
Collection Peter Blum, New York

78 **Bad Habits** 1970
Oil on canvas
73 × 78 inches (185.5 × 198.2 cm)
Collection National Gallery of Australia,
Canberra

79 **Courtroom** 1970
Oil on canvas
67 × 129 inches (170.2 × 327.7 cm)
Robert and Jane Meyerhoff, Phoenix,
Maryland

80 **Dawn** 1970
Oil on canvas
67 $\frac{1}{4}$ × 108 inches (170.8 × 274.3 cm)
Private Collection

81 **Flatlands** 1970
Oil on canvas
70 × 114 $\frac{1}{2}$ inches (177.8 × 290.8 cm)
Collection Byron R. Meyer, San Francisco

82 **Scared Stiff** 1970
Oil on canvas
57 × 81 inches (144.8 × 205.7 cm)
Private Collection, Well, N. Yorkshire

83 **Window** 1970
Graphite on paper
18 × 21 inches (45.7 × 53.3 cm)
Collection of Harry W. and
Mary Margaret Anderson

84 **Painter's Table** 1973
Oil on canvas
77 $\frac{1}{4}$ × 90 inches (196.2 × 228.6 cm)
National Gallery of Art, Washington
Gift (partial and promised) of
Ambassador and Mrs. Donald M. Blinken
in memory of Maurice H. Blinken and in
honor of the 50th Anniversary of the
National Gallery of Art, 1991.69.1

85 **Painting, Smoking, Eating** 1973
Oil on canvas
77 $\frac{1}{2}$ × 103 $\frac{1}{2}$ inches (196.8 × 262.9 cm)
Collection Stedelijk Museum, Amsterdam
Purchased with support of the
Vereniging "Rembrandt"

86 **Pantheon** 1973
Oil on panel
45 × 48 inches (114.3 × 121.9 cm)
The Estate of Philip Guston
Courtesy of McKee Gallery, New York

87 **Four Heads** 1974
Ink on paper
18 × 24 inches (45.7 × 61 cm)
The Edward R. Broida Collection

88 **Lamp and Chair** 1974
Ink on paper
19 × 25 $\frac{1}{4}$ inches (48.3 × 64.1 cm)
The Edward R. Broida Collection

89 **Self-Portrait** 1974
Ink on paper
13 $\frac{3}{4}$ × 16 $\frac{3}{4}$ inches (34.9 × 42.5 cm)
Private Collection

90 **Smoking in Bed** 1974
Ink on paper
19 × 24 inches (48.3 × 61 cm)
Collection of Jasper Johns

91 From the Phlebitis Series 1975
Ink on paper
19 × 24 inches (48.3 × 61 cm)
Private Collection

92 From the Phlebitis Series 1975
Ink on paper
24 × 19 inches (61 × 48.3 cm)
Private Collection

93 From the Phlebitis Series 1975
Ink on paper
24 × 19 inches (61 × 48.3 cm)
Private Collection

94 Head 1975
Oil on canvas
69^1/$_4$ × 74^1/$_2$ inches (175.9 × 189.2 cm)
Private Collection, London

95 San Clemente 1975
Oil on canvas
68 × 73^1/$_4$ inches (172.7 × 186.1 cm)
Private Collection

96 Web 1975
Oil on canvas
67 × 97^1/$_4$ inches (170.2 × 247 cm)
The Edward R. Broida Collection

97 Web 1975
Ink on paper
19 × 24 inches (48.3 × 61 cm)
Private Collection

98 Source 1976
Oil on canvas
76 × 117 inches (193 × 297.2 cm)
The Edward R. Broida Collection

99 Pit 1976
Oil on canvas
74^1/$_2$ × 116 inches (189.2 × 294.8 cm)
Collection National Gallery of Australia,
Canberra

100 Wharf 1976
Oil on canvas
80 × 116 inches (203.2 × 294.6 cm)
Collection of the Modern Art Museum
of Fort Worth
Museum Purchase, The Friends of Art
Endowment Fund

101 Green Rug 1976
Oil on canvas
94 × 68^1/$_2$ inches (238.8 × 174 cm)
The Edward R. Broida Collection

102 Ancient Wall 1976
Oil on linen
80 × 93^5/$_8$ inches (203.2 × 237.8 cm)
Hirshhorn Museum and Sculpture
Garden, Smithsonian Institution
Regents Collections Acquisition Program,
1987

103 The Painter 1976
Oil on canvas
74 × 116 inches (188 × 294.6 cm)
Jane Lang Davis

104 Cherries 1976
Oil on canvas
69 × 116 inches (175.3 × 294.6 cm)
The Edward R. Broida Collection

105 Frame 1976
Oil on canvas
74 × 116 inches (188 × 294.6 cm)
Collection of Robert Lehrman,
Washington, D.C.

106 Cherries II 1976
Oil on canvas
78 × 115 inches (198.1 × 292.1 cm)
Lyn and Jerry Grinstein

107 Sleeping 1977
Oil on canvas
85 × 70 inches (215.9 × 177.8 cm)
Private Collection

108 Couple in Bed 1977
Oil on canvas
81^1/$_8$ × 94^5/$_8$ inches (206.2 × 240.3 cm)
The Art Institute of Chicago,
Through prior bequest of Frances W. Pick
and Memorial Gift from her daughter,
Mary P. Hines, 1989.435

109 The Night 1977
Oil on canvas
68 × 120^1/$_4$ inches (172.7 × 305.4 cm)
Daniel W. Dietrich II

110 Back View 1977
Oil on canvas
69 × 94 inches (175.3 × 238.8 cm)
San Francisco Museum of Modern Art
Gift of the artist
© Estate of Philip Guston

111 To I.B. 1977
Oil on canvas
67^1/$_4$ × 80 inches (170.8 × 203.2 cm)
The Estate of Philip Guston
Courtesy of McKee Gallery, New York

112 Cabal 1977
Oil on canvas
68 × 116 inches (172.7 × 294.6 cm)
Whitney Museum of American Art,
New York
50th Anniversary Gift of Mr. and
Mrs. Raymond J. Learsy, 81.38

113 The Street 1977
Oil on canvas
69 × 110^3/$_4$ inches (175.3 × 281.3 cm)
The Metropolitan Museum of Art,
New York
Purchase, Lila Acheson Wallace and
Mr. and Mrs. Andrew Saul Gifts, Gift of
George A. Hearn, by exchange, and
Arthur Hoppock Hearn Fund, 1983
(1983.457)

114 **Pyramid and Shoe** 1977
Oil on canvas
68 × 116 inches (172.7 × 294.6 cm)
David and Renee McKee, New York

115 **Curtain** 1977
Oil on canvas
69 × 106 inches (175.3 × 269.2 cm)
The Estate of Philip Guston
Courtesy of McKee Gallery, New York

116 **Street II** 1977
Oil on canvas
67 ^{1}/$_2$ × 72 ^{1}/$_2$ inches (171.4 × 184.1 cm)
The Estate of Philip Guston
Courtesy of McKee Gallery, New York

117 **Ladder** 1978
Oil on canvas
70 × 108 inches (177.8 × 274.3 cm)
The Edward R. Broida Collection

118 **Hinged** 1978
Oil on canvas
68 ^{1}/$_2$ × 73 ^{1}/$_2$ inches (174 × 187 cm)
Flick Collection

119 **Feet on Rug** 1978
Oil on canvas
80 × 104 inches (203.2 × 264.2 cm)
The Estate of Philip Guston
Courtesy of McKee Gallery, New York

120 **Red Sky** 1978
Oil on canvas
82 × 105 ^{1}/$_2$ inches (208.3 × 268 cm)
Private Collection

121 **Painter's Forms II** 1978
Oil on canvas
75 × 108 inches (190.5 × 274.3 cm)
Collection of the Modern Art Museum
of Fort Worth
Museum Purchase, The Friends of Art
Endowment Fund

122 **The Line** 1978
Oil on canvas
71 × 73 ^{1}/$_4$ inches (180.3 × 186.1 cm)
Private Collection
Courtesy of McKee Gallery, New York

123 **Friend—To M. F.** 1978
Oil on canvas
68 × 88 inches (172.7 × 223.5 cm)
Purchased with funds from the Coffin
Fine Arts Trust; Nathan Emory Coffin
Collection of the Des Moines Art Center,
1991.48

124 **Aegean** 1978
Oil on canvas
68 × 126 inches (172.7 × 320 cm)
The Estate of Philip Guston
Courtesy of McKee Gallery, New York

125 **Plain** 1979
Oil on canvas
69 × 93 inches (175.3 × 236.2 cm)
Carnegie Museum of Art, Pittsburgh
Fellows Fund, 1980

126 **Group in Sea** 1979
Oil on canvas
68 × 88 ^{1}/$_2$ inches (172.7 × 224.8 cm)
Private Collection
Courtesy Timothy Taylor Gallery, London

127 **Talking** 1979
Oil on canvas
68 ^{1}/$_2$ × 78 inches (174 × 198.1 cm)
The Edward R. Broida Collection

128 **Flame** 1979
Oil on canvas
48 × 60 inches (121.9 × 152.4 cm)
Private Collection

129 **Wheel** 1979
Oil on canvas
48 × 60 inches (121.9 × 152.4 cm)
Private Collection

130 **Large Brush** 1979
Oil on canvas
32 × 36 inches (81.3 × 91.4 cm)
Aaron I. Fleischman

131 **The Hand** 1979
Oil on linen
32 × 36 inches (81 × 91.5 cm)
Kunstmuseum Winterthur, Inv. Nr. 1581

132 **Untitled** 1980
Ink on paper
23 × 29 inches (58.4 × 73.7 cm)
Private Collection

133 **Untitled (Cherries)** 1980
Acrylic and ink on paper
20 × 30 inches (50.8 × 76.2 cm)
Private Collection

134 **Untitled (Head)** 1980
Acrylic and ink on paper
20 × 30 inches (50.8 × 76.2 cm)
Private Collection

135 **Untitled (Hillside)** 1980
Acrylic and ink on paper
23 × 29 inches (58.4 × 73.7 cm)
Private Collection

136 **Untitled (Kettle)** 1980
Acrylic and ink on paper
20 × 30 inches (50.8 × 76.2 cm)
Private Collection

137 **Untitled (Ladder)** 1980
Acrylic and ink on paper
20 × 30 inches (50.8 × 76.2 cm)
Private Collection

138 **Untitled (Sandwich)** 1980
Acrylic and ink on paper
20 × 30 inches (50.8 × 76.2 cm)
Private Collection

Chronology

This biographical outline incorporates information found in the following publications: *Philip Guston*, San Francisco Museum of Modern Art, 1980; *Philip Guston*, Robert Storr, 1986; *Philip Guston: La Raíz del Dibujo*, Sala Rekalde, Bilbao, 1993; and *Philip Guston Gemälde 1947–1979*, Kunstmuseum Bonn, 1999. Supplemental information was provided by the McKee Gallery archives.

1913

Philip Goldstein born June 27th in Montreal, Canada, the youngest of seven children. Parents Louis and Rachel are Russian immigrants from Odessa.

1919

Goldstein family moves to Los Angeles.

1923/24

Finds father dead, the result of suicide by hanging.

1926

Begins to withdraw to closet lit by single light bulb hanging from ceiling to practice copying cartoon strips, like George Herriman's *Krazy Kat* and Bud Fisher's *Mutt and Jeff*. Mother enrolls him in correspondence course from Cleveland School of Cartooning.

1927

Enrolls in Manual Arts High School in Los Angeles; becomes friends with Jackson Pollock and Manuel Tolegian. Teacher Frederick John de St. Vrain Schwankovsky introduces them to Oriental philosophy, the teachings of mystics Ouspensky and Krishnamurti, and modern European art. Creates drawings for student publication *Weekly*. Wins drawing contest sponsored by Los Angeles *Times*.

1928

Expelled, along with Pollock, for distributing leaflets satirizing English department and criticizing popularity of sports in the school. Pollock is readmitted, Guston does not return.

1929

Paints and studies art independently nights and weekends. Becomes aware of Mexican mural movement through January issue of *Creative Art* magazine. Visits Ojai Valley in May with Pollock, Tolegian, and Schwankovsky to see Hindu mystic Krishnamurti.

1930

Awarded yearlong scholarship to Otis Art Institute in Los Angeles; meets future wife, Musa McKim. Quits Otis Art Institute after three months. Through Jackson

Guston and Musa McKim in
New York loft, 1936

PHILIP GUSTON RETROSPECTIVE

Pollock, meets painter Reuben Kadish. Begins to study reproductions of Italian Renaissance masters Piero della Francesca, Giotto, Mantegna, and Michelangelo. Through Kadish, meets Los Angeles Surrealist painter Lorser Feitelson. At invitation of Feitelson, visits Walter and Louise Arensberg's collection in their home, designed by Frank Lloyd Wright. Introduced there to several modern European paintings bought at 1913 Armory Show, as well as works by Pablo Picasso and Giorgio de Chirico, which profoundly impact his work. Visits Pomona College in Los Angeles with Pollock to observe José Clemente Orozco painting his mural *Prometheus* in Frary Dinner Hall. Produces first drawing featuring hooded figure, leading to creation of painting *Conspirators* (1930, now lost). Pollock leaves for New York in the fall to attend Art Students League and enrolls in Thomas Hart Benton's classes.

1931

First solo exhibition, organized by artist Herman Cherry, takes place in Los Angeles at Stanley Rose bookshop and gallery, where *Conspirators* is sold. Becomes increasingly interested in political and social issues. Joins John Reed Club, a Marxist group encouraging artists to abandon concept of "art for art's sake." Working with other members of club, creates several portable murals, including his own submission depicting "Scottsboro Boys" case. Murals eventually destroyed by group of para-police called the "Red Squad." Hired for minor role as artist in John Barrymore movie *Trilby*.

1932

Becomes more familiar with Mexican mural movement, due to local activities of Orozco and David Alfaro Siqueiros, who is painting controversial murals in Chouinard Art Institute and Plaza Art Center in Los Angeles.

1933

Exhibits in a museum for first time, in *XIV Annual Exhibition of Painters and Sculptors* at Los Angeles Museum. *Mother and Child*, a work revealing influence of Picasso, Parmigianino, de Chirico, and Piero della Francesca, is included in exhibition.

1934

Travels with Reuben Kadish and poet/critic Jules Langsner to Morelia, Mexico in late spring. With help from Siqueiros, they are commissioned to paint a mural in the Palacio de Maximilian (now the University of Michoacan) entitled *The Struggle Against Terror* addressing the fight against fascism and war (mural is later illustrated and titled *The Struggle Against War and Fascism* in *Time* magazine, April 1, 1935). Returns to California to complete mural commissioned by International Ladies Garment Workers Union for City of Hope Sanitarium for Tuberculosis in Duarte.

1935

Moves to New York City at urging of Pollock. Lives temporarily with Pollock and Pollock's brother Sande McCoy. Contracted by murals department of Works Progress Administration (WPA), organization created by Roosevelt's New Deal Program and Federal Arts Project

(FAP) to provide jobs and economic support for artists. WPA/FAP, under direction of Holger Cahill, also hires Arshile Gorky, Adolph Gottlieb, Willem de Kooning, Lee Krasner, and Mark Rothko.

1936

Meets James Brooks, Burgoyne Diller, Gorky, de Kooning, Conrad Marca-Relli, and Stuart Davis while working for WPA/FAP. Visits exhibition *Cubism and Abstract Art* at MoMA and A. E. Gallatin collection of modern European art at Museum of Living Art, New York University, where he sees *The City* by Fernand Léger and *Three Musicians* by Picasso. Attends de Chirico exhibition at Pierre Matisse Gallery.

1937

Marries artist/poet Musa McKim on February 4th, with Sande McCoy as witness. Travels to Dartmouth College with Pollock and McCoy to see Orozco's mural *The Epic of American Civilization* (1932–34). Paints *Bombardment* in response to war in Spain and German bombing raids of April.

1938

Paints murals *Early Mail Service* and *Construction of the Railroad* for post office in Commerce, Georgia, demonstrating compositional influence of Piero della Francesca's frescoes in Arezzo and Uccello's works on equestrian combat. Spends summer in Ferndale, Bucks County, Pennsylvania near McCoy and Pollock.

1939

Paints *Maintaining America's Skills* (destroyed 1940) for facade of WPA Building at New York World's Fair; wins first prize in contest based on public opinion. Creates *Work and Play/Cultural and Recreational Activities of a Community Center*, mural commissioned by WPA/FAP for Queensbridge Housing Project, New York; considers it to be first important pictorial work. Sees Max Beckmann exhibition at Curt Valentin's Buchholz Gallery, New York.

1940

Quits WPA after completion of Queensbridge mural. Moves to Woodstock, New York and begins transition back to easel painting, a shift culminating in *Martial Memory* (completed 1941), which presents child's play as allegory of war. Attends Picasso retrospective at MoMA.

1941

Creates murals for President Steamship Lines in *S.S. Monroe*, *S.S. Hayes*, and *S.S. Jackson* (removed when employed for WWII). Produces two murals in collaboration with Musa entitled *New Hampshire Pulpwood Logging* and *Wildlife in the White Mountains* for United States Forestry Building in Laconia, New Hampshire. Takes position as art teacher for University of Iowa, Iowa City (at that time known as the State University of Iowa). Focuses on studio painting, especially compositions containing figures and objects, as well as portraits and cityscapes. Completes first mature easel painting, *Martial Memory*.

Philip's panel is on the left,
Musa's is on the right

1942

Included in *Annual Exhibition of American Painting
and Sculpture* at Art Institute of Chicago (also in 1943,
1944, 1945, 1946, 1951, and 1959). Finishes last mural,
Reconstruction and Well-Being of the Family (installed
1943), for Social Security Building auditorium,
Washington, D.C.

1943

Daughter, Musa Jane, born January 18th. Receives
commission from *Fortune* magazine to illustrate articles
on defense industry and Central Training Command's
army air-training programs. Visits airfield training
centers in Texas for assignment. Creates series of
drawings used for training U.S. Navy fighter pilots.
Attends classes in celestial navigation to complete set
of murals used as visual aids for pre-flight training
by Naval Air Force. Included in *The Biennial Exhibition
of Contemporary American Oil Paintings* at Corcoran
Gallery of Art, Washington, D.C. (also in 1945, 1949,
and 1955).

1944

Holds solo exhibition of paintings and drawings at
University of Iowa. Participates in *The Annual Exhibition
of Painting and Sculpture* organized by Fine Arts
Academy of Pennsylvania in Philadelphia.

1945

Sentimental Moment (1944) wins First Prize in *Painting
in the United States* from Carnegie Institute, Pittsburgh.
Holds first solo exhibition in New York at Midtown
Galleries. Leaves University of Iowa to accept teaching

position at Washington University, St. Louis until 1947,
after which Max Beckmann fills position. Paints *Porch I*
and *If This Be Not I*.

1946

Awarded John Barton Payne Medal and Purchase Prize
from *The Fifth Biennial Exhibition of Contemporary
American Paintings, 1946* at Virginia Museum of Fine
Arts, Richmond for *The Sculptor* (1943).

1947

Moves to artists' colony in Byrdcliffe, New York near the
Overlook Mountain area after receiving Guggenheim
Fellowship. Moves to Woodstock soon after. Receives
Joseph Pennel Award from Pennsylvania Academy of
Fine Arts and Altman Award in *121st Annual Exhibition
of Contemporary American Painting, Sculpture, Water
Color, and Graphic Art* from National Academy of Design,
New York for *Holiday* (1944). Finishes *Porch No. 2*,
containing depictions of legs and studded shoe soles,
images appearing throughout later works. Excepting
The Tormentors (completed 1948), abandons painting
and focuses on drawing with an interest in exploring
abstraction. Befriends painter Bradley Walker Tomlin.

1948

Awarded $1,000 grant from American Academy of Arts
and Letters, New York; Purchase Prize from University
of Illinois; and Prix de Rome from American Academy,
Rome. Travels to Europe for first time; studies Italian,
French, and Spanish masters firsthand. During yearlong
stay, contacts composer John Cage and artist Conrad

Marca-Relli in Rome. From travels, gains new outlook toward drawing, including new techniques, such as drawing views from hotel windows. *Ischia* and other landscape drawings further suggest an increasing interest in abstraction. Settles in Woodstock, New York after returning.

1949

Mother dies in Los Angeles. Befriends critics Thomas Hess and Harold Rosenberg and artists Barnett Newman, Mark Rothko, and Robert Motherwell, who encourages study of existential writings by Camus, Kafka, Kierkegaard, and Sartre. Meets composer Morton Feldman through John Cage. Briefly shares studio in New York City with Tomlin and James Brooks. Lives with Robert Phelps and his wife, the painter Rosemarie Beck, before moving into Studio Building on West 10th Street. Completes painting *Review*.

1950

Teaches at University of Minnesota in Minneapolis for spring semester. Moves back to New York and joins "Eighth Street Club," a group of artists sharing ideas and concerns in attempt to form sense of community.

Takes position as Professor of Art, New York University. Teaches one class a week and visits Cedar Street Tavern, an Abstract Expressionist "hangout," after class. Attends conferences with Cage and Feldman organized by Zen master D. T. Suzuki. Focuses on abstract ink-on-paper drawings such as *Small Quill Drawing*, in which built-up marks suggest influence of Oriental calligraphy. Completes *Red Painting*, signaling shift from figuration to abstraction.

1952

Holds first solo exhibition of abstract works at Peridot Gallery, New York; participates in *Expressionism in American Painting* at Albright Art Gallery, Buffalo, New York. Joins Charles Egan Gallery, New York, also representing Franz Kline, de Kooning, Robert Nakian, George McNeil, and Isamu Noguchi. Meets art critic Dore Ashton, who later writes several extensive essays concerning his life and work. Begins another period in which focus is directed toward drawing. Preparatory drawings such as *Drawing Related to Zone* (completed 1954) contain grid-like compositions.

1953

Holds solo exhibition at Egan Gallery. Included in *Abstract Expressionists* at Baltimore Museum of Art. Begins teaching for Pratt Institute, Brooklyn (until 1958). Sees Federico Fellini's films *Lo sceicco bianco* (*White Sheik*, 1952) and *I Vitelloni* (*The Young and the Passionate*, 1953); becomes lifelong admirer.

Guston drawing in the gardens of the American Academy in Rome, 1960

1954

Completes *Zone*, featuring large red areas. Leads to *Painting*; *For M* (completed 1955); and *The Room* (completed 1955). Paintings are influential, in school described briefly as "Abstract Impressionism."

1955

Joins Sidney Janis Gallery, New York; shows until 1962 along with other Abstract Expressionists, including Kline, de Kooning, Pollock, and Rothko. Increases use of impasto, resulting in centralized areas of intensely colored amorphous shapes that emerge in a series of gouaches and paintings, such as *To Fellini* (1958).

1956

Included in *12 Americans* at MoMA and *Modern Art in the United States* at Tate Gallery, London. Sells *Painting* (1954) to Philip Johnson for MoMA. Jackson Pollock dies in car accident.

1957

Participates in *IV Bienal de São Paulo.* Executes *Native's Return* and *Oasis*, examples in a series with strong use of blue. Produces *Fable II* and *Cythera*. Continues to draw; begins producing large number of small oil paintings and gouaches.

1958

Included in *The New American Painting*, exhibition organized by MoMA to introduce Abstract Expressionists to Europe, and *Nature in Abstraction* at the Whitney. Begins new period of drawing using a more fluid line. *Head—Double View* and *Forms in Change* demonstrate beginning of disenchantment with abstraction and anticipate works inspired by figuration and landscape. Makes statement that questions abstraction, which appears in first issue of *It Is: A Magazine of Abstract Art*. Becomes friends with writer Edward Estlin Cummings and poet Stanley Jasspon Kunitz, who wins Pulitzer Prize this year and who later becomes critic under pseudonym "Dilly Tante."

1959

Leaves teaching profession (until 1973) after receiving $10,000 fellowship from Ford Foundation. Wins Flora Mayer Witkowsky Prize in *63rd American Exhibition, Painting, Sculpture* from Art Institute of Chicago for *The Street* (1956). Participates in *Documenta II*, Kassel, Germany and *V Bienal de São Paulo*. Completes *The Painter*.

The 1962 Philip Guston
retrospective at the Solomon R.
Guggenheim Museum, New York

PHILIP GUSTON RETROSPECTIVE

Guston with Willem de Kooning in de Kooning's Long Island studio, 1965

Guston in his New York studio, c. 1965

1960

Participates in symposium moderated by Harold Rosenberg with Motherwell, Ad Reinhardt, and Jack Tworkov at Philadelphia Museum School of Art in March. *It Is* magazine publishes transcription of event in article "The Philadelphia Panel." Sends thirteen paintings to Venice Biennale as part of United States Pavilion. Spends summer traveling in Europe with wife and daughter. Visits Rome, Florence, Paris, and London. Stays in Umbria to study nearby frescoes by Piero della Francesca. Creates drawings *Sortie*, *Celebration* (completed 1961), and *Pleasures*, which include elements of landscape and figuration. Returns to New York; works with forms that resemble heads while simultaneously limiting coloration to gray, blue, and pink tones. Begins to explore lithographic techniques.

1961

Included in *American Abstract Expressionists and Imagists* at Guggenheim and MoMA exhibition *Modern American Drawing*, which travels to Europe and Israel. Exhibition *Philip Guston/Franz Kline* held at Dwan Gallery, Los Angeles. Invited to serve as Guest Critic for Yale Summer School in Norfolk, Connecticut (invited back in 1963, 1970, 1971, 1973, and 1974). Completes "dark" painting *North*.

1962

Leaves Sidney Janis Gallery with other Abstract Expressionists in protest of their hosting a Pop art exhibition. Major retrospective organized by the Solomon R. Guggenheim Museum; travels to Amsterdam, Brussels, London, and Los Angeles. Begins friendship with poet Bill Berkson.

1963

Joins Marlborough-Gerson Gallery with Gottlieb, Motherwell, Rothko, and David Smith. In September, daughter marries Daniel Kadish, son of Reuben Kadish (divorced 1972). Returns home to New York after attending Guggenheim retrospective in Los Angeles. Travels to Montreal with wife to see childhood home. Creates series of dark gouaches, including *Departure*, *Untitled*, and *Dark Form*, containing more figurative elements.

1964

Participates in *Painting and Sculpture of a Decade: 1954–1964* at Tate Gallery, London; *The American Contemporary Drawing* at Guggenheim; and *An International Exhibition of Drawing* in Mathildenhöhe, Darmstadt. Grandson David born. Spends Christmas with family at the Rothkos'.

1965

Helps create New York Studio School for Drawing and Painting, established in original Whitney Museum. Included in *New York School: The First Generation of Paintings of the 1940s and 1950s* at Los Angeles County Museum of Art. Publishes two articles revealing fascination with process of painting: "Piero della Francesca: The Impossibility of Painting" in May *Art News* and "Faith, Hope, and Impossibility" in *Art News Annual* XXXI (1966). Begins to focus solely on drawing at end of year. Executes pen-and-ink drawings depicting simple forms using fine contour lines, seen in *The Stone* and *The Scale*. Leaves Marlborough-Gerson Gallery. Second grandson, Jonathan, born.

1966

Philip Guston: Recent Paintings and Drawings, solo exhibition of abstract paintings, drawings, and gouaches from 1958–65 held at The Jewish Museum, New York; *Philip Guston, A Selective Retrospective Exhibition: 1945–1965* held at Rose Art Museum at Brandeis University in Waltham, Massachusetts; solo exhibition held at Santa Barbara Museum of Art. Provides illustrations for poem "Ode to Michael Goldberg" in MoMA curator Frank O'Hara's book *In Memory of My Feelings*. Begins two series of minimal drawings called "pure drawings." Rejoins Marlborough-Gerson Gallery with Conrad Marca-Relli. Travels with Renate Ponsold to Europe. Separates from Musa for one year. Buys house in Siesta Key, Florida. Musa moves to McDowell Colony in Peterborough, New York in summer. Reconciles with Musa in the winter.

1967

Returns to Woodstock and continues friendship with Marca-Relli and next-door-neighbor, sculptor Raoul Hague, who creates small museum among several different buildings. Portrait of Musa McKim part of collection. *Six Painters: Mondrian, Guston, Kline, de Kooning, Pollock, Rothko*, organized by Morton Feldman and Dominique de Menil, held at University of St. Thomas, Houston. Conducts seminars for New York Studio School until 1973. Begins relationship with David McKee at the Marlborough-Gerson Gallery. Creates drawings *Edge* and *Mark*.

1968

Receives second Guggenheim Fellowship. Spends summer in Saratoga Springs, New York as Artist in Residence, Skidmore College. Continues to re-engage figuration through drawings of everyday objects. Forms friendship with poet Clark Coolidge, who later publishes exchanges with Guston along with drawings in the book *Baffling Means* (1991).

Guston in 1977

1969

Included in *New York Painting and Sculpture: 1940–1970* to celebrate centenary of Metropolitan Museum of Art. Guest Critic for Graduate School of Fine Arts, Columbia University (also in 1970 and 1972). Returns to painting, first by transfixing drawings onto small panels and later by executing large paintings like *City* and *City Limits*. Initiates friendship with writer Philip Roth.

1970

Receives Honorary Doctorate in Fine Arts from Boston University. Selected as Trustee of American Academy in Rome. Holds first exhibition of new figurative works, including those with Ku Klux Klan imagery, in October at Marlborough Gallery. Although Rosenberg responds favorably in *The New Yorker*, show receives mostly negative reaction. Travels to Europe for nine months shortly after Marlborough opening. Holds solo exhibition of new works at Boston University. Ends friendship with Feldman after Feldman brings critic Robert Hughes to see new works, who later claims they

demonstrate "clumsy figuration." Publishes theories on art in article "Philip Guston: A Day's Work, 1970" in *Art Now: New York*.

1971

Travels with wife to Orvieto, Siena, Arezzo, Florence, San Gimignano, Venice, Sicily, Greece, and Crete. Asked to serve as Artist in Residence at American Academy in Rome. Begins *Roma* series of oils on paper depicting formal gardens of Italy and Etruscan and Roman excavation sites. Returns to Woodstock at end of summer after Musa develops meningitis. Executes series of caricature drawings entitled *Poor Richard*, inspired by dinner conversations with Philip Roth, who is working on *Our Gang*, a satirical comment on the Nixon administration.

1972

Leaves Marlborough Gallery in October. Transports all
works in Marlborough Gallery's storage to Woodstock.
Elected member of National Institute of Arts and
Letters. Filmed by Michael Blackwood for West German
Television. Begins *Painting, Smoking, Eating* (completed
1973), self-portrait lying in bed performing signature
acts. Excessive eating habits and smoking three packs of
unfiltered Camel cigarettes a day begin to affect health.

1973

Begins position teaching once a month at Boston
University (until 1978). Participates in *American Art at
Mid-Century 1*, organized by Dr. William Seitz for
National Gallery of Art, Washington, D.C.; Henry
Geldzahler curates *Philip Guston: Drawings 1938–1972*
at Metropolitan Museum of Art. Article in autumn issue
of *Boston University Journal* contains quote by Guston
on subject of drawing. Executes *Painter's Table* and
Smoking I. Introduces one-eyed, "lima bean–shaped"
(self-portrait) heads as dominant theme.

1974

Joins David McKee and Renee Conforte's new gallery on
second floor of Barbizon Hotel for Women on East 63rd
Street, New York. Exhibition of new paintings opens the
David McKee Gallery. Large exhibition of new work held
at Boston University School of Fine and Applied Arts
Gallery. Publishes two articles written with Harold
Rosenberg: "Conversations: Guston's Recent Paintings"
in *Boston University Journal* and "On Cave Art, Church
Art, Ethnic Art, and Art" in December *Art News*. Paints
Smoking in Bed II and *Head and Bottle* (completed 1975).

1975

Honored with Distinguished Teaching of Art Award
from College Art Association. Solo show of *Roma* series
held at Makler Gallery, Philadelphia. Begins examination
of "deluge" theme in drawings *Current* and *Lower Level*.
Begins to depict piles of objects from studio in drawings
and paintings like *Allegory*, which portrays Morton
Feldman as music, Raoul Hague as sculpture, Musa as
poetry, and himself as painting.

1976

Hospitalized for short time due to exhaustion.
Participates in *Drawings by Five Abstract Expressionist
Painters* with de Kooning, Gorky, Kline, and Pollock at
Massachusetts Institute of Technology Hayden Gallery.
Solo exhibition at David McKee Gallery includes *Deluge*
paintings. In prolific burst, creates key works *Pit, Wharf,
Source, Green Sea, Floor, Monument, Frame, Green Rug*.
Daughter Musa marries Tom Mayer in Ohio. Dore
Ashton publishes *Yes, But . . . : A Critical Study of Philip
Guston*. Befriends poet/novelist Ross Feld.

1977

Two-part exhibition in March at David McKee Gallery includes key works from 1976. Musa hospitalized from stroke in April. Anxiety and severe depression lead to complete withdrawal from the New York art world. Leaves McKee Gallery in May; returns in December. In response to Musa's illness, paints series of intimate portraits, *Couple in Bed*, *Sleeping,* and *Head*, featuring a fantasy portrait of Musa's condition. San Francisco Museum of Modern Art purchases the triptych *Blue Light*, *Red Sea*, *The Swell*.

1978

Elected member of American Academy of Arts and Sciences in Boston. Becomes Professor Emeritus at Boston University. Paints *Tomb*, *Friend—To M. F.*, and *Ladder*.

1979

Six large late works included in *New Work—New York* at Hayward Gallery, London. Suffers near-fatal heart attack after traveling to San Francisco in March. Admitted to Coronary Care Unit at Benedictine Hospital, Kingston, New York. Recovers, but productivity slows as a result. Begins to create small-format paintings in summer. Paints *East Coker—T. S. E.* after re-reading T. S. Eliot's *Four Quartets*. Produces lithographs, with Gemini Prints, using aluminum and transfer paper.

1980

Honored with Creative Arts Award for Painting from Brandeis University. Featured in "A Talk with Philip Guston," published by Mark Stevens in March 15 issue of *New Republic*. Large retrospective opens May 16th, organized by SFMOMA; travels to Corcoran Gallery of Fine Art, Washington, D.C.; Museum of Contemporary Art, Chicago; Denver Art Museum; and Whitney Museum, New York. *Pit* and *Bad Habits* purchased by the National Gallery of Australia, Canberra. On June 7th, suffers heart attack and dies while eating dinner in Woodstock at home of Sylvia and Fred Elias, his doctor. Buried in Woodstock Artists' Cemetery.

Selected Bibliography

Writings, Statements, and Illustrations by the Artist

1943

Illustrations for "Brave New World, F.O.B.," *Fortune* (August 1943): 124, 126–27.

Illustrations for "Troop Carrier Command," *Fortune* (October 1943): 130–35.

1944

Illustrations for "The Air Training Program," *Fortune* (February 1944): 147–52, 174.

Statement in "Types—by American Artists," *Art News Annual* (December 1944): 88.

1955

Illustrations for Delmore Schwartz, "Fulfillment: Poem," in "Poets and Pictures," *Art News Annual XXIV* (November 1955): 90–91.

1956

"Four Drawings," *The Black Mountain Review* (Spring 1956): 171–74.

Statement in Dorothy C. Miller, ed., catalogue for *12 Americans* (New York: The Museum of Modern Art, 1956): 36.

1957

Sam Hunter, "Interview with Philip Guston," *Playbill* (November 1957): 52–53.

Joan Pring, "Interview with Guston in His Studio at 113 East Eighteenth Street, New York, June 25, 1957," Archives of The Museum of Modern Art, New York.

"Notes on the Artist," in John I. H. Baur, catalogue for *Bradley Walker Tomlin* (New York: Whitney Museum of American Art, 1957): 9.

1958

Statement in John I. H. Baur, catalogue for *Nature in Abstraction* (New York: Whitney Museum of American Art, 1958): 69.

Statement in *It Is* (Spring 1958): 44.

1959

Statement in catalogue for *The New American Painting* (New York: The Museum of Modern Art, 1959): 40–43.

1960

Statement in Philip Pavia and Irving Sandler, eds., "The Philadelphia Panel," *It Is* (Spring 1960): 34–38, 40. Panel discussion with Guston, Robert Motherwell, Ad Reinhardt, Harold Rosenberg, and Jack Tworkov.

1961

"In Support of the French Intellectuals," *Partisan Review* (January–February 1961): 144–45. Group statement signed by Guston and others.

1965

"Piero della Francesca: The Impossibility of Painting," *Art News* (May 1965): 38–39.

"Faith, Hope, and Impossibility," *Art News Annual XXXI*, 1966 (October 1965): 101–3; 152–53.

Bill Berkson, "Dialogue with Philip Guston, November 1, 1964," *Art and Literature: An International Review* (Winter 1965): 56–69.

1966

"Brandeis University Talk," unpublished, unedited dialogue with Joseph Ablow (Brandeis University, 1966).

Philip Guston, "Philip Guston's Object: A Dialogue with Harold Rosenberg," in Sam Hunter, catalogue for *Philip Guston: Recent Paintings and Drawings* (New York: The Jewish Museum, 1966).

1970

Anonymous, "Philip Guston: A Day's Work," *Art Now: New York* 2, no. 8 (1970); reproduced in catalogue for *Philip Guston* (New York and San Francisco: George Braziller in association with the San Francisco Museum of Modern Art, 1980).

1972

Cover and six drawings in *Big Sky* 4 (Bolinas, California, 1972).

1973

Illustrations for David Aronson, "Philip Guston: Ten Drawings," *Boston University Journal* (Autumn 1973). Features quote by Guston on the subject of drawing.

Drawings and notes in *Big Sky* 5 (Bolinas, California, 1973).

1974

With Harold Rosenberg, "Conversations: Guston's Recent Paintings," *Boston University Journal* (Fall 1974): 43–58.

With Harold Rosenberg, "On Cave Art, Church Art, Ethnic Art, and Art," *Art News* (December 1974): 36–41.

1978

"Philip Guston Talking," lecture at the University of Minnesota, 1978, transcribed by Renee McKee, in Nicholas Serota, ed., catalogue for *Philip Guston: Paintings 1969–1980* (London: Whitechapel Art Gallery, 1982): 50.

Joan Pring, "Interview with Guston in His Studio at 113 East Eighteenth Street, New York, June 25, 1978," Archives of The Museum of Modern Art, New York.

1980

Mark Stevens, "A Talk with Philip Guston," *The New Republic* (March 15, 1980): 25–28.

Jan Butterfield, "Philip Guston— A Very Anxious Fix," *Images and Issues* (Summer 1980): 30–35.

Joanne Dickson, "Transcript of a Conversation with Philip Guston, May 14, 1980," *National Arts Guide* (November–December 1980): 38.

Statement in *Philip Guston* (Los Angeles: Gemini G.E.L., 1980–83).

Articles and Reviews about the Artist

1935

Anonymous, "On a Mexican Wall," *Time* (April 1, 1935).

1938

"'Project' Mural Avoids 'Sweetness and Light,'" *Art Digest* (June 1, 1938): 15.

1939

Anonymous, "Mural on WPA Building Judged Best Outdoor Art," *The New York Times* (August 7, 1939): 3. (New York World's Fair)

Alfred Frankfurter, "Directions in U.S. Painting," *Art News* (1939).

Ruth G. Harris, "Public Taste in Murals," *The New York Times* (1939).

1940

Ruth Reeves, "Art Forms in Architecture: Murals," *Architectural Record* (October 1940): 74.

1941

Chandler de Brossard, "Mural Designs for American Ships: A Federal Art Project," *The Studio* (London, February 1941): 63.

Frank Caspers, "The Field of American Art Education: Guston Goes to Iowa," *Art Digest* (September 1, 1941): 29.

Anonymous, "Our Own Choices from the Carnegie Awards," *Art News* (November 1, 1941): 10.

1942

H. W. Janson, "'Martial Memory' by Philip Guston and American Painting Today," *Bulletin of the City Art Museum of Saint Louis* (December 1942): 34–41.

1943

Anonymous, "Guston's Social Security Mural: Completed Despite War," *Art News* (March 1943): 8.

Anonymous, "The Passing Shows," *Art News* (October 1943): 29.

1944

Emily Genauer, "Excellent Examples of American Art," *New York World-Telegram* (August 12, 1944).

1945

Margaret Breuning, "Philip Guston Impresses in New York Debut," *Art Digest* (January 15, 1945): 12.

Howard Devree, "Among the New Exhibitions," *The New York Times* (January 21, 1945): 8.

Rosamund Frost, "Guston: Meaning out of Monumentality," *Art News* (February 1945): 24.

Edward Alden Jewell, "Annual Carnegie Survey," *The New York Times* (October 14, 1945): 7.

Anonymous, "Prize Winners," *Time* (October 22, 1945): 77.

Anonymous, "Critics' Choice, The Armory," *Art News* (October 1945): 19, 25, 26.

Edgar Kaufmann, "Coming Home to the Carnegie," *Art News* (October 1945): 10, 12–13.

John O'Connor, Jr., "Painting in the United States, 1945," *Carnegie Magazine* (November 1945): cover, 139–40.

1946

Anonymous, "Philip Guston: Carnegie Winner's Art is Abstract and Symbolic," *Life* (May 27, 1946): 90–92.

1947

Anonymous, "Philip Guston Wins $1,200 Art Award," *The New York Times* (January 3, 1947): 19.

H. W. Janson, "Philip Guston," *The Magazine of Art* (February 1947): 54–58.

Anonymous, "Philip Guston Visits the Institute," *Munson-Williams-Proctor Institute Bulletin* (November 1947): n.p.

1948

Emily Genauer, "This Week in Art," *New York World-Telegram* (July 13, 1948).

Mary Holmes, "Metamorphosis and Myth in Modern Art," *Perspective* (Louisville, Winter 1948): 77–85.

1950

Anonymous, "Mural Painter is Named to NYU Professorship," *The New York Times* (March 4, 1950): 18.

1952

Paul Brach, "A New Non-Objective Guston Poses Questions of Degree," *Art Digest* (January 1, 1952): 18.

A. L. Chanin, "Controversial Show by Philip Guston," *New York Compass* (January 6, 1952): 24.

Howard Devree, Review of Peridot Gallery exhibition, *The New York Times* (January 6, 1952): 9.

"One Explanation," *Time* (January 7, 1952): 56.

Dorothy Seckler, "Reviews and Previews," *Art News* (January 1952): 44.

Harold Rosenberg, "The American Action Painters," *Art News* (December 1952): 22–23, 48–50. Reprinted in H. Rosenberg, *The Tradition of the New* (New York: Horizon, 1959).

1953

Paul Brach, "New York: Affirmation," *Art Digest* (January 15, 1953): 13.

Fairfield Porter, "Philip Guston," *Art News* (February 1953): 55.

1954

Robert Rosenblum, "Varieties of Impressionism," *Art Digest* (October 1954): 7.

Sam Hunter, "Philip Guston," *Art in America* (December 1954): 291–95.

1955

S. Macdonald Wright, "Art News from Los Angeles," *Art News* (October 1955): 59.

1956

Ivan C. Karp, "Philip Guston," *The Village Voice* (February 15, 1956): 7.

Betty Chamberlain, "Philip Guston," *Art News* (February 1956): 47.

Dore Ashton, "Art: The Age of Lyricism," *Arts and Architecture* (March 1956): 14–15, 43–44.

Louis Finkelstein, "New Look: Abstract-Impressionism," *Art News* (March 1956): 36–39, 66–68.

Patrick Heron, "The Americans at the Tate Gallery," *Arts* (March 1956): 15.

Leo Steinberg, "Fritz Glarner and Philip Guston Among '12 Americans' at The Museum of Modern Art," *Arts Magazine* (June 1956): 42–45.

Dore Ashton, "Art," *Arts and Architecture* (September 1956): 4, 5, 13, 35–36.

Robert Creely, "Philip Guston: A Note," *The Black Mountain Review* (1956): 171–74.

1957

Warren R. Dash, "Philip Guston," *Arts* (April 1957): 60.

1958

Anonymous, "Review," *New York Post* (February 1958).

Parker Tyler, "Philip Guston," *Art News* (April 1958): 12.

Dore Ashton, "Art," *Arts and Architecture* (May 1958): 5, 28–29.

1959

Dore Ashton, "Art," *Arts and Architecture* (March 1959): 8, 28–29.

Irving Sandler, "Guston: A Long Voyage Home," *Art News* (December 1959): 36–39, 64–65.

John Canaday, "Art: Stylistic Poles Apart," *The New York Times* (December 30, 1959): 44.

Dore Ashton, "Some Lyricists in the New York School," *Art News Review*.

Harold Rosenberg, "Tenth Street: A Geography of Modern Art," *Art News Annual* 1959: 120–43.

1960

Carlyle Burrows, "Style Change Best for Guston," *New York Herald Tribune* (January 3, 1960).

John Canaday, "Two American Painters," *The New York Times* (January 3, 1960): B18.

Dore Ashton, "Art," *The New York Times* (February 5, 1960): 24.

Sidney Tillim, "Philip Guston's Restlessness," *Arts* (February 1960): 51.

Dore Ashton, "Art," *Arts and Architecture* (March 1960): 10–11.

John Canaday, "Word of Mouth: Four Abstract Painters Make a Brave Try at Explaining Their Ideas," *The New York Times* (April 3, 1960): II, 3.

Anonymous, "The 30th Venice Biennale: A Selection of Pictures . . . ," *Art International* (Lugano, September 25, 1960): 38–39.

Dore Ashton, "Philip Guston," *Evergreen Review* (September–October 1960): 88–91.

1961

Emily Genauer, "Masson and Guston," *New York Herald Tribune* (February 17, 1961).

Robert M. Coates, "The Art Galleries," *The New Yorker* (February 25, 1961): 90, 93.

Thomas B. Hess, "Reviews and Previews," *Art News* (March 1961): 10–11.

Irving Sandler, "Philip Guston," *Art News* (March 1961): 10.

Gerald Nordland, "De Kooning, Kline, and Guston," *Frontier* (April 1961): 23–24.

Sidney Tillim, "Month in Review," *Arts* (April 1961): 49.

Lawrence Alloway, "Ashton on Guston," *Arts Review* (July 29–August 12, 1961): 17–20.

Lawrence Alloway, "Easel Painting at the Guggenheim," *Art International* (Lugano, Christmas 1961): 33.

Dore Ashton, "Philip Guston. Paradox. Irony. The Mirror. The Traffic. The Comic. Finale," *Metro* 3 (Milan, 1961): 33–41.

1962

Emily Genauer, "Guston's Switch from Meaning," *New York Herald Tribune* (May 6, 1962).

Max Kozloff, "Art," *The Nation* (May 19, 1962) 453–55.

Irving Sandler, "In the Art Galleries," *The New York Post* (May 27, 1962): 12.

Anonymous, "One Man Show by Philip Guston at Guggenheim," *Art Students League News* (May 1962): 1–2.

Sam Hunter, "Philip Guston," *Art International* (May 1962): 62–67.

Frank O'Hara, "Growth and Guston," *Art News* (May 1962): 31–33, 51–52.

Henry P. Raleigh, "Image and Imagery in Painting," *Art Journal* (Spring 1962): 156–64.

Vivien Raynor, "Guston," *Arts* (September 1962): 50.

Lawrence Alloway, "Notes on Guston," *Art Journal* (Fall 1962): 8–11.

Bill Berkson, "Art Chronicle," *Kulchur* (New York, Fall 1962): 36–38, 42.

Hilton Kramer, "Art Chronicle," *Hudson Review* (Autumn 1962): 418–19.

1963

Roger Coleman, "Philip Guston at Whitechapel," *Art News and Review*.

Nigel Gosling, "Another Pilgrim from America," *The Observer* (January 20, 1963).

John Russell, "Beyond Nature," *The Sunday Times* (London, January 20, 1963).

Guy Burn, "Guston," *Arts Review* (January 26–February 9, 1963): 10.

Norbert Lynton, "London Letter," *Art International* (February 1963): 69–70.

David Sylvester, "Philip Guston: Luxurious," *New Statesman* (February 15, 1963): 247–48.

Edwin Mullins, "Guston and the Imaginative Experiment," *Apollo* (March 1963): 229–30.

Keith Roberts, "Exhibition at the Whitechapel Gallery," *Burlington Magazine* (March 1963): 136.

Jane Harrison, "Retrospective at Whitechapel," *Arts* (April 1963): 27.

Henry Seldis, "Giant Retrospective of Philip Guston's Works," *Los Angeles Sunday Times* (June 9, 1963): 13.

Gerald Nordland, "Review at Mid-Life," *Frontier* (July 1963): 23–25.

Peter Yates, "Philip Guston at the County Museum," *Arts and Architecture* (September 1963): 4–5, 31–32.

1965

Hilton Kramer, "Abstractions of Guston Still Further Refined," *The New York Times* (January 1, 1965): 22.

Dore Ashton, "The American Vision at the Marlborough," *Studio International* (February 1965): 64–67.

Dore Ashton, "Philip Guston, the Painter as Metaphysician," *Studio International* (February 1965): 64–67.

Morton Feldman, "Philip Guston: The Last Painter," *Art News Annual XXXI*, 1966 (October 1965): 97–100.

Francine du Plessix, ed., "Painters and Poets," *Art in America* (October–November 1965): 39.

1966

William Berkson, "Philip Guston: A New Emphasis," *Arts Magazine* (February 1966): 15–18.

Dore Ashton, "An Evolution Illuminated: New York Commentary," *Studio International* (March 1966): 112–13.

Dore Ashton, "Art," *Arts and Architecture* (April 1966): 6, 7–8.

Dore Ashton, "Exhibition at The Jewish Museum," *Arts and Architecture* (April 1966): 6–8.

Michael Benedikt, "Abstract Expressionism and After," *Art International* (April 1966): 79–80.

1967

Morton Feldman, "Some Elementary Questions," *Art News* (April 1967): 54–55, 74.

Helmut Wohl, "Philip Guston and the Problems of Painting," *Harvard Art Review* (Spring/Summer 1967): 28–30.

1970

Hilton Kramer, "A Mandarin Pretending to be a Stumblebum," *The New York Times* (October 25, 1970): B27.

Bill Berkson, "The New Gustons," *Art News* (October 1970): 44–47, 85.

John Perreault, "Art," *The Village Voice* (November 5, 1970): 26.

Harold Rosenberg, "Liberation from Detachment," *The New Yorker* (November 7, 1970): 136–41.

John Gruen, "Demons and Daisies," *New York Magazine* (November 9, 1970): 62.

Robert Hughes, "Ku Klux Komix," *Time Magazine* (November 9, 1970): 62–63.

Willis Domingo, "Galleries," *Arts* (November 1970): 59.

Musa Jane Kadish, "Art Mailbag: A Personal Vendetta against Guston?" *The New York Times* (December 6, 1970): B30. Response to article by Hilton Kramer, 1970.

Robert Pincus-Witten, "New York," *Artforum* (December 1970): 74–75.

Henry Gerrit, "New York," *Art International* (Lugano, Christmas 1970): 79–80.

1971

Morton Feldman, "Give My Regards to Eighth Street," *Art in America* (March–April 1971): 96–99.

Jacob Kainen, "Philip Guston's Work Goes Deeply against the Grain of Current Art Practice," *The Washington Post* (May 23, 1971): 36–37.

Marilyn Haegberg, "Guston's Political Hoods," *San Diego Magazine* (August 1971): 20, 22, 24, 28.

Morton Feldman, "After Modernism," *Art in America* (November–December 1971): 68–77.

1973

Barbara Rose, "Art," *New York* (July 30, 1973): 70.

Morton Feldman, "The Anxiety of Art," *Art in America* (September–October 1973).

Al Brunnelle, "Reviews and Previews, 'Philip Guston Drawings 1938–1972,'" *Art News* (October 1973): 93.

David Aronson, "Philip Guston: Ten Drawings," *Boston University Journal* (Autumn 1973): 21.

1974

Robert Taylor, "Guston: The Raw & the Refined," *Boston Sunday Globe* (March 24, 1974): A42.

Kenneth Baker, "Art: Guston's Bleeding French Fries," *Boston Phoenix* (April 2, 1974): II, 13.

Kay Larson, "From Abstraction to the Absurd: The Transformation of Philip Guston," *The Real Paper* (Boston, April 3, 1974): 20–21.

Kenneth Baker, "Philip Guston at Boston University," *Art in America* (May–June 1974): 115.

John Russell, "Guston's Last Tape Mislaid," *The New York Times* (November 23, 1974): 58.

Lawrence Alloway, "Art," *The Nation* (November 30, 1974).

Thomas B. Hess, "The Abstractionist Who Came in from the Cold," *New York Magazine* (December 9, 1974): 102–3.

Noel Frackman, "New York: Philip Guston at David McKee," *Arts* (December 1974): 19.

1975

Lawrence Campbell, "Philip Guston (McKee)," *Art News* (January 1975): 90.

Roberta Smith, "Philip Guston," *Artforum* (February 1975): 65–66.

Kay Larson, "Identity Crisis," *Art News* (May 1975): 71.

Eila Kokkinen, "Five Abstract Expressionists: Willem de Kooning, Jackson Pollock, Arshile Gorky, Philip Guston, Franz Kline," *Boston University Journal* 23: 32, 36, 37.

1976

April Kingsley, "Philip Guston: David McKee Gallery," *Soho Weekly News* (March 18, 1976): 30–34.

Thomas B. Hess, "Dumb Is Beautiful," *New York Magazine* (March 29, 1976): 86–87.

Carter Ratcliff, "New York Letter," *Art International* (Lugano, April–May 1976): 54–55.

Ross Feld, "Philip Guston," *Arts Magazine* (May 1976): 9.

Peter Frank, "New York Reviews," *Art News* (May 1976): 134.

Phil Patton, "Reviews," *Artforum* (May 1976): 62–63.

Fred Orton and Gavin Bryars, "Morton Feldman: Interview," *Studio International* (November/December 1976): 244–48.

1977

Norbert Lynton, "From Mandarin to Stumblebum," *Times Literary Supplement* (January 7, 1977): 5.

Hilton Kramer, "Art: New Works by Philip Guston," *The New York Times* (March 25, 1977): III, 18.

William Zimmer, "Philip Guston Part II: David McKee Gallery," *Soho Weekly News* (April 28, 1977): 23–24.

Kenneth Baker, "Philip Guston's Drawings: Delirious Figuration," *Arts Magazine* (June 1977): 88–89.

Carter Ratcliff, "New York Letter," *Art International* (July–August 1977): 73–74.

Malcolm Quantrill, "London Letter," *Art International* (December 1977): 61–62.

1978

Roberta Smith, "The New Gustons," *Art in America* (January–February 1978): 100–105.

Ross Feld, "Philip Guston's 'Wharf,'" *Arts Magazine* (April 1978): 146–47.

Rene Ricard, "Philip Guston at David McKee," *Art in America* (November–December 1978): 157.

Alfred Frankenstein, "The Master of Delicacy Goes Rough and Tough," *San Francisco Chronicle* (December 28, 1978): 41.

Kay Larson, "New York Reviews," *Art News* (December 1978): 141.

1979

Mary Stofflet-Santiago, "Philip Guston: A Thorough Preview," *Artweek* (January 13, 1979).

Edgar Buonagurio, "Philip Guston," *Arts Magazine* (February 1979): 31.

Merle Schipper, "Kline and Guston: Phases of Drawing," *Artweek* (August 11, 1979): 1, 16.

"Philip Guston at David McKee," *Soho News* (October 18, 1979).

Carrie Rickey, "What Becomes a Legend Most?" *The Village Voice* (October 22, 1979): 91.

Dore Ashton, "A Response to Philip Guston's New Paintings," *Arts* (December 1979): 130–31.

1980

Albright, Thomas, "A Survey of One Man's Life," *San Francisco Chronicle* (May 15, 1980).

Grace Glueck, "Philip Guston, Painter, 66, Dead: An Abstract Expressionist Leader," *The New York Times* (June 10, 1980): D19.

Carrie Rickey, "Dreaming with His Eyes Open: Philip Guston 1913–1980," *The Village Voice* (June 23, 1980): 73.

Mark Stevens, "Diamond in the Rough," *Newsweek* (June 23, 1980): 88–89.

April Kingsley, "Philip Guston's Endgame," *Horizon* (June 1980): 34–41.

Thomas Albright, "Philip Guston: 'It's a Strange Thing to be Immersed in the Culture of Painting,'" *Art News* (September 1980): 114–16.

Kenneth Baker, "Breaking the Silence," *Artforum* (September 1980).

Roberta Smith, "Philip Guston, 1913–1980," *Art in America* (September 1980): 7–19.

Carrie Rickey, "Gust, Gusto, Guston," *Artforum* (October 1980): 32–39.

Paul Brach, "Looking at Guston," *Art in America* (November 1980): 96–101.

1981

Lewis Kachur, "Philip Guston," *Arts Magazine* (January 1981): 9.

John Russell, "Art: Philip Guston in Retrospect," *The New York Times* (July 3, 1981).

John Perreault, "Guston Winds," *Soho Weekly News* (July 8, 1981): 51.

Peter Schjeldahl, "Self-Abuse on Parade," *The Village Voice* (July 15, 1981): 72.

Kay Larson, "Painting from Ground Zero," *New York Magazine* (July 20, 1981): 58–59.

Robert Hughes, "Reflections in a Bloodshot Eye," *Time* (August 1981).

Dore Ashton, "Philip Guston: Different Subjects," *Flash Art* (December 1981–January 1982): 20–25.

1983

Michael Brenson, "Art: Assessing Guston by His Late Paintings," *The New York Times* (October 21, 1983): C28.

1984

Paul Brach, "Paint Remover: The Late Guston," *Art in America* (February 1984): 118–21.

1985

Stuart Morgan, "Bread and Circuses," *Artforum* (March 1985): 82–86.

1986

Ablow, Joseph, "The Nature of Identity: Metamorphosis of an Artist," *Bostonia Magazine* (April/May 1986): 14–19.

Adam Gopnik, "The Genius of George Herriman," *The New York Review of Books* (December 18, 1986): 19–28.

1987

Robert Zaller, "Philip Guston and the Crisis of the Image," *Critical Inquiry* (Fall 1987): 59–94.

1988

John Yau, "Philip Guston," *Artforum* (January 1988): 114.

Joann Moser, "Forum: Philip Guston's 'Hovering,'" *Drawing* (March–April 1988): 132.

Vivien Raynor, "Three Artists Who Abandoned Abstraction," *The New York Sunday Times* (July 17, 1988).

Musa Mayer, "My Father, Philip," *The New York Times Magazine* (August 7, 1988): 24, 55, 58.

Roberta Smith, "Retrospective Covers Guston's Two Careers," *The New York Times* (September 9, 1988).

Hilton Kramer, "Guston at MoMA: What was 'In' Drove This Artist Compulsively," *The New York Observer* (September 19, 1988).

Kay Larson, "Waiting for the Light," *New York Magazine* (September 26, 1988).

Theodore F. Wolff, "Philip Guston's Wide-Ranging 50-Year Career in Art," *The Christian Science Monitor* (September 26, 1988).

Arlene Raven, "Seeing and Believing," *The Village Voice* (September 27, 1988).

Kenneth Baker, "A Giant Emerges," *San Francisco Chronicle* (October 2, 1988).

Adam Gopnik, "Cyclops," *The New Yorker* (October 3, 1988).

Jack Flam, "The Gallery: Philip Guston," *The Wall Street Journal* (October 17, 1988).

Dore Ashton, "This Is Not What I Mean at All," *Arts Magazine* (November 1988): 69–71.

William Corbett, "What a Miracle Images Are!" *Arts Magazine* (November 1988): 51–54.

Ross Feld, "Guston in Time," *Arts Magazine* (November 1988): 40–45.

Alison de Lima Greene, "The Artist as Performer," *Arts Magazine* (November 1988): 55–61.

Marjorie Welish, "I Confess: The Drawings of Philip Guston," *Arts Magazine* (November 1988): 46–50.

Eleanor Heartney, "The Drawings of Philip Guston," *Art News* (December 1988): 143.

1989

Paul Brach, "An Act of Salvation," *Art in America* (January 1989): 130–35.

John Yau, "The Phoenix of the Self," *Artforum* (April 1989).

Jordi Costa, "Tras su colección de dibujos, llega la obra pictórica de Philip Guston a la Virreina," *ABC* (May 26, 1989).

Olga Spiegel, "Una completa retrospectiva de la obra pictórica de Guston inaugurada en la Virreina," *La Vanguardia* (May 26, 1989).

Anonymous, "El pintor Philip Guston, influenciado por Goya, expone en Barcelona," *El Correo de Andalucía* (May 27, 1989).

Marie-Clarie Uberquoi, "La carrera singular d'un pintor inquiet," *Diari de Barcelona* (May 27, 1989).

Hugh McFarlane, "Museum of Modern Art," *The Oxford Times* (June 2, 1989).

Abel Figueres, "Les relacions entre contigut forma," *AVUI* (June 9, 1989).

Tim Hilton, "Ghosts of the Past," *The Guardian* (June 9, 1989).

Francesc Miralles, "Guston, la lucha a contracorriente," *La Vanguardia* (June 17, 1989).

Josep Miguel García, "Philip Guston," *Guía del Ocio* (July 2, 1989).

Aidan Dunne, "Staying the Same by Changing," *The Sunday Tribune* (August 13, 1989).

Brian Fallon, "Drawing Close to the Edges of Nightmares," *Irish Times* (August 17, 1989).

Brian Fallon, "Philip Guston at Douglas Hyde Gallery," *Irish Times* (August 17, 1989).

Kat Robinson, "Guston: Satire and the Threat of Violence," *Sunday Independent* (September 1989).

1993

Philip Roth, "Breast Baring," *Vanity Fair* (October 1989): 94–99. Reprinted in P. Roth, *Shop Talk*, 2001 (see page 270).

Janet Kutner, "The Guston Looks," *The Dallas Morning News* (November 18, 1989).

William Corbett, "Philip Guston Drawing Poems," *Notus* (Fall 1989): 3.

1990

Peter Schjeldahl, "Painted Words," *7 Days* (February 1990).

Debra Bricker Balken, "Combined Aesthetics: Philip Guston and Clark Coolidge," *Art New England* (March 1990): 13–14.

Jeremy Gilbert-Rolfe, "Unmade in America," *Arts Magazine* (September 1990).

Kay Larson, "Pop Goes the Easel," *New York Magazine* (October 1990).

Michael Brenson, "Philip Guston: Paintings," *The New York Times* (November 9, 1990).

1991

Andrew Graham-Dixon, "Laughing in the Dark," *The Independent* (February 23, 1991).

Musa Mayer, "Under the Influence," *Mirabella* (March 1991).

Meyer Raphael Rubenstein, "Philip Guston and Clark Coolidge at Galerie Lelong," *Art in America* (July 1991): 123.

William Corbett, "Philip Guston/Clark Coolidge," *Arts Magazine* (Summer 1991): 67.

Nicholas Jenkins, "Philip Guston at David McKee," *Art News* (December 1991): 12.

Karen Wilkin, "At the Galleries," *Partisan Review* (Winter 1991).

José Luis Merino, "Guston," *El Mundo* (May 1993).

A. Okariz, "Los dibujos de Philip Guston," *Egin* (May 1993).

Xabier Sáenz de Gorbea, "La raíz del dibujo y sus rutas," *Arte* (May 1993).

M. J. Gandariasbeitia, "135 dibujos mostrarán en Bilbao la trayectoria del pintor norteamericano Philip Guston," *Cultura* (May 9, 1993).

Francisco Chacón, "Philip Guston, Obsesión por el dibujo," *El Mundo* (May 11, 1993).

Francisco Chacón, "La 'investigadora' de Guston," *El Mundo* (May 14, 1993).

Robert Hughes, "The View from Piccadilly," *Time* (October 4, 1993).

1994

Roberto Ohrt, "Dreck in Farbe: der Maler Philip Guston," *Da* (March 1994): 90–97.

Debra Bricker Balken, "Afterword to 16 Poems for Philip Guston," *TO* (Spring 1994): 53–54.

William Corbett, "Guston's Guston: How One Bold Artist Saw His Place in the Universe," *The Boston Phoenix* (September 1994).

Debra Bricker Balken, "Double Billings: Philip Guston's Poem-Pictures," *The Print Collector's Newsletter* (September–October 1994).

Michael Edward Shapiro, "Philip Guston: The War Years," *The Print Collector's Newsletter* (September–October 1994).

Robert Taylor, "Philip Guston's Poem-Pictures Rise above Art Lingo," *The Boston Sunday Globe* (October 2, 1994).

Nancy Stapen, "Philip Guston Exhibit at B.U. Offers Profound Rewards," *The Boston Sunday Globe* (October 2, 1994).

Joseph Ablow, "Ordered Terror: The Art of Philip Guston," *Bostonia Magazine* (Fall 1994).

Nancy Stapen, "Philip Guston, Boston University Art Gallery," *Art News* (December 1994): 145.

William Corbett, "Philip Guston: Drawing Poems," *Art New England* (December 1994–January 1995).

1995

Roberta Smith, "A Philip Guston Decade Colored by Red and Pink," *The New York Times* (April 28, 1995).

Sabine Russ, "Die Suche nach der Mitte," *Aufbau* (May 26, 1995).

Joel Lewis, "Guston Gets Another Go," *Forward* (June 9, 1995).

Didier Ottinger, "Acquisition d'un tableau de Philip Guston par le Musée des Sables d'Olonne," *La Revue du Louvre* (June 1995): 73–75.

Philippe Dagen, "Philip Guston aux Sables: l'abstraction aller et retour," *Le Monde* (July 4, 1995).

Holland Cotter, "A Painter Who Collaborated with Poets," *The New York Times* (July 7, 1995).

Marie-Gaëlle Chabot, "Guston reconnu aux Sables," *Presse-Océan* (July 24, 1995).

Anonymous, "Le musée des Sables expose Guston," *Ouest France* (July 1995).

Nicola Kalinsky, "Exhibition Review: Drawing the Line," *Burlington Magazine* (July 1995).

"Philip Guston ou la modernité revisitée," *Le Journal des arts* 16 (July–August, 1995).

Marielle Ernould-Gandouet, "Philip Guston: Oeuvres sur papier 1975–1980," *L'Oeil* (July–August 1995).

R. J., "L'étrangeté inquiétante des choses," *Ouest France* (August 18, 1995).

Jean-Louis Pradel, "L'apocalypse triviale de Philip Guston," *L'Événement du Jeudi* (August 24–30, 1995).

Anonymous, "Philip Guston," *Art Press* (September 1995).

Manuel Jover, "L'art impur de Philip Guston," *Beaux Arts Magazine* (September 1995).

Leslie Laidet, "Philip Guston: Oeuvres sur papier," *Critique d'art* (September 1995): 56.

Raphael Rubenstein, "Ars poetica," *Art in America* (September 1995): 100–103, 121.

Paul Brach, "Philip Guston at McKee," *Art in America* (October 1995): 131–32.

Ronald Jones, "Philip Guston's Poem-Pictures," *Frieze* (November 1995).

1996

Michael Kimmelman, "Philip Guston: Paintings from the 70s," *The New York Times* (October 11, 1996).

Ursula Bode, "Alte Manner sind gefahrlich: Das Spatwerk von Guston, de Kooning, Miró, und Picasso in Bremen," *Die Zeit* (November 20, 1996).

Peter Winter, "Schwung, Volumen und Dichte: Vier Maler mit ihrem Spätwerk in der Bremer Weserburg: Picasso, Miró, de Kooning, and Guston," *Frankfurter Allgemeine Zeitung für Deutschland* (November 25, 1996).

Heiner Stachelhaus, "Die Krise des Alters malend gemeistert: das Weserburg-Museum konfrontiert Zeitgenössisches mit dem Spätwerk von vier Klassikern," *St. Gallener Tageblatt* (1996).

1997

Grady T. Turner, "Philip Guston," *Art News* (November 1997).

1998

Suzanne Muchnic, "The Shock of the Old," *Los Angeles Times* (June 7, 1998).

1999

Ruth Händler, "Trying Racism On," *Ausstellungen* (September 1999).

Samuel Herzog, "Stiller Abscheid vom Absoluten, Ausstellung Philip Guston im Kunstmuseum Bonn," *Neue Züricher Zeitung*, Feuilleton (October 15, 1999).

David Anfam, "Bonn, Philip Guston," *The Burlington Magazine* (December 1999).

2000

Gerog Von Leiston, "Zurück zur Figuration," *Stuttgarter Zeitung* (February 18, 2000).

Claudia Von Ihlefeld, "Kraftstrotzender Kulturpessimist," *Heilbronner Stimme* (February 19, 2000).

Volker Bauermeister, "Der Vorturner des Stilbruchs," *Badische Zeitung* (February 26, 2000).

Nikolai B. Von Forstbauer, "Malerei der offenen Faust oder Die Form ist die Farbe," *Stuttgarter Nachirchten* (February 29, 2000).

Christoph Bannat, "Heimlicher Vater, Tabubruch: Philip Guston kehrte von der Abstraktion zurück zur Figur," *Vogue* Deutschland (February 2000).

Christian Marquar, "Der Ku-Klux-Klan ist immer dabei," *Kunst* (March 2, 2000).

Carmela von Thiele, "Kapuzen und das Böse im Ich," *Badische Neueste Nachrichten* (March 2, 2000).

Carmela von Thiele, "Mich interessiert das Böse," *Der Tagesspiegel* (March 5, 2000).

Robert C. Morgan, "Philip Guston: Small Paintings and Drawings 1968–1980," *Review* (March 15, 2000).

Holger Steinemann, "Weg zurück zur Gegenständlichkeit," *Staatsanzeiger für Baden-Württemberg* (March 20, 2000).

Rosanne Altstatt, "Philip Guston im Kunstverein," *Kunstbulletin* (April 2000).

Jennifer Couëlle, "Philip le Grand," *Le Presse* (Montreal, June 17, 2000).

Geneviève Breerette, "Au Centre Georges Pompidou, Philip Guston le désenchanté," *Le Monde* (September 15, 2000).

Emmanuelle Lequeux, "La Peinture Existentialiste De Philip Guston," *Le Monde* (September 27–October 3, 2000).

Michael Gibson, "Philip Guston: A Rage to Paint," *International Herald Tribune* (September 30–October 1, 2000).

Philippe Regnier, "Un Expressionniste Militant, Philip Guston, un Abstrait Hanté par la Figure," *Le Journal des arts* (September 2000).

Annie Cohen-Solal, "L'art américain mine de rien," *Le Journal Des Arts* (October 6, 2000).

Marie-Christine Stephan, "Les combats de Philip Guston," *Kultur* (October 17, 2000).

Lieven Van den Abeele, "Schilderen tegen Ku Klux Klan," *De Standaard* (October 17, 2000).

Anonymous, "Philip Guston. Peintures 1947–79," *Descubrir el Arte* (October 2000).

Richard Leydier, "The Heresies of Philip Guston," *Art Press* (October 2000).

A. G., Centre Georges Pompidou, "Philip Guston: peintures, 1947–1979: Le rire de la liberté," *Zurban* (November 8, 2000).

Deborah Everett, "Philip Guston—Paintings and Drawings from the 1970s," *NY Arts* International Edition (Winter 2000).

Alain Delaunois, "Philip Guston, un peintre en liberté," *Arts Plastiques*.

Fran Krijk, "Philip Guston," *AuxiPress*.

2001

Francine Koslow Miller, "Philip Guston, Fogg Art Museum," *Artforum* (February 2001).

David Kauffman, "'A Vast Precaution to Avoid Immobility': Philip Guston's 'To I. B.' (1977)," *The Burlington Magazine* (May 2001).

Arthur C. Danto, "Dick (Nixon) Heads," *The Nation* (October 1, 2001).

Mario Naves, "The Life and Times of Richard Nixon," *The New York Observer* (October 1, 2001).

Harry Cooper, "Philip Guston's 'Poor Richard,'" *Bookforum* (Fall 2001).

2002

Sarah Boxer, "Drawings are Still Kicking Nixon Around," *The New York Times* (June 17, 2002).

Exhibition Catalogues and Books

1944

State University of Iowa, catalogue for *Paintings and Drawings by Philip Guston* (Iowa City: Student Union Board, 1944).

1945

Midtown Galleries, catalogue for *Philip Guston* (New York, 1945).

1947

H. W. Janson, *Modern Art in the Washington University Collection* (Saint Louis: City Art Museum of Saint Louis, 1947): 11, 27.

Hugo Weisgall, *Advancing American Art* (Prague: U.S. Information Agency, 1947): n.p.

1950

H. H. Arnason, catalogue for *Contemporary American Painting* (Minneapolis: Walker Art Center, 1950). 5th Biennial Purchase Exhibition.

University of Minnesota, catalogue for *Philip Guston* (Minneapolis, 1950).

1951

Robert Motherwell and Ad Reinhardt, eds., *Modern Artists in America: First Series* (New York: Wittenborn, Schultz, 1951): 80.

Ninth Street Gallery, catalogue for *Exhibition of Painting and Sculpture* (New York, 1951).

Peridot Gallery, catalogue for *Paintings 1948–1951 by Philip Guston* (New York, 1951).

Andrew C. Ritchie, catalogue for *Abstract Paintings and Sculpture in America* (New York: The Museum of Modern Art, 1951).

Sidney Janis Gallery, catalogue for *American Vanguard Art for Paris Exhibition* (New York, 1952).

1953

The Baltimore Museum of Art, catalogue for *Abstract Expressionists* (Baltimore, 1953).

1954

The Solomon R. Guggenheim Museum, catalogue for *Younger American Painters* (New York, 1954).

1955

Munson-Williams-Proctor Institute, catalogue for *Italy Re-Discovered* (Utica, 1955).

1956

Dorothy C. Miller, ed., catalogue for *12 Americans* (New York: The Museum of Modern Art, 1956).

Sidney Janis Gallery, catalogue for *Philip Guston* (New York, 1956).

Sidney Janis Gallery, catalogue for *7 Americans* (New York, 1956).

1957

Catalogue (São Paulo, Brazil: Museu de Arte Moderna, September 1957).

Sidney Janis Gallery, catalogue for *8 Americans* (New York, 1957).

1958

John I. H. Baur, catalogue for *Nature in Abstraction: The Relation of Abstract Painting and Sculpture to Nature in Twentieth-Century American Art* (New York: Whitney Museum of American Art, 1958).

1959

Dore Ashton, *Philip Guston* (New York: Grove Press, 1959).

Kassel, catalogue for *Kunst Nach 1945. II. Documenta* (Cologne, 1959).

The Museum of Modern Art, catalogue for *The New American Painting, As Shown in Eight European Countries 1958–1959* (New York, 1959).

Sidney Janis Gallery, catalogue for *8 American Painters* (New York, 1959).

Sidney Janis Gallery, catalogue for *Guston* (New York, 1959).

Sidney Janis Gallery, catalogue for *Sidney Janis Presents an Exhibition of Recent Paintings by Philip Guston* (New York, 1959).

1960

Werner Haftmann, *Painting in the Twentieth Century* (London: Lund Humphries, 1960): vol. 1, 353, 391–92; vol. 2, 450, 510.

Herbert Read, *The Forms of Things Unknown: Essays Towards an Aesthetic Philosophy* (New York: Horizon Press, 1960): 165.

Kenneth B. Sawyer, *Quattro Artisti Americani: Guston, Hofmann, Kline, Roszak* (Venice: XXX Biennale, 1960).

Sidney Janis Gallery, catalogue for *9 American Painters* (New York, 1969).

1961

H. H. Arnason, catalogue for *Abstract Expressionists and Imagists* (New York: The Solomon R. Guggenheim Museum, 1961).

Dwan Gallery, catalogue for *Philip Guston, Franz Kline* (Los Angeles, 1961).

Sidney Janis Gallery, catalogue for *10 American Painters* (New York, May 1961).

1962

H. H. Arnason, catalogue for *Philip Guston* (New York: The Solomon R. Guggenheim Museum, 1962).

Dore Ashton, *The Unknown Shore: A View of Contemporary Art* (Boston: Little, Brown, and Co., 1962): 65–71.

John Canaday, "Their Separate Ways: Jack Levine and Philip Guston," *Embattled Critic: View on Modern Art* (New York: Noonday Press, 1962): 137–41.

1963

Kevin Levin, "Philip Guston," in Lee Nordess, ed., *Art USA Now* (New York: Viking Press, 1963): vol. 1, 218–21.

1964

Harold Rosenberg, *The Anxious Object: Art Today and Its Audience* (New York: Horizon Press, 1964): 26, 49, 83.

1965

Gladys Shafron Kashdin, "Abstract Expressionism: An Analysis of the Movement Based Primarily on Interviews with Seven Participatory Artists," PhD dissertation (Florida State University, 1965).

1966

Sam Hunter (Introduction), Harold Rosenberg (dialogue with the artist), catalogue for *Philip Guston: Recent Paintings and Drawings* (New York: The Jewish Museum, 1966).

William Seitz, catalogue for *Philip Guston: A Selective Retrospective Exhibiton: 1945–1965* (Waltham, Mass.: Brandeis University, 1966).

1967

Morton Feldman, catalogue for *Six Painters: Mondrian, Guston, Kline, de Kooning, Pollock, Rothko* (Houston: Art Department, University of St. Thomas, 1967); text reprinted as Feldman, "After Modernism," *Art in America* (November/December 1971): 68–77.

Frank O'Hara, *In Memory of My Feelings* (New York: The Museum of Modern Art, 1967).

Barbara Rose, *American Art Since 1900: A Critical History* (New York: Praeger, 1967): 126, 189, 206, 209.

Santa Barbara Museum of Art, catalogue for *Philip Guston* (Santa Barbara, 1967).

1969

Edward Lucie-Smith, *Late Modern: The Visual Arts Since 1945* (New York: Praeger, 1969): 43, 47.

Barbara Rose, *American Painting, the 20th Century* (Lausanne: Skira, 1969): 80, 86.

Harold Rosenberg, *Artworks and Packages* (New York: Dell, 1969): 216, 218, 222.

1970

Marlborough Gallery, catalogue for *Philip Guston* (New York, 1970).

Irving Sandler, *The Triumph of American Painting: A History of Abstract Expressionism* (New York: Praeger, 1970): 6, 96, 219, 233, 234, 258, 261, 264, 265.

1971

La Jolla Museum of Contemporary Art, catalogue for *Philip Guston, Recent Work* (La Jolla, 1971).

Maurice Tuchman, ed., *New York School: The First Generation* (Greenwich: New York Graphic Society, 1971): 75–81; revised edition of catalogue for *New York School: The First Generation* (Los Angeles: Los Angeles County Museum of Art, 1965).

1972

Contemporary Art 1942–72: Collection of the Albright-Knox Art Gallery (New York: Praeger, 1972): 18–19, 21, 54, 56, 417, 454.

B. H. Friedman, *Jackson Pollock: Energy Made Visible* (New York: McGraw-Hill, 1972): xviii, 9, 10, 26, 37, 39, 46, 84, 111–12, 188, 194, 213, 222–23.

John Gruen, *The Party's Over Now* (New York: Viking Press, 1972): 128, 129, 154, 181, 248, 249–50, 251.

Francis V. O'Connor, ed., *The New Deal Art Projects: An Anthology of Memoirs* (Washington, D.C.: Smithsonian Institute Press, 1972): 37, 41, 100, 235, 253, 254, 255, 256, 286, 292.

Harold Rosenberg, *The De-definition of Art* (New York: Macmillan, 1972): 43, 130, 132–40, 193, 194.

Leo Steinberg, *Other Criteria: Confrontations with Twentieth-Century Art* (New York: Oxford University Press, 1972): 282–85.

1973

Dore Ashton, *The New York School: A Cultural Reckoning* (New York: Viking Press, 1973).

Gertrude Kasle Gallery, catalogue for *Philip Guston: Major Paintings of the Sixties* (Detroit, 1973).

Francis V. O'Connor, ed., *Art for the Millions: Essays from the 1930s by Artists and Administrators of the WPA Federal Art Project* (Boston: New York Graphic Society, 1973): 22, 23.

Brian O'Doherty, *American Masters: The Voice and the Myth* (New York: Random House, 1973): 89.

William Stott, *Documentary Expressionism and Thirties America* (New York: Oxford University Press, 1973): 118.

John Wilmerding, ed., *The Genius of American Painting* (New York: William Morrow, 1973): 261, 263, 267, 298, 300, 301, 325, 326, 330, 331.

1974

Dore Ashton (Introduction), catalogue for *Philip Guston: New Paintings* (Boston: Boston University, 1974).

Matthew Baigell, *The American Scene: American Painting of the 1930s* (New York: Praeger, 1974): 78, 81.

David McKee Gallery, catalogue for *Philip Guston* (New York, 1974).

1975

Bill Berkson, *Enigma Variations* (Bolinas, Calif.: Big Sky, 1975). Cover and drawings by Guston.

Michèle Cone, *The Roots and Routes of Art in the 20th Century* (New York: Horizon Press, 1975): 170–71, 173, 187–88, 193, 198.

Eila Kokkinen, catalogue for *Drawings by Five Abstract Expressionist Painters: Arshile Gorky, Willem de Kooning, Jackson Pollock, Franz Kline, Philip Guston* (Cambridge: Hayden Gallery, Massachusetts Institute of Technology, 1975).

Nancy Dustin Wall Moure and Phyllis Moure, *Artists' Clubs and Exhibitions in Los Angeles Before 1930*, Publications in Southern California Art, no. 2 (Los Angeles: Privately Printed, 1975): n.p.

Frank O'Hara, *Art Chronicles 1954–1966* (New York: George Braziller, Inc., 1975): 134–41.

Harold Rosenberg, *Art on the Edge* (New York: Macmillan, 1975): 73, 81, 83, 99, 231, 237.

1976

Dore Ashton, *Yes, But . . . : A Critical Study of Philip Guston* (New York: Viking Press, 1976); revised edition, *A Critical Study of Philip Guston* (Berkeley, Los Angeles, and Oxford: University of California Press, 1990).

David McKee Gallery, catalogue for *Philip Guston: Paintings 1975* (New York, 1976).

1977

Alfred H. Barr, Jr., *Painting and Sculpture in The Museum of Modern Art 1929–1967* (New York: The Museum of Modern Art, 1977): 334, 547–48.

David McKee Gallery, catalogue for *Philip Guston: Paintings 1976* (New York, 1977).

Barbaralee Diamonstein, ed., *The Art World: A Seventy-Five-Year Treasury of Art News* (New York: Rizzoli, 1977): 194, 264, 295, 298, 354.

Colin Naylor and Genesis P-Orridge, eds., "Philip Guston," in *Contemporary Artists* (London: St. James Press, 1977): 371–72.

1978

Allan Frumkin Gallery, catalogue for *Philip Guston, Major Paintings 1975–76* (Chicago, 1978).

Lois Craig and the Staff of the Federal Architecture Project, *The Federal Presence: Architecture, Politics, and Symbols in United States Government Buildings* (Cambridge: MIT Press, 1978): 408.

David McKee Gallery, catalogue for *Philip Guston: Drawings 1947–1977*, with statement by Philip Guston (New York, 1978).

Francis V. O'Connor, "Philip Guston and Political Humanism," in Henry A. Milton and Linda Nochlin, eds., *Arts and Architecture in the Service of Politics* (Cambridge: MIT Press, 1978): 62–68.

Irving Sandler, *The New York School: The Painters and Sculptors of the Fifties* (New York: Harper & Row, 1978).

1979

David McKee Gallery, catalogue for *Philip Guston, Paintings 1978–1979* (New York, 1979).

1980

John Coplans, "The Private Eye of Philip Guston," *Philip Guston* (Los Angeles: Gemini G.E.L., 1980).

San Francisco Museum of Modern Art, catalogue for *Philip Guston*, with essays by Ross Feld and Henry Hopkins (New York and San Francisco: George Braziller in association with the San Francisco Museum of Modern Art, 1980).

Philip Verre, catalogue for *Return to the Figure: Three Studies—Philip Guston, Jean Hélion, Irene Rice-Pereira* (New York: Bronx Museum of the Arts, 1980).

1981

Morton Feldman, catalogue for *Philip Guston, 1980/The Last Works* (Washington, D.C.: Phillips Collection, 1981).

Henry T. Hopkins, *Philip Guston: His Last Years* (San Francisco: San Francisco Museum of Modern Art, 1981).

1982

Nicholas Serota, ed., with Norbert Lynton, catalogue for *Philip Guston: Paintings, 1969–1980* (London: Whitechapel Art Gallery, 1982).

1984

Peter Schjeldahl, "Philip Guston," in *Art of Our Time: The Saatchi Collection* (London and New York: Lund Humphries in association with Rizzoli, 1984) 12–14.

Robert Storr with Joseph Ablow, John Buckley, and Edward F. Fry, *Philip Guston: The Late Works* (National Gallery of Victoria, Melbourne under the auspices of the International Cultural Corporation of Australia, 1984).

1985

Stanley Kunitz, "Remembering Guston," in *Next-to-Last Things: New Poems and Essays* (New York: Atlantic Monthly Press, 1985): 73.

1986

Robert Storr, *Philip Guston* (New York: Abbeville Press, 1986).

1987

David McKee Gallery, catalogue for *Philip Guston: "Roma" 1971* (New York, 1987).

1988

Magdalena Dabrowski, catalogue for *Drawings of Philip Guston* (New York: The Museum of Modern Art, 1988–89).

Musa Mayer, *Night Studio: A Memoir of Philip Guston by His Daughter* (New York: Alfred A. Knopf, 1988); second edition (New York: Penguin Books, 1990).

1989

Mark Rosenthal, with Dore Ashton, Carrie Rickey, and Francisco Calvo Serraller, catalogue for *Philip Guston: Retrospectiva de Pintura* (Madrid: Centro de Arte Reina Sofia, 1989).

1990

Debra Bricker Balken, catalogue for *Drawings from the Philip Guston and Clark Coolidge Exchange* (Pittsfield: The Berkshire Museum, 1990).

Bill Berkson, "The Dark Pictures" in catalogue for *Philip Guston 1961–65* (New York: McKee Gallery, 1990): n.p.

Sanford Schwartz, *Artists and Writers* (New York: Yarrow Press, 1990): n.p.

1991

Clark Coolidge, *Baffling Means*, with drawings by Philip Guston (Stockbridge: O-blek Editions, 1991).

1993

Kosme María de Barañano, catalogue for *Philip Guston: La Raíz del Dibujo—Roots of Drawing* (Bilbao: Rekalde, 1993).

Robert Natkin, "Epilogue—Letter to David McKee," *Subject Matter and Abstraction—in Exile* (Herts: The Claridge Press, 1993).

1994

Debra Bricker Balken, *Philip Guston's Poem-Pictures*, with contributions by Bill Berkson, Clark Coolidge, William Corbett, and Stanley Kunitz (Seattle: University of Washington Press, 1994).

William Corbett, *Philip Guston's Late Work: A Memoir* (Cambridge, Mass.: Zoland Books, 1994).

Musa McKim, *Alone with the Moon* (Great Barrington: The Figures, 1994).

1995

Didier Ottinger, catalogue for *Philip Guston* (Les Sables d'Olonne: Musée de l'Abbaye Saint-Croix, 1995): 10–168.

Kevin Power, "Guston: The Late Paintings," in *Picasso, Guston, Miró, de Kooning: Painting for Themselves: Late Works* (Bremen: Neues Museum Weserburg, 1996): 72.

1996

Michael E. Shapiro, catalogue for *Philip Guston: Working through the Forties* (Iowa City: University of Iowa Museum of Art, 1996).

1997

Robert Hughes, *American Visions: The Epic History of Art in America* (New York: Alfred A. Knopf, 1997).

1998

Sally Radic with Renee McKee and Manuel Padorno, *Línea y Poesía: Philip Guston/Musa McKim* (Lanzarote: Funación César Manrique, 1998).

1999

Kosme de Barañano, catalogue for *Diskurs um Philip Guston* (Düsseldorf: Kunstmuseum Winterthur and Richter Verlag, 1999).

Christoph Schreier, with Michael Auping and Martin Hentschel, catalogue for *Philip Guston: Gemälde 1947–79* (Bonn: Hatje Cantz and Kunstmuseum Bonn, 1999).

2000

Didier Ottinger with Philip Roth and Philip Guston, catalogue for *Philip Guston, Peintures 1947–1979* (Paris: Éditions du Centre Pompidou, 2000).

Joanna Weber with Harry Cooper and Laura Greengold, catalogue for *Philip Guston: A New Alphabet* (New Haven: Yale University Art Gallery, 2000).

2001

Debra Bricker Balken, *Philip Guston's Poor Richard* (Chicago: The University of Chicago Press, 2001).

Kosme de Barañano and Mª Jesús Folch, catalogue for *Philip Guston: One-Shot Painting* (Valencià: ALDESA—Institut Valencià d'Art Modern, 2001).

Albrecht Kastein, ed., *Philip Guston*, with essays by Jutta Koether, Roberto Ohrt, and William Corbett (Köln: BQ, 2001).

Philip Roth, *Shop Talk: A Writer and His Colleagues and Their Work* (New York and Boston: Houghton Mifflin Company, 2001): 131–38.

Films

Interview with David Sylvester (British Broadcasting Company, London, 1963).

The New York School (Michael Blackwood Productions, New York, 1973).

Philip Guston: A Life Lived, 1913–1980 (Michael Blackwood Productions, New York, 1980).

Photograph Credits

Brian Albert: plate 94

Courtesy Albright-Knox Art Gallery, Buffalo: page 47; from Michael Auping, *Abstract Expressionism: The Critical Developments* (New York and Buffalo: Harry N. Abrams in association with the Albright-Knox Art Gallery, 1987).

Arthur Ames: page 17 (left)

Image © The Art Institute of Chicago: plate 108

Ben Blackwell: plates 54, 74

Dan Budnik: pages 51 (© 1964 Magnum Photos), 250

A. Burger: plate 118

Bevan Davies: plate 36

© Virginia Dortch: pages 59, 249

Mark Edwards: page 254 (left)

Lee Fatherree: plate 83

Sidney B. Felsen: pages 255, 256

Philip Gagliani: plate 28

Gamma One Conversions, Inc.: plate 1

© 2002 Artists Rights Society (ARS), New York / DACS, London; photograph by David Heald, © The Solomon R. Guggenheim Foundation, New York: figure 11

Denise Hare: pages 20, 67

Tom Jenkins: plates 90, 121

Peter Juley: figures 4, 7

Michael Korol, New York: plates 5, 8, 9, 17, 20, 24, 26, 34, 52, 55, 58, 59, 60, 61, 62, 75, 80, 86, 89, 91, 92, 93, 97, 132; figures 8, 9, 17

D. James Lee: plate 10

Photograph © 2002 Museum Associates / Los Angeles County Museum of Art: plate 39

Renee McKee: pages 19, 253, 254 (right)

The Metropolitan Museum of Art: plate 30 © 1992; plate 51 © 1985; plate 113 © 1984

Digital Image © The Museum of Modern Art / Licensed by SCALA / Art Resource, NY: plates 35, 45

Photograph © 2002 Board of Trustees, National Gallery of Art, Washington: figure 5

© 1986 Douglas M. Parker Studio: plates 6, 21, 29, 73, 87, 98, 104

Eric Pollitzer, New York: plate 71

Renate Ponsold: pages 45, 251 (right and left)

F. Raux; © Réunion des Musées Nationaux / Art Resource, New York: figure 20

© Mondrian / Holtzman Trust, c/o Beeldrecht / Artists Rights Society (ARS), New York; Photograph © San Francisco Museum of Modern Art: figure 6

© Steven Sloman, New York: plates 40, 108, 112; pages 12, 54, 252

© Barbara Sproule: page 89

Lee Stalsworth: plate 102

Photo Courtesy of Gerard Tempest: page 76

Time magazine: page 25

Michael Tropea, Chicago: plate 123

Sarah Wells, New York: plates 19, 25, 27, 50; figure 3

Edward Weston, *Philip Guston*, 1930, © 1981, Arizona Board of Regents, Center for Creative Photography: page 243

David Wharton: figures 12, 14, 16

Graydon Wood: figures 10, 18, 19

Imprint

First published in hardback in the United States of America in 2003 by Thames & Hudson Inc., 500 Fifth Avenue, New York, New York 10110.

thamesandhudsonusa.com

Library of Congress Catalog Card Number 2002102624
ISBN 0-500-09308-3

Printed and bound in Italy by Conti Tipocolor

Published on the occasion of the exhibition *Philip Guston Retrospective*, organized by the Modern Art Museum of Fort Worth in 2003.

Edited by Pam Hatley,
Modern Art Museum of Fort Worth
Designed by Peter B. Willberg
Produced by Thames & Hudson

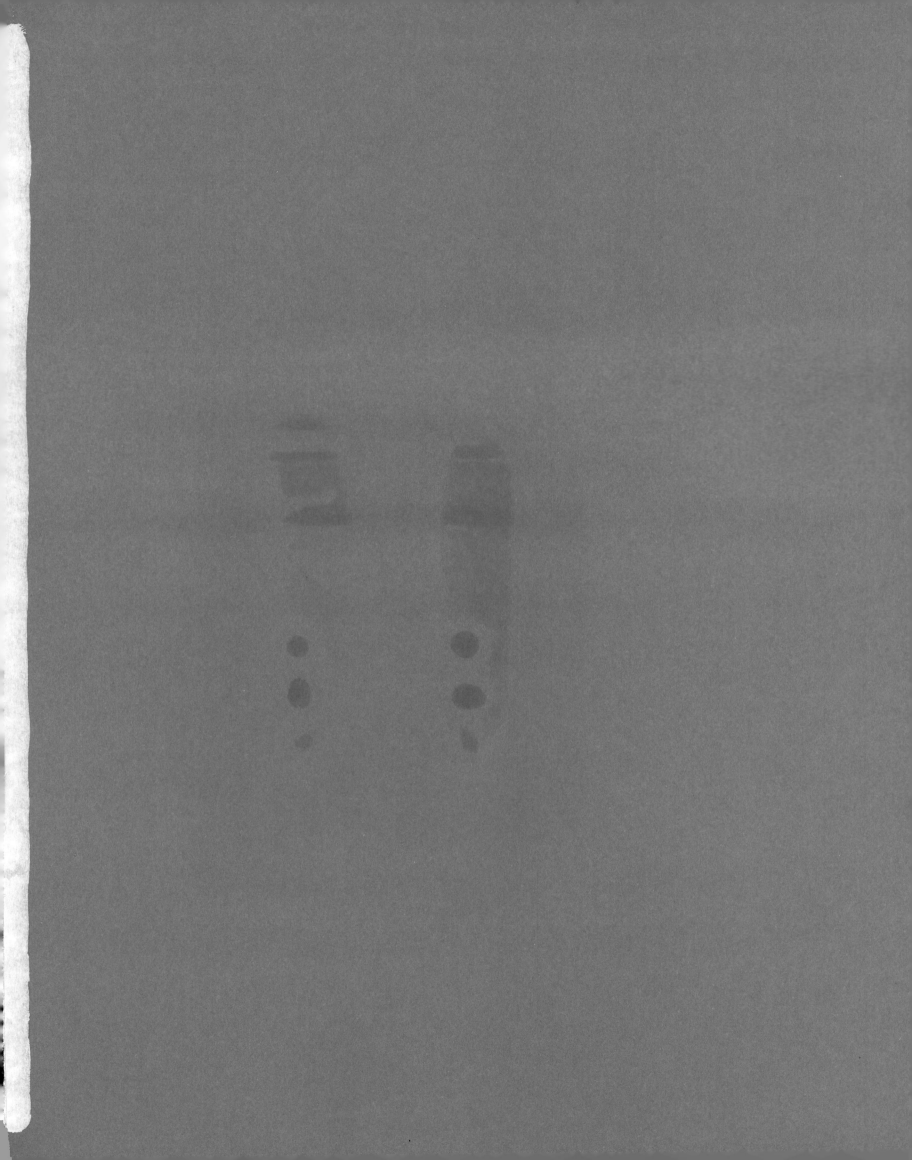